T0366939

Statesmanship and Party Government

HARVEY C. MANSFIELD

Statesmanship
and
Party Government

A Study of Burke and Bolingbroke

THE UNIVERSITY OF CHICAGO PRESS

Chicago and London

The University of Chicago Press, Chicago 60637
The University of Chicago Press, Ltd., London
© 1965 by The University of Chicago
All rights reserved. Published 2013.
Paperback edition 2013
Printed in the United States of America

22 21 20 19 18 17 16 15 14 13   2 3 4 5 6

978-0-226-02217-8 (paperback)
978-0-226-02220-8 (e-book)
10.7208/9780226022208

Library of Congress Cataloging-in-Publication Data

Mansfield, Harvey C.
      Statesmanship and Party Government : a study of Burke and
      Bolingbroke / Harvey C. Mansfield.
         p. cm.
      Includes bibliographical references and index.
      ISBN-13: 978-0-226-02217-8 (paperback : alk. paper)
      ISBN-10: 0-226-02217-X (paperback : alk. paper)
1. Bolingbroke, Henry St. John, Viscount, 1678–1751. 2. Burke,
Edmund 1729–1797. 3. Great Britain—Politics and government—18th
century I. Title

JN1119 .M3

♾ This paper meets the requirements of ANSI/NISO z39.48-1992
(Permanence of Paper).

To my father and mother

Acknowledgments

My thanks are due first of all to Professor Samuel Beer of Harvard University, who has guided my interest in Britain and in political parties ever since he first aroused it. Professor William Y. Elliott, formerly of Harvard and now of American University, helped this book with his unpitying criticism and, in general, has shown me what courage of the intellect demands. Professor Leo Strauss of the University of Chicago gently and powerfully suggested many of the arguments in this book.

My father has always set my standard for the political scientist, and he has lent much more than his name to this undertaking. It is my good fortune to be formed by his unobtrusive education.

For help with the manuscript I am greatly indebted to David Lowenthal, Roger C. Moulton, and Joseph Cropsey; and for help with typing, to Mrs. Joan Erdman.

"*All acting in Corps tends to reduce the consideration of an individual who is of any distinguished Value.*"

Burke, Letter to Shackleton, May 25, 1779

"*When bad men combine, the good must associate; else they will fall, one by one, an unpitied sacrifice in a contemptible struggle.*"

Burke, "Thoughts on the Cause of the Present Discontents."

Contents

CHAPTER ONE

The Origins of Party Government

In considering the origins of party government, we face this problem: parties are universal, but party government is recent. Parties are universal because in politics men act for motives which can be and are stated in opinions. Opinions are disputable, especially opinions about the most important topics, opinions on which citizens and regimes stake their lives. Being disputable, such opinions attract and repel: they create partisans. Politics seems to be essentially partisan. There have been many regimes without visible parties and perhaps some entirely without parties. But partyless regimes are not non-partisan. They may suppress the parties which might dispute the opinions they have established, but they cannot suppress the disputability of their opinions. Parties are potential in every regime where they are not actual; and where they are actual, there are also potential parties lurking beneath every opinion taken for granted by the actual parties. The secret records of all regimes reveal private parties of politicians or courtiers not visible to the citizens or subjects, and historians have exposed the disputable assumptions of regimes which believed themselves to be founded on rock.

Since politics is essentially partisan, and since the essence of politics is clear to any unbiased observer, it is not surprising that party government is now almost ubiquitous. There is almost no regime which does not claim to have party government—which does not use, avow its use, and praise its use of a party or parties. There is almost no regime which is not proud of having a party or parties. Party is understood to be the birthright of new regimes, and the conflict of our times between Western liberalism and communism seems not to involve the existence of party government, but only the practice of essentially different party regimes. Thus assured that party government is accepted almost everywhere, political scientists have studied those problems of party which presuppose the existence of party government: the selection of leaders by a party, the representativeness of different kinds of parties, the functions of party, the nature of a "party system," and so forth. These complex and sophisticated problems arise because the simple reason for partisanship—the holding of disputable opinions—seems to be sufficient justification for party government.

Yet if party government seems inevitable, it is perplexing that it should be so recent. Two centuries ago there was no party government, and the few early examples of party government have been widely imitated only recently. The origins of party government are not coeval with Western civilization, nor with modern political philosophy, nor even with the founding of contemporary regimes. In America, party was begun by a founder of the regime, Jefferson, in opposition to other founders and as a modification of their work. In Britain, party was first praised by a statesman, Burke, who claimed to be defending the regime of the Whig revolution, but who defended it by modifying it. Burke and Jefferson, as founders of party government, were at first alone in their praise of party. Famous men—the Federalists in America, the Old Whigs in Britain—men whom we rightly regard as the founders of our contemporary regimes, men who are not otherwise so remote from contemporary beliefs, opposed party government with a vehemence equal to the energy with which they upheld the cause of liberty. If it is perplexing that party government is so recent, it is startling that earlier advocates of liberty and founders of free constitutions opposed party government. Indeed, it is too mild to say that they opposed party government; they would have been astounded to see it taken for granted by sober men living under free constitutions. We must appraise the near-ubiquity of party government today in the light of its complete absence in the past.

On this evidence it seems necessary to distinguish parties from party government. Parties are universal, but party government is the result of the recent discovery that parties can be respectable. Because the reason for partisanship is so simple and compelling, the respectability, not the existence, of party is the distinguishing mark of party government. In 1769, the year before Burke published his "Thoughts on the Cause of the

Present Discontents," he wrote that "party divisions whether on the whole operating for good or evil, are things inseparable from free government."[1] By contrast, in the "Thoughts" he presented a *defense* of party, as a worthy and necessary instrument of free government under certain conditions. If Burke thought in 1769 that parties were inseparable from free government, why did he make so long an argument in 1770 to recommend them? By "party divisions," Burke in 1769 meant the small groups contending in Parliament, within view of the people; in 1770, he defended these groups as "on the whole operating for good." It was one thing for Burke to identify an institution as inseparable from free government, whether or not it was a deformity, and another thing for him to argue that an institution long considered a deformity was really a beauty of free government.

The respectability of party can be better understood if one distinguishes between the public and the private constitutions of a country. The public constitution is the arrangement of rule which appears to the public and is taught in the schools; the private constitution is the way in which the regime "really works" behind the scenes. Honest men often find a perplexing discrepancy between the two, for the distinction between the public and private constitutions does not quite correspond to the distinction between public and private ends. Honest men wrongly believe that what cannot be avowed in public cannot be for the good of the public. Those who seek only private advantage can be plausible in public, however; and unpublicized action may be necessary to prevent the success of private association for private advantage. Parties have perhaps always existed in the private constitutions of countries, more openly in free constitutions; and some have acted for private advantage and some for the public good. Only very recently have parties been awarded status in the public constitution by a change in the public estimation of party. It is true that no party, not even the Communist party of the Soviet Union, has full status in the public constitution. However much the law may recognize and regulate party activity, no party has the legal status of a legislature or an executive, by which its program would count as law or decree. Nevertheless, a party or parties are now held everywhere to be essential to the law and thus allowed to reflect some of the majesty of the law. It is certainly no longer public decorum to deplore parties to the point of wishing for their disappearance.

Party government has spread everywhere as a result of the revolution of opinion regarding party. This striking change must impress the student of politics. When he reflects upon it, he will seek its origin, for the origin is a possible source of understanding which he cannot overlook. Some changes occur inadvertently and may be understood best by those who can use hindsight. Other changes are intentional, and may be understood better by their makers than by those who live with the result but do not reflect on the original alternative. The "founders of party," if we use the term precisely, would be the makers of this striking change, but we cannot decide whether they merit the title unless we know who they were and what their intentions were.

The purpose of this study is to explain the reasons why Edmund Burke undertook to present the first argument in Britain for the respectability of party. Burke's "Thoughts" contains the first such argument anywhere since Machiavelli's *Discourses on Livy*.[2] We do not intend to make a psychological analysis of Burke's argument or to seek out reasons for his argument other than those he gave or implied. If Burke's reasons are inadequate, their inadequacy should appear after full consideration, and they should be replaced by a better argument. Nor do we intend to trace the influence of his argument in British politics from its appearance to its adoption by the Foxite Whigs and the successors of Pitt. Since this study is about Burke's political philosophy and the origins of party government, its premise must be that these two topics are connected. The premise is that party government is chiefly a matter of opinion regarding party, and that being a matter of opinion, it is a cause of argument. It follows that in order to understand the origins of party government in Britain, one must give the most studious attention to Burke's argument in favor of party.

Previous studies of the origins of party government in Britain have not accepted this premise and have not adequately considered Burke's argument. They have sought the origins of party government in the origins of the Whigs and Tories or in the coming of democracy to Britain or in the first toleration of opposition. Although these opinions will be treated in the interpretation of Burke's argument, it is proper to introduce them here as challenges to the premise of this study.

Whigs and Tories

The names "Whig" and "Tory" date from the Exclusion Bill crisis of 1680–81. In the attempt to exclude the Duke of York from the throne, the Earl of Shaftesbury gathered his adherents in Parliament and led them in the elections fought on this issue. The King organized his forces in defense of his prerogative, and the two parties collided in full view of the public. "Never before had political clubs existed with so elaborate an organization or so formidable an influence," says Macaulay; and henceforth "Whig" and "Tory" "spread as widely as the English race," to "last as long as the English literature." Churchill says, more explicitly, "There had been *sides* in the Great Rebellion; henceforward there would be *parties,* less picturesque, but no less fierce."[3] The careful organization, the demagogic tactics, and the discipline of the first Whigs under Shaftesbury have recently been described by J. R. Jones, and the Whigs' anticipation of modern methods made clear. But these first Whig partisans were too eager and their Tory opponents too reluctant for the settled impermanence and comfortable oscillation of party government. Neither party was willing to accept the right of the other party; and no party leader, Shaftesbury included, meant to sustain permanently the organization and the discipline required for the success of the event.[4] The Whigs brought forth the Exclusion Bill to meet an emergency, and always meant their party to die when success had been achieved. Charles II copied the Whigs in their methods and in this intention. For both sides, party was an emergency resource never intended as a fixture in the public constitution.

Moreover, this issue was resolved in 1689, when a bill excluding Catholics from the throne was passed as part of the Revolution Settlement. The issue had been lost to the King's party in 1682, but it was not then resolved. James II, using his prerogative to advance the cause of Catholicism, strained the loyalty of the Tories and made the Whigs rebellious. After three years of such rule, having disgusted his friends and emboldened his enemies, he quit the throne and left the makers of the Revolution a rare opportunity—the opportunity of resolving the issue on which the Whigs and Tories had first arisen instead of securing a partisan victory for the Whigs. It is generally recognized by historians that the Revolution Settlement was not a victory for Shaftesbury: for Macaulay, the hero of the Revolution is William of Orange, while, for Trevelyan, the spirit of the Revolution is the spirit of the "Trimmer"—of Lord Halifax, the celebrated antipartisan. Indeed, the Whig historians are disinclined to give credit to the makers of the Revolution for their artful use of this opportunity, and they do not sufficiently explain the secular principles which made possible a non-partisan resolution of the religious issues between the parties.[5]

In his "Thoughts" Burke presented the first argument in Britain for party government, but at the beginning of this pamphlet he alluded to the welcome fact that "the great parties which formerly divided and agitated the kingdom are known to be in a manner entirely dissolved."[6] The great parties to which he refers are the seventeenth-century parties which were divided on the issues of the divine right of kings, and of papacy and episcopacy. Burke implies that the dissolution of these great parties was necessary to the respectability of parties. It could not be respectable for gentlemen to join a party, much less to join different parties, until the parties had resolved these crucial issues. For Burke, respectable party government meant government by parties which were not great. Party government was based on the disappearance of the great parties. Although the party names and some of their practices continued, their essence was new: they were now, in some sense, small parties. To the extent that the Whigs and Tories accepted the Revolution Settlement, as they did increasingly through the first half of the eighteenth century, they disowned their inheritance from the Exclusion Bill crisis and became small parties.

The Revolution Settlement was the foundation of party government in Britain because it destroyed the basis of the great parties. The great parties did not just subside to the size and temper of the parties which are factors in party government; they did not become small merely because British statesmen were exhausted and disgusted by civil war and had decided to dispute over lesser matters for lesser prizes. They were made small by the settling of religious controversy and the plain rejection of the divine right of kings. The Sacheverell trial in 1710 showed that the issues resolved in 1688–89 could be raised again, and that *if* they were raised, they would be as hot as ever. The eighteenth-century parties were not lukewarm seventeenth-century parties; they were made on a new foundation.[7]

But only the foundation of party government was made by the Revolution Settlement. Although the eighteenth-century parties were small parties, they were not said to be respectable until the publication of Burke's pamphlet, some eighty years after the Revolution. Nor did this pamphlet immediately succeed in giving a better reputation to party. For a time the Rockingham party (and not all of its members at that) stood alone as the party whose doctrine was partisanship, making a record to show that parties can be lacking in greatness. It was not enough to destroy the basis of the great parties; it was necessary also to demonstrate two further points: that small parties would not become great by heating up the issues they raised; and that there was no harm in small parties—indeed, that there was even positive good in them. Burke's "Thoughts" is based on the Revolution Settlement, and on this basis he argues the two further points necessary to justify and to begin party government.

The Coming of Democracy

Another opinion sees the origin of party government in the coming of democracy to Britain. This is the opinion of M. Ostrogorski, a pioneer student of the history of party government, and of Max Weber.[8] They argue that the *ancien régime* in Britain was destroyed neither in 1688 nor in 1746 (the last defeat of the Stuart Pretender); it was destroyed in 1832, when the middle class first made its separate power felt in the passage of the Reform Act. Before 1832 there were parties of aristocratic groups (Weber calls them parties of notables), which were so restrained that their divisions did not disturb the harmony of society.[9] These aristocratic parties were sometimes annoyed by maverick Radicals in Parliament, but from 1750 to 1850 they were challenged by extra-Parliamentary reform movements such as the Wilkesite Society for the Defence of the Bill of Rights, the Protestant Association, the Catholic Association, Dr. Price's Revolution Society, the Anti-Corn-Law League, and many others. Historians have produced many studies of these movements, taking them to be precursors of democratic and socialist parties or early substitutes for such parties. Democracy and socialism were not willingly embraced by the aristocratic parties in Parliament, but had to be forced upon them. For some reason, however, the aristocratic parties did not resist to the point of civil war, as had the seventeenth-century parties. Instead, they accepted the opportunity to reach for votes from among those who had agitated against them, and they accepted the necessity of extra-Parliamentary organization to effect this purpose. According to Ostrogorski and Weber, the origin of party government is not to be found in the origin of the parties themselves but in the origin of extra-Parliamentary organization in the parties. They consider the origin of party government in the light of democracy and socialism and hence place emphasis on the organization of parties. Ostrogorski's book is entitled *Democracy and the Organization of Political Parties*.

Although this argument has been the occasion for many useful works on parties, it is unhistorical and misleading. It neglects the overriding concern of British statesmen in the seventeenth and eighteenth centuries regarding parties. Ostrogorski and Weber remark that there was an aristocratic party government in the eighteenth century, and they are not ignorant that there was no such party government in the seventeenth century. But they proceed as if this difference were made insignificant by the coming of democracy and socialism. Ostrogorski and Weber make the same error in regard to British politics that Anglo-Saxons are accused of making in regard to politics on the Continent: they underestimate the importance of the religious issue. They underestimate the importance of the settlement of the religious issue in 1688–89.

On the contrary, Burke referred to the religious issue when he called the seventeenth-century parties "the great parties." Hume also meant religious parties when he said: "Parties from principle, especially abstract speculative principle, are known only to modern times, and are, perhaps, the most extraordinary and unaccountable *phenomenon* that has yet appeared in human affairs."[10] With this uncharacteristic vehemence, Hume contrasted the parties of interest, found at all times, with the parties of (religious) principle, found only in modern times. The writings of Aristotle and Thucydides and of the ancient historians of the Roman Republic are full of the conflicts of the rich and poor, but almost silent about religious parties.[11] In a way, Ostrogorski and Weber, with their emphasis on democracy and socialism, are closer to the ancient view of parties than to the viewpoint of the early modern statesmen and political philosophers. But neither Greece nor Rome knew party government: even though the conflicts of the rich and the poor were the central issue of politics, their parties were never allowed respectability in the public constitution. Parties were considered fatal, not vital to the health of the regime; and the party conflict was fought fiercely in the belief that the bane of party could be removed with the defeat of the opposing party.[12] The philosophers who proposed a solution to the party conflict of the rich and the poor chose the remedy of mixed government, not party government. They mixed the parties into the constitution, hoping to settle their conflict by yielding something to the interest and opinions of each. In their proposals they tried to settle the conflict, not merely to reduce its scope; and they gave concessions to the parties in order to acquire their allegiance and to induce them to be parties no longer.[13]

Modern party government was made possible, in Burke's view, by the settling of the religious issue. Therefore modern party government presupposes the *raising* of the religious issue. It presupposes the existence, before the destruction, of "the most extraordinary and unaccountable" great parties, "known only to modern times." Further, we shall see by an examination of Bolingbroke's thought on natural religion that the religious issue, once raised, had to be settled in a certain way so that it would not be raised again. In regard to the religious issue, the "aristocratic" British parties of the eighteenth century were liberal; on this fundamental point they were all opponents of the *ancien régime*. It is generally agreed that in Britain both liberalism and party government preceded democracy and socialism and that the first British liberals were converted aristocrats.

When, on the Continent, the religious issue still lives to complicate party divisions on the social issue, how can it be supposed that in Britain the settling of the religious issue had no important effect on the consequent divisions over the social question? The *settling* of the religious issue in modern Britain could not be expected to have had the same effect as the *absence* of the religious issue in ancient party politics. According to Burke, the settling of the religious issue made party government possible in modern Britain. When considering the problem of party government, Ostrogorski and Weber begin with the derivative issues of democracy and socialism, issues which took their shape from the settling of the religious issue. Their study of the organization of parties needs to be supplemented by studies of early opinions about party government.

It may seem hard to accuse Max Weber of overlooking the importance of the religious issue in the coming of party government. He was the leader of the school of opinion which teaches that the modern world as a whole, including party government, grew from Protestantism or from certain Puritan sects. The "formal" freedom of modern government permits and encourages parties based on differences of principle which may develop from followings of charismatic leaders and which take the place of traditional groupings in traditional societies. Weber agrees with Hume that parties of principle are known only to modern times, but denies that they are unaccountable; instead, he argues that they are characteristic of modern government. Modern government is a consequence of modern beliefs, and in Britain modern beliefs are an outgrowth or an inheritance (it is not clear which)[14] of *one* of the great parties. Since modern British government has emerged from one of the great parties, the settlement of the religious issue in 1688–89 did not itself dissolve the great parties. It was merely the sign that the Puritan doctrine had been transformed. The doctrinal basis of party government was present in certain Puritan doctrines of religious toleration that had only to be secularized, somehow, in order to appeal to both of the great parties. These doctrines were, of course, not secularized by the religious Puritans, who were fanatics for toleration; nor were they secularized in the Revolution Settlement, which presupposed that they were secularized. Although Weber looked for this secularization in the doctrines of certain Puritan sects, he might have considered that a secular doctrine is needed to secularize a religious belief.[15] Because he believed that modern government results from an inner transformation of Protestantism, he did not consider the settling of the religious issue decisive. To Weber, the settlement merely signaled the success of the transformation.

The Toleration of Opposition

This argument leads to a third opinion: that party government arose when toleration of opposition was established. In this view, toleration of opposition is the secular product of religious toleration, and parties are secularized sects or congregations. The great religious parties became the parties of party government just as the idea of toleration was extended from religious to political freedom. The great parties were not dissolved but were rather worn down by the general disgust with the effect of theological rancor and enervated by the growing diffidence of their own members. Party government, in this view, is the result of disgust and diffidence—in sum, of disillusionment. The fanatics of the great parties opened their eyes to the consequences of their divine-right principles, for example, the threat of French domination in Europe, and began to doubt them. At first they did not abandon their principles, but they began to question their right to destroy opponents for the sake of their principles and began to concede the right of opponents to oppose.

At the same time, turning their attention to opportunities for commercial profit and to thoughts of secure advancement in the professions, the former partisans gave a calculating allegiance to a new political science of balance and maneuver. While partisan energies were otherwise employed, Locke, Halifax, and Bolingbroke took control of the opinions of statesmen and partisans and quietly stifled the source of partisanship, the Puritan and Stuart principles of divine right. Managerial politicians like Harley and Walpole replaced the thunderous statesmen of the seventeenth century and seduced the disillusioned partisans with petty favors and pettier promises. The Tories gradually lost their courtly principles as they joined in the general revulsion against James II. But in the new regime they held their old grudge against the Whigs, while they inconsistently clamored for equal privileges with the Whigs. The result was a composite: they kept enough old Toryism to maintain the two-party dualism of the seventeenth century but dropped their divine-right principles to insure the loyalty and harmlessness of their opposition.

Kurt Kluxen has made the most recent and complete presentation of this view.[16] It is on the whole a true picture, but it has two difficulties. In the first place, having accurately represented the managerial realism of the new political science, it neglects the confidence of that political science. The aim of Bolingbroke, on whom Kluxen concentrates his study, was not merely to quiet the conflict of the seventeenth-century parties; that would have been the aim of any reasonable statesman ruling a distracted people. Bolingbroke's aim was to make a society on rational principles, a new society not liable to the partisan conflicts inspired by prejudice, especially religious prejudice. The confidence of this purpose, in its way, was as high as the fanaticism of the seventeenth-century parties. As will be explained, Bolingbroke opposed the privileges of the ruling Whigs, not because he wanted similar privileges, but because he really believed that such privileges were unnecessary to the working of the constitution. He did not plan his opposition party as the first in a long succession of opposition parties, nor did he mean to be only the first opponent of government with the deliberate intent not to make himself a hero of the constitution. His party was, on the contrary, planned as the *last* party, the party whose aim was to destroy every future excuse for party.

Burke thought he saw the danger of this high confidence, and brought forth his argument for party government to prevent its evil effects. Thus in Britain the first argument for party government *was* produced by disillusionment, or by anticipated disillusionment. Burke was disillusioned with Bolingbroke's program for preventing all potentially partisan prejudices from influencing the British constitution. Instead of being disgusted with religious civil war, he was fearful of this thorough attempt to make religious civil war impossible. Kluxen's view does not account for the confidence which the first attempt to be thoroughly and unashamedly realistic inspired. Men who had this confidence led the opposition to party government as well as the opposition to the ruling Whigs.

Second, even if opposition be recognized as loyal and legal, this is not enough to establish party government. Opposition is loyal and legal in a free constitution, but not every free constitution has party government. Parties have been held by many to be the bane of free constitutions. After 1688 it was usual to look for methods by which opposition could be prevented from becoming party opposition. In the eighteenth century there was a distinction, familiar to readers of Namier, between legitimate opposition and "formed," or party, opposition.[17] Since Britain had a free constitution, it was thought respectable for a politician to oppose the king's policy; in Parliament he could speak to persuade others to his opinion and gather their votes against the king's policy. But in his dealings with the king, he was expected to grieve or sulk by himself. Any attempt to act with others in a "formed opposition" was considered an attack on the discretion of the king and was thought to be prompted by a desire for "place" or a disaffection with the constitution. A man should not obscure his own merit and the merit of his opinions by adding to them the influence of other men and their opinions; if he did, he confessed that he loved himself more than his merit. Not all politicians held this belief with full strictness, nor did all practice it. In a well-known constitutional incident in 1746; the Pelhams agreed to resign together, having secured the support of Pitt; and George II was forced to take them back on better terms.[18] But certainly a permanent or sine die organization of opposition was not considered respectable.

As long as these beliefs were dominant, the king could act more or less independently as his own prime minister, and the cabinet, led by *its* prime minister, could at best make an isolated attack on a particular position.[19] The Rockingham party, under the direction of Burke, was the first party to challenge the dominant opinion and adopt the permanent respectability of formed opposition. For Bolingbroke, formed opposition was justified only by the intent to remove every cause of such opposition. Thus the relation of opposition to party government is not simple; it is complicated by the difference between a tolerated, legal opposition and a respectable, formed opposition. Bolingbroke's program against the respectability of parties was an early and enthusiastic exercise of the right of legal opposition, which developed after the Settlement of 1688-89.

These three opinions, all contrary to the premise of this study, agree that the justification of party is only a response to the particular circumstances of the seventeenth and eighteenth centuries. Party government was not intended or planned or founded, they assert. It grew out of the conflict of the Whigs and Tories, or perhaps out of the conflict of the Roundheads and Cavaliers. It grew out of the secular democratic movements of the late eighteenth century and ultimately from the religious democratic movements of the seventeenth century. It grew out of the attempt of Tory politicians to make a place for themselves and their ideas in the essentially Whig regime established in 1688. From this common conclusion that party government is a response to circumstances, it follows that the study of the origin of party government is no great help to the study of party government now. Circumstances are different today, and we could only learn the extent of the difference by studying the origin of party government. In particular, the *opinions* of statesmen and political philosophers regarding party government would be impertinent today.

But if, on the other hand, the respectability of party did not simply succeed the practice of party, it may be allowed that party government was deliberately founded. If party government was founded when party was shown to be respectable and when this conclusion was agreed to by the ruling authorities, the opinions of the founders may be relevant today. If party government was at first an object of choice and chosen for particular reasons, those reasons may tell us something of the character of party government today. Our premise that opinions about party were once important implies that party government has an intelligible character and that because it has an intelligible character, it has in some degree a permanent character. In the American presidential election of 1960, for example, the religious issue was raised in the competition of the two parties. This was widely regarded as unfortunate, but why should it be so? An understanding of the religious issue in the origin of party government may provide an answer, not so much because we directly inherit that former experience as because the problem is similar. In any case, we do not wish to force the premise of this study on the reader by means of these brief objections to three contrary opinions. The purpose is only to gain his attention for the study which follows.

The Traditional View of Party

If it is maintained that party government was only a response to circumstances, there is still a possible argument for the importance of opinions on party. The decisive factor in the practice of parties before Burke's "Thoughts" was the operation of the traditional view of party. This view frowns upon party, but does not exclude the occasional use of party. It is compatible even with the habitual toleration of parties. Hence it may be inferred that the respectability of party was not a necessary response to the practices of parties, whether occasional or usual. The practices of parties could be understood and justified according to the traditional view without the respectability of party and without party government.

Rarely can one speak of *the* traditional view, but it is possible here. It is remarkable that before the late eighteenth century, statesmen and political philosophers were nearly unanimous in the opinion that party was evil. They thought that every society must be substantially free from dissent on some most precious topics; if opinions on those topics are questionable and liable to partisan division, it is vital that they be settled. But serious or "great" parties will be concerned precisely with those topics, and they must be avoided at any cost, save the sacrifice of principle. On the other hand, frivolous or "small" parties are dangerous and corrupting. They are dangerous because great divisions can grow from small beginnings, as, for example, in the disputes between the High-Heels and the Low-Heels and the Big-Endians and their opponents in the land of Lilliput.[20] Parties which manage to remain frivolous are distracting to serious statesmen, degrading to the innocent politicians whom they entice, and ultimately subservient to the irresponsible ambition of the politicians who profit from them. It is not where the serious issues are settled that frivolous parties cause no harm, but where there are no serious matters from which men can be distracted. Jefferson once expressed his hostility to light-hearted partisanship and doubted that it could remain light-hearted: "The good are rare enough at best. There is no reason to subdivide them by artificial lines. But whether we shall ever be able so far to perfect the principles of society, as that political opinions shall, in its intercourse, be as inoffensive as those of philosophy, mechanics, or any other, may well be doubted."[21] In sum, according to the traditional view parties are trouble, or they make trouble; and if not, they are inexcusable.

But the traditional view is not entirely opposed to partisanship. Party was excluded, as we have said, from the public constitution; but it was allowed a place in the private constitution, as a dangerous instrument which might serve the public good. Party was held to be an evil always, since, even at best, when it is adopted for good motives, it causes dissension and sets a bad example.[22] But there might come an occasion when this evil would have to be accepted in order to save the most precious principles of the regime. In 1757, Lord Hardwicke wrote that opposition parties are "the most wicked combinations that men can enter into, worse and more corrupt than any administration that I ever yet saw."[23] But he provided for an exception to this principle in case of absolute necessity, and he must have had in mind the conspiracy of the Whig and Tory lords against James II in 1688.

This must be a silent exception. Because early writers on party were so fulsome about its general evil and so reticent about its very infrequent necessity, they leave an impression of stuffiness and artlessness very annoying to modern students of party. Some modern students have therefore accepted the honor of having discovered party for contemporary political science.[24] But these students do not see the subtlety of the traditional view, whereby no responsible person would broadcast the workings of a dangerous instrument which he knew was likely to be misused—although he might have to use it himself. Such a person could *study* party, and thus, by separating himself from those who simply shun evil, become in a sense a member of a party. But he would not publish the results of his study, for they would indeed be useful to all, to good men and traitors alike. Yet good men, in the traditional view, would use party only to abolish the occasion for party. An open defense of party in general would therefore destroy the usefulness of party to good men and would serve uniquely the interests of evil men. In order to serve its occasional good purpose, party must be kept out of the public constitution. The traditional view of party was based on a naïvely strict distinction between public and private, as if what is for the public good could always be avowed in public; but it included a silent exception to serve knowing statesmen in emergencies. It was a view attuned to the practice of politics in a less confiding and less organized age.

Within this view there was a difference of opinion on what to do about parties, assuming that they were generally evil. The older opinion, described above, was that they should be suppressed; but certain modern political philosophers, Hume for example, argued that in a free country parties must probably be tolerated. Hume said: "To abolish all distinctions of party may not be practicable, perhaps not desirable in a free government."[25] *The Federalist* No. 10 similarly maintained that since the causes of faction are latent in human nature, factions cannot be suppressed without loss of liberty; they must be moderated in their effects. In both cases the opinion that parties may be tolerated is accompanied by an argument to show that they may be made and kept tolerable. Moderated factions and tolerable parties give free men a place to spend their energy while distracting them from worse mischief. From this standpoint, a society of moderated factions is far preferable to a lethargic, factionless society whose subjects grow dull or resentful.

But this toleration of parties is not the same as a belief in the respectability of party.[26] Even when the toleration of parties is thought to bring strength to a free state, the difference remains, for many a necessary activity is not considered respectable or fit for the public eye. The strength generated from tolerated parties is in any case not accountable to the parties themselves, which merely express the energy of free men, but to freedom as a principle. If the great parties could be made small and kept small by the extension of principles which allay and distract religious fervor, men could live freely without holding parties to be respectable. They could praise freedom without praising its most unfortunate by-product, parties; and they could be as alert to the dangers which come from the very principles of freedom as to those which come from outside enemies.

Acknowledging the difference between toleration of parties and respectability of parties, one might still assert that Hume's opinion is a temporary station in a progression from the suppression to the respectability of party. But Hume's opinion on the toleration of party is a *substitute* for the respectability of party; rather than a tentative new view, it is an accommodation to the traditional view of party. By demonstrating that parties could be tolerated without being held respectable, Hume's opinion made Burke's argument for the respectability of party harder, not easier. As we shall see, Burke's argument was directed against Bolingbroke's conviction that parties should not be tolerated; Burke thus seems to take Hume as an ally. But Hume repudiated the modern parties of religious principle. He tried to show that a difference of principle makes partisanship dangerous more surely than a conflict of ambition, whereas Burke tried to show that statesmen could act on principle only if they combined in parties. Both men desired a free constitution, which Hume thought must be defended *against* parties and which Burke thought could be defended only *with* parties.

One must therefore distinguish the foundation of party government from the beginning of party government. The foundation of party government, the Revolution Settlement which reduced the great parties to small parties, could justify Bolingbroke's opinion that parties were now intolerable, Hume's that they were now tolerable, and Burke's that they were now respectable. We conclude that the traditional view of party could hold its own against the practice of party and even against the developments which provided the foundation for party government. It had to be opposed successfully by a contrary view. That Burke's view of party succeeded the traditional view is no proof of its truth, since opinions do not always become dominant by superior argument. But after this introductory investigation one cannot say that argument was irrelevant to the origin of party government. The aim of this study is to know the arguments for and against party government as they were presented at its origin.

Moreover, the argument about party government is not settled, for the traditional view of party has not yet been overcome. It lives today in popular opinion, which distinguishes between "statesman" and "politician," and often uses "political" (in the United States) or "party political" (in Britain) as terms of opprobrium. Modern students of party oppose such usage as "an anomaly," "fashionable denigration" or sneering, and as showing a "moral bias."[27] Indeed, they offer their justification of party chiefly against its popular disrepute. One political scientist has said: "It was not until the present century that a sizable body of expert, respectable opinion arose confidently to assert that parties are a necessary feature of responsible popular government."[28] This statement has the character of a reassurance to popular doubts, suggesting that the people should bow to an opinion which is sizable, respectable, confidently stated in the twentieth century, and expert. The last quality seems to be decisive: the people are told that experts in political science have found that parties are necessary to responsible popular government. One may consider the truth of this expert finding by examining the political philosophy of Burke, who knew politics before party was respectable.

Statesmanship and Party Government

Burke so insisted on the distinction between reform and innovation that we dare not, without investigation, describe his argument for the respectability of party as one or the other. But if the existence of a change is established and its importance sufficiently suggested, we may inquire into the character of the change. The change Burke promoted was from statesmanship to party government. Statesmanship is the capacity to do what is good in the circumstances, a capacity in which men, as individuals, are variously accomplished. Since they are variously accomplished in this, they are unequal; and statesmanship is essentially an unequal capacity. As such, it must be defined by its best example, not by an average sample; for we cannot know what a statesman can do unless we know the limit of human capacity, that is, what a great man would do. The study of statesmanship is therefore chiefly the study of great men, and reliance on statesmanship is a reliance on the performance and example of great statesmen. The replacement of statesmanship by party is an attempt to avoid dependence on great men.

Burke was writing about Chatham when he said that acting in a corps tends to reduce the value of a distinguished individual, but he could have been writing about himself. He was a great statesman who sought not merely to reduce Britain's reliance on his single capacity, but to reduce her reliance on the capacity of any great statesman. He promoted this change by introducing parties into the public constitution, by making party government the respectable instrument of honest men of principle. Defining "party" as a body of men united on some particular principle, he made parties available to good men in association against bad men. But a principle on which good men can agree to associate publicly must be an honest principle, a principle which shocks no sensibilities and which sacrifices some of the clear discernment of an "individual who is of any distinguished value" to procure the association of good men. It is not that a statesman is unprincipled or above principle; it is rather that his principle loses its refinement in the translation to public speech, and thence to party program. In such translation, a principle must be defensible as well as practicable; and defensible not to a public ready to be impressed by great statesmen, but to a party eager to correct a seeming unconformity and to a public taught to reward partisanship. A party principle is necessarily attuned to lesser capacities than is a statesman's principle. Burke conceived the respectability of party because he was willing to accept the less exact principle in exchange for a lessened reliance on statesmen; for great statesmen are unreliable, at least in the sense that they may not always be available. Burke believed that the regularity of honest men could compensate for their lack of discrimination, and that party government could substitute for statesmanship.

The reputation Burke deserves as a founder of party government casts a shadow upon the argument he made for the respectability of party; for the founding of party government is not a partisan act, but an act of statesmanship. To understand this act, one must make a careful interpretation of Burke's "Thoughts," beginning with the surface appearance of the pamphlet. At the start Burke stated his reservations about intervening to divulge the cause of the present discontents, with some appearance of vagueness. Upon reflection, however, one may conclude that Burke's delicacy and vagueness are related and that he perpetrated a legend upon his eighteenth-century readers in order to make them act— not to a narrowly partisan end, but for the amendment of the constitution. He has used a statesman's rhetoric in describing a danger with a view to its remedy. But the essence of his remedy is to reduce dependence on statesmanship. Burke's argument in the "Thoughts" moves from statesmanship to party government, from its subtle and tentative beginning to the broad confidence and blunt proposal at its end.

The "Thoughts" is a reply; it offers a remedy to a danger of tyranny. Burke brought party to view as a defensive tactic. His antagonist is not named and has to be identified; we have supposed him to be Bolingbroke, through his influence upon "a certain political school" active in the 1760's. To know Bolingbroke's influence means to know his intention, and we find that his intention was to use party as an *offensive* tactic. But since the program of his party was hostility to partisanship, he intended only the respectability of his own party, and that only for as long as the corrupt aristocratic parties survived. Burke proposed the respectability of party to counter the menace of a party whose program was hostility to partisanship. His defensive conception of party more nearly resembles the modern democratic party system than does the single-party reform espoused by Bolingbroke. Yet in the conflict of Bolingbroke and Burke, implied in the defensive argument of Burke, is found the origin of party government in Britain. The programmatic aspiration of Bolingbroke's party and the settled responsibility of Burke's party system have endured as opposite and complementary elements in the modern democratic party system.

Having identified and examined Burke's antagonist, we can proceed to show how Burke's defense of party results from his participation in modern political philosophy, from his adherence to the doctrine of the natural rights of man. We find his conception of the British constitution to be popular government surprisingly like the popular government of *The Federalist*—modified, made elegant, and effected by the rule of gentlemen. Party, or the party system, is a remedy for the weaknesses of popular government and is suited to the modest political capacity of gentlemen.

But Burke the statesman, who introduced this change, did not consider that the constitution could continue indefinitely without other interventions from superior statesmen; the "rules of prudence" which permit the respectability of party are not so certain and effectual. Although there is a movement in the "Thoughts" from statesmanship to party government, there remains a tension between the two. In the last chapters we attempt to discover in Burke's other writings a reconciliation of these two principles, which Burke calls "actual virtue" and "presumptive virtue." Nowadays the problem of statesmanship and party government remains, but is hidden under the dominance of party government. The party system gets credit for statesmanship because statesmen must act in parties, and partisans believe that they have satisfied the claim of greatness when they have demanded party leadership. Let it be suggested that this problem is best studied at the time of the origin of party government, when the alternative was clearer.

CHAPTER TWO

The Statesman's Presumption

In studying the origins of party government one cannot overlook or treat lightly its original justification. For at its origins, party government is bound to be the conclusion of an analysis. Those who consider party to be a necessary instrument of free government must admit, as others will assert, that its necessity was first reached as a conclusion. Burke's "Thoughts" contains an analysis of a danger to the British constitution, and proposes remedies for the danger, of which party is the chief remedy. My interpretation will follow the course of Burke's argument from the danger to the remedy. In beginning a discussion of the danger, we shall suppose that Burke considers the British constitution to be a limited or constitutional monarchy, but a closer understanding of Burke's conception of the constitution will be required later.

Some interpreters and historians believe that Burke presents the danger to the constitution exactly as he sees it. But while they observe that his presentation is exaggerated, they conclude that his purpose is narrowly partisan.[1] According to our interpretation, Burke presents the danger as a "plan" by the court cabal, but he truly believes the danger to be the plausibility of a new theory of government. He exaggerates the "plan," but not for a narrowly partisan purpose. Burke's presentation (and that followed in this chapter) moves from a discussion of the particular danger of a plot, to the general danger of a harmful theory.

The first sentence of the "Thoughts" declares: "It is an undertaking of some degree of delicacy to examine into the cause of public disorders." The first impression one gets of the whole of the "Thoughts" is that Burke's description of the danger is vague. We believe Burke's "delicacy" to be the

20

cause of his vagueness, which is not, therefore, accidental, but intended and studied. His delicacy results from his conception of the statesman's presumption, that a danger be remediable. To present a danger as general may destroy the confidence (both of statesmen and in statesmen) required for the remedy of the danger; yet to present a general danger as particular invites ineffective and even exacerbating attempts at remedy. Burke's solution to this problem seems to be the vague presentation of a particular danger. His statesmanship must lack candor and use rhetoric.

Burke would admit that his pamphlet is rhetorical. It is not "honest history" or "scientific history" because Burke does not present what he sees as he sees it. Nevertheless, one must examine the court "plan" which Burke reveals as if he had meant it literally, in order to prove the existence and manner of his rhetoric. One must show that the "plan" is literally impossible. The more rhetoric uncovered by inquiry into the literal meaning, the further such inquiry must proceed, for well-made rhetoric has an exact relation to the truth, and contains more, not less, than honest history. Good rhetoric conveys the paramount practical problems of the time to its entire audience; and to the careful observer, it conveys also the background of these problems, the opinions taken for granted, and the things considered unchangeable. Its presentation is part of its content. For example, the "Thoughts" makes little reference to the relation between religion and party; yet, as we have seen, the very presentation of a general argument in defense of parties reflects Burke's confidence that the religious settlement of 1688–89 has succeeded.

A good contemporary political writing, because it is contemporary, distinguishes the paramount practical problems from their background. The contemporary writer is not tempted by hindsight, as is the historian, to blame statesmen for not doing the impossible or to excuse them for not doing the achievable. The contemporary writer keeps his attention on action, and hence on the limits of action. By engaging in politics, he reproduces the setting of politics for his later readers. They note, as we have noted, that after Burke welcomes the dissolution of "the great parties which formerly divided and agitated the kingdom," he proceeds to justify parties formed upon "some particular principle" to promote "the national interest." Such justifiable parties must therefore, in Burke's opinion, be small parties. His pamphlet does not have to be put in historical context; rather, the context of which Burke was aware, the dissolution of "the great parties," need only be revealed.

Burke's perspective may have been limited or erroneous, but one cannot properly substitute another perspective for it until his has been thoroughly examined. His mistakes may be enlightening; for they are mistakes within a political setting. It is well to know that parties were first defended in the belief that the serious conflict of religious parties could be avoided. The conflict of religious parties in Europe in the seventeenth century was succeeded by the conflict of racial and class parties in the nineteenth and twentieth centuries. In opposing Bolingbroke's influence, Burke partly foresaw the rise of class parties after the settlement of religious conflict. But if he had known the future course of party government toward racial and class conflict, it is very unlikely that he would have defended the respectability of party. He reacted against Bolingbroke's confident program for the abolition of party, but he confidently supposed that a system of parties would protect the British constitution from the danger of Bolingbroke's antiaristocratic program. One must reproduce Burke's confidence from his own account, in order to judge whether he was unfortunate or mistaken in what he expected from party government. He could conceivably have foreseen the coming of racial and class parties, which he would have abhorred; and if he ought reasonably to have foreseen them, his political setting was not as he supposed it. In studying Burke's account of the political setting of his time, as conveyed in the assumptions of his rhetoric, one learns to question that account and to seek the true limits of action in the eighteenth century.

The honest historian has the rewarding duty of reading Burke's pamphlet, even if it is rhetorical. He also has the duty of reporting that Burke's rhetoric is honest in its way. For while it is agreed that honesty demands speaking the truth, it is also admitted that not speaking the full truth is not necessarily dishonest or narrowly partisan. This must be recognized in order to understand Burke's "Thoughts." An honest historian can tell what he knows, but an honest statesman may well discover that "it is an undertaking of some degree of delicacy to examine into the cause of public disorders." One cannot dismiss Burke's rhetoric as misleading and prejudiced. One must be exact in order to prove its studied vagueness.

The Statesman's Presumption

In considering the delicacy, or difficulty, of Burke's enterprise, we find that he gives his own explanation:

> If a man happens not to succeed in such an inquiry, he will be thought weak and visionary; if he touches the true grievance, there is a danger that he may come near to persons of weight and consequence, who will rather be exasperated at the discovery of their errors, than thankful for the occasion of correcting them.[2]

But the "first study of a statesman" ought to be "the temper of the people." As the "temper" of the people might seem to be equivalent to the "opinion" of the people, Burke next examines their opinion:

> To complain of the age we live in, to murmur at the present possessors of power, to lament the past, to conceive extravagant hopes of the future, are the common dispositions of the greatest part of mankind; indeed the necessary effects of the ignorance and levity of the vulgar. Such complaints and humours have existed in all times; yet as all times have not been alike, true political sagacity manifests itself in distinguishing that complaint which only characterizes the general infirmity of human nature, from those which are symptoms of the particular distemperature of our own air and season.

The characteristic defects of the people's opinion explain further the delicacy of Burke's duty. The statesman, or the private man acting (in the spirit of the Riot Act) as statesman, will be thought weak and visionary if he mistakes those complaints of the people which are produced by the "general infirmity of human nature" for the symptoms of a "particular distemperature." Yet when he has found a particular distemperature, and seeks the cause of it, he risks offending persons of weight and consequence. Burke simply dismisses the complaints of the people as a guide to the cause of the present discontents. Such complaints are a hazard for the statesman if he takes them seriously, but they are not a cause of the delicacy of his duty. The complaints, or opinions, of the people are constant and indiscriminate; they cannot be the same as the temper of the people, which is the first study of the statesman.

Having dismissed popular complaints, Burke turns to the opinions of statesmen "in or out of power." All agree that there is "something particularly alarming in the present conjuncture." Next he lists some typical causes of distemper that do not exist in the present—the great parties, external calamity, new taxation, unsuccessful war. Hence the present distemper is strange. Burke asks the opinion of the ministers as to its cause, and in this case refutes them. He seriously considers their opinion, but not the people's opinion.

The ministers cite general, not particular, causes—those which pertain to general movements of events, not to single accidents. The causes they cite are so general that nothing can be done about them; even consummate wisdom is ineffectual against them. The increase of trade and manufacturing and the growth of empire have brought wealth to the British, making them a free people, insolent when they possess wealth, guilty when they lack it. Fortunately, it is beyond the power of the ministers to make the constitution unfree in order to restrain economic activity and colonization; and international events beyond their control have required the conquest of extra territories. A few libelers and disappointed politicians, who will be found in any society and whom a free society must tolerate, have been the immediate cause of the present distemper, according to the ministers. This analysis of the cause of the present distemper leads the ministers to "absolute despair," if they understand the extent of their assertions, or to "particular punishments," if they do not. In the latter case, the ministers foolishly suppose that by punishing "a few puny libellers," they can repair the deep flaws in the constitution which they have uncovered by their analysis. They are wrong, because "particular punishments are the cure for accidental distempers in the state."

Burke's treatment of the ministers' opinions can be regarded as an elaboration of the earlier explanation he gave of his delicacy. The ministers cite general causes without remedy, which ought to produce "absolute despair." They are "weak and visionary" in their attempts to understand the present discontents, because, like the people, they mistake the constant sources of complaint for the efficient cause of the discontents. They do not appear so weak as a private man like Burke, since, having power, they can disguise their weakness in harshness to the "few puny libellers." Guided by such an analysis, their remedy will fail. What is then the true cause of the present discontents, whose successful discovery will bring danger from persons of weight and consequence?

In the next two pages, Burke opposes the opinions of the ministers in every way except by proving them wrong. To understand the need for his delicacy, one must appreciate that the ministers' opinions are in a sense only too true. Burke objects, indeed, to the practical effect of their opinions. If their opinions are true, then the present temper of the people is very perverse indeed, and can only be remedied by poverty, renunciation of empire, and despotism. Particular punishments will not suffice to hold down this perversity, but will only inflame it. The practical effect of the ministers' opinions is to paralyze truly remedial action and to exacerbate the evil. According to Burke, the ministers hold their opinions "without much observation of our present disposition, and without any knowledge at all of the general nature of mankind."[3] The ministers, it seems, are more ignorant of the effects of their opinions than of the facts they observe. Indeed, their opinions may be partly right, to the extent that they point to a general cause of the present distemper. This distemper has a general cause, it can be supposed, but not exactly the one the ministers ascribe to it. They are not far wrong, however, for Burke takes seriously the opinion that the growth of wealth has brought dangers to the constitution. He seems to be in partial agreement with the ministers.

This impression is strengthened by considering the two apparent contradictions which next appear in Burke's introductory remarks. Burke says, in the discussion of the practical effect of the ministers' opinions, that particular punishments inflame "those heats which arise from a settled mismanagement of the government, or from a natural indisposition in the people"; this must be reconciled with his statement on the next page, and his assumption throughout the pamphlet, that there is settled mismanagement in the government as a result of the "court system." Is there settled mismanagement in the government? If so, how will any statesman's plans, including Burke's, help to cure it? If none will, why not rely on inconstancy as the "natural corrective of folly and ignorance"?

Between these two statements Burke inserts a discussion of the people's disputes with their rulers. In such disputes, he says, one's presumption must favor the people, for the people, unlike their rulers, have no interest in disorder. Their rulers "may act ill by design as well as by mistake." Burke does not explain this difficult distinction, but proceeds to cite the view of a ruler who was good by design, that government "foible et dérangé" brings on revolution by great men and that popular uprisings come from impatience with suffering rather than a desire to attack. That is, though the consequences are dreadful, on neither side is the intention wicked. This citation from Sully makes a suggestion contrary to Burke's introduction of it, for Burke implies that it is to illustrate a ruler's acting ill by design. Instead, it suggests that a well-meaning ruler, if "foible et dérangé," may bring on revolution. This quotation could also refer to a case of "settled mismanagement," since feeble rule might not arise from the accidental ineptitude of some ruler, but from a defective system. Burke then says: "If this presumption in favor of the subjects against the trustees of power be not the more probable, I am sure it is the more comfortable speculation; because it is more easy to change an administration than to reform a people."[4] Here Burke sets aside the truth of his presumption in favor of its comfort; he says that it is made for the sake of another presumption, the statesman's. When he attempts to understand events the statesman must presume that the events may be altered by possible action, like changing an administration, rather than impossible or very difficult action, like reforming a people. General causes of distemper seem to be the least remediable; therefore the statesman's presumption will especially conceal general causes by disguising them as particular causes. If Burke did ascribe general causes to the present discontents, we might expect him to disguise them in this way.

Two indications of such ascription have been uncovered so far: the phrase "without much observation" and the quotation (in French) from Sully. The phrase hints at Burke's agreement with the ministers that one general cause of the present discontents is the freedom of British society, combined with a "natural indisposition in the people." The quotation from Sully suggests that another general cause is feeble government, or "settled mismanagement." This general cause is disguised by Burke's introductory statement that rulers "may act ill by design, as well as by mistake." Feeble government makes great men revolt; Sully does not directly state that it also makes the people revolt. But "impatience of suffering" could be brought on by greater evils or by greater awareness of constant and general evils. A feeble government could increase the people's impatience by increasing the awareness of general evils—for example, by blaming the corruption of the people for their present distemper. Such blame renders the government more feeble both by paralyzing its will and by increasing the reaction of the people. If the people are told that they are corrupt from general causes, they may believe this and relax, or refuse to accept this and assign their discontent to false particular causes, with dangerous results. To act requires an interpretation of the cause of distress which permits a successful remedy. It is here that the ministers are wrong. To the extent that they speak the truth about present conditions, they worsen those conditions and paralyze possible remedies. They give an "easy" general view, which makes the appropriate political remedy difficult.

Of course remedial action must be truly possible for the statesman's presumption to be well founded. But what is truly possible may not be so if it is truly described in public. The use of rhetoric is clearly dangerous, as much to the good of the statesman who departs from the habit of true description as to the good of the country which he presumes to protect. Yet all practical men, and especially all statesmen, use rhetoric and sense its beneficial effects. The danger of rhetoric only enhances its beneficial effects.

The other rhetorical contradiction in the introductory section of the "Thoughts" concerns this statement: "It is very rare indeed for men to be wrong in their feelings concerning public misconduct; as rare to be right in their speculation upon the cause of it."[5] But we were told earlier that "to complain of the age that we live in, to murmur at the present possessors of power . . . are . . . the necessary effects of the ignorance and levity of the vulgar."

There is then more truth in the complaints of the people than Burke at first seemed to admit; their slight and ignorant *opinions* are simply misleading, but their *feelings* are accurate. The statesman must therefore judge their temper from their feelings. "The people have no interest in disorder"; their feelings are dependable when statesmen know to depend on them. Every people has its temper, its disposition, but it cannot be said that every people, or any people, has a natural indisposition. Any general cause of distemper that pretends to find a "natural indisposition in the people" identifies a danger impossible to remedy if it did exist. Thus the statesman who cites such a general cause invites failure and frustration. But in a limited monarchy, statesmen cannot blame the king, a person of weight and consequence, without seeming to undermine the constitution, and the temptation to blame the people is thereby the greater. A statesman should interpret every distemper as curable by something like a change in administration, because he can and must presume that the people are good.

This conception of the statesman's field of competence is more restricted than the classical conception of Plato and Aristotle. In one passage in the *Laws*, Plato makes a mythical presumption that rule is not dissolved except by the mistakes of the rulers. He does not wish to display the kinds of occasions on which rulers are helpless, since in displaying them, he would be offering the rulers a basket of excuses. Thus, in order to emphasize the responsibility of rulers, Plato argues the self-sufficiency of good policy—as if good policy did not have to be supplemented by good luck. Burke does not presume the self-sufficiency of virtuous rulers; he presumes that the people are sufficiently virtuous if they live under a free constitution. According to Plato, statesmen are blameable because it is presumed that every distemper of the people is curable. Plato's presumption is more exacting than Burke's, for Plato makes the statesmen responsible for producing a good people. Burke's statesman is held responsible for good policy because the people are already sufficiently virtuous.

According to Aristotle, the statesman, being superior in prudence to the people, sees more than they; in understanding and treating their problems, he is not bounded by their horizon. But the statesman's competence, in Burke's view, seems to be limited by the accuracy of the people's feelings; he may not and need not question this accuracy in his remedies for popular distemper. It follows that the statesman must presume more according to Burke than according to Plato and Aristotle. Since Burke's statesman cannot form the people's feelings, he must presume a good effect from actions which do not attempt to form or to educate the people.[6]

Hence the delicacy of Burke's duty. He himself is not an ordinary statesman; he is a private man acting as a statesman on an extraordinary occasion. The occasion is extraordinary because the usual remedy—a change in administration—is not sufficient; one symptom of the distress, indeed, is found in the very frequent changes of administration in the 1760's, seven in ten years. The general cause of distemper, "settled mismanagement," is not the result of a "natural indisposition in the people," but is beyond the usual recourse of ordinary statesmen. Burke seems to imply a distinction between ordinary and extraordinary statesmanship. His delicate task is to make an unusual problem seem usual, but to do so without denying the need for an unusual remedy. It is a problem beyond the competence of ordinary statesmanship, but he, a private man, must bring it within that competence. He himself does not require the statesman's presumption, which translates general causes into particular causes; but he must use it.

He must use it because "the generality of people are fifty years, at least, behind-hand in their politics."

There are but very few, who are capable of comparing and digesting what passes before their eyes at different times and occasions, so as to form the whole into a distinct system. But in books everything is settled for them, without the exertion of any considerable diligence or sagacity. For which reason men are wise with but little reflection, and good with little self-denial, in the business of all times except their own.[7]

"The whole train of circumstances" is given to men, "from the trifling cause to the tragical event," in a kind of authoritative history of the past. Using history as precept, the people speculate wrongly, relying confidently upon the absence (or shouting up the reappearance) of past symptoms of tyranny, such as ship-money, forest laws and the *droit du seigneur*. History might seem to solve the problem which the statesman's presumption uncovers by showing general causes as precedents, in the clothes of circumstance and patriotic remembrance. In this way history would "serve admirably to reconcile the old quarrel between speculation and practice." But those who have faith in the precepts of history seek to soothe the false despair induced by easy generalities with a mistaken confidence in the efficacy of precedent. The general causes of the present discontents, to which the ministers reason so quickly, can be stripped of their desperate import by reference to these precedents.

Belief in the authority of history results in a form of theoretical delusion, in which historical precedent serves the same misleading function as general causes do in the ministers' opinions. It restates rather than solves the problem of the statesman's presumption. It is the statesman's duty to avoid misleading historical precepts and to see the cause of *present* misconduct. But ordinary statesmen will not always be able to see this cause, since there are "but very few" who can "form the whole into a distinct system." Ordinary statesmen sense the need for rhetoric and for a diagnosis which will permit proper action. But they share the confidence in history which the people have and cannot supply the need for rhetoric that they sense. Burke's duty is to fulfil the statesman's duty when the ordinary statesman cannot fulfil it. In doing so, he must allow for the propensity of both ordinary statesmen and the people to understand present events in the terms of authoritative books. He must present the menace of "influence" in terms of the menace of "prerogative"—that is, as a cabal. "A great deal of the furniture of ancient tyranny is worn to rags; the rest is entirely out of fashion." Burke's rhetorical task is to make some furniture of tyranny, credible for the present because wrought in a recognizable style of the past, yet not so familiar as to dispel alarm.

To summarize: The beginning of the "Thoughts" subtly develops the subject of the delicacy of the statesman's duty; at the same time, it is a rhetorical *repetitio* on that subject, reiterating the need for caution. The development occurs by a kind of dialectic between particular and general, through three stages of explanation of the need for delicacy: first Burke's insistence on the need for delicacy, then the people's opinion of the cause of the present discontents, and finally the ministers' opinion. In discussing the delicacy of his task, Burke says that success in defining the cause of the present discontents is possible; he distinguishes the appearance of failure (seeming weak and visionary) from the consequence of success (coming near to persons of weight and consequence). The alternative is a feeble generality or a dangerous particular. He dismisses the people's opinion of the cause of the present discontents because it does not distinguish between the general infirmity of human nature and the particular causes of distemperature. And he refutes the ministers' opinion because it produces a dilemma—either general causes without remedies, leading to despair, or particular causes met by punishments, leading to frustration. The *present discontents*" are manageable because they seem to be temporary and because they have one "cause." In Burke's seemingly uncontrived "Thoughts," the single cause of the present discontents is between particular and general: it is "settled mismanagement," as he says so precisely. Burke must allow for the unreliability of the people's opinions on the cause of public misconduct by supplying a particular recital of signs of this mismanagement that the people can interpret. Thus, in the beginning, Burke has established distinctions between the people and the statesmen, and between Burke (or those like himself) and ordinary statesmen.

The Plan of the Court Cabal

The introductory part of the "Thoughts" consists of Burke's remarks on current opinions about the cause of distempers; his own analysis of the cause occupies the body of the pamphlet. This analysis identifies the cause as a "plan" or "project" by a "court cabal," "a certain set of intriguing men." But Burke is reluctant to identify the planners and concludes only that the court cabal has instituted a new system of policy. He supplies a vague narrative of the plan, which hints at occurrences known to all public men of the time, as though the new court system were a particular distemper, curable by something like a change in administration. Such a change would of course have re-established the Rockingham party in power, as an appropriate remedy for a particular distemper. But Burke's remedy is in fact a general recommendation of party, and he recommends the Rockingham party only as an example of a true party. The historians who think that Burke actually believed the new court system to be the instrument of a squad of plotters, ambitious in the ordinary way, reduce the generality of his suggested remedy and identify his motive as narrowly partisan.

It can be shown, on the contrary, that Burke was proposing a constitutional remedy for a general danger produced by a new theory. This theory, not the malevolence of plotters, has created the new court system. This theory threatens the constitution by virtue of its plausibility to both the people and public men. The "plan" is a rhetorical device contrived by Burke in accordance with the statesman's presumption that the people are good or good enough. Instead of attacking their gullibility, he represents the plausible theory by a "legend" (to use Namier's term) so that they can understand its evil intent and effect. The legend reads like a plot, in order to respect the statesman's presumption; yet the plot is never so specific that the Rockingham party can think to oppose it merely by replacing the present administration. The legend appears to be particular but only vaguely so. It is impossible if taken literally; yet it is carefully constructed for this delicate rhetorical effect. To prove this interpretation it is necessary to regard briefly the surface of Burke's whole analysis of the cause of the present discontents.

We return to the beginning of that analysis. Contrary to the misleading assurance of history, there are now new means and objects of ambition. We have to do with the politics of our own age only, or with particular evils. Yet the examples Burke gives of particular evils—ship-money, forest laws, and the *droit du seigneur*—are signs of tyranny so obsolete as to cause us to wonder whether more consequential evils may be more enduring. The constitution is now mature, but even so it might suffer from the same kind of attempt that was made on it while it was maturing, if not from the same attempts. Burke next compares the power of the crown as "prerogative" with its power as "influence," and the very comparison supports this supposition. The "power of the Crown" is the obvious similarity in "prerogative" and "influence"; but Burke chooses to state the differences between them. Surprisingly, he says that influence is now stronger and less odious than prerogative, which was the instrument of tyranny in the seventeenth century. Moreover, Burke seems to account influence as the more general danger, since it is based on "the interest of active men," while prerogative requires the support of "antiquated prejudices." "The ignorance of the people is a bottom but for a temporary system; the interest of active men in the state is a foundation perpetual and infallible."[8] Indeed, it is accidental, he says, that influence has *not* been a danger since the Revolution, after which the new court was obliged to seek support from the established aristocracy. Thus Burke introduces a new form of an old evil by emphasizing the difference between the new and the old, and yet manages to suggest the similarity. By following Burke's rhetoric, the reader would begin to understand the cause of the present discontents so as to seek the remedy that Burke has in mind. The reader would say that the present danger is influence, which is dangerous in the same way as the cabal that encouraged abuse of the king's prerogative, but which is remediable only in some new way.

Burke then describes a plan aimed at the fortunate partition of influence, since the Revolution, between the king and the great aristocratic party leaders. "To get rid of all this intermediate and independent importance, and *to secure to the court the unlimited and uncontrolled use of its own vast influence, under the sole direction of its own private favour*, has for some years past been the great object of policy."[9] In what follows, Burke is almost obtrusively vague. He continues to describe this "plan," always in the passive voice, often in a conditional tense, usually omitting any reference to the "planners." But who are they? "This project, I have heard, was first conceived by some persons in the court of Frederic of Wales." Burke identifies them by hearsay and to this extent only. Frederick is now dead, and his is the only name mentioned.

Is Lord Bute, the King's favorite, the planner? Consider this statement:

The earliest attempt in the execution of this design was to set up for minister, a person, in rank indeed respectable, and very ample in fortune; but who, to the moment of this vast and sudden elevation, was little known or considered in the kingdom [Bute]. To him the whole nation was to yield an immediate and implicit submission.

It looks as though Bute is not the planner; others have set him up. But then the plan is curious, indeed foolish. Others set up Bute, but Bute receives the "immediate and implicit submission." Bute is then in a position to remove these mystic planners when they become embarrassing and dangerous to him—a result that they could have easily foreseen. True, they abandoned this "earliest attempt," but not because it was foolish in this way. We may note that the foolishness in this gift of submission applies to any plan that seeks to make a puppet of the apparent wielder of power by giving him real power (that is to say, without retaining a greater terror against him). Any such "planner" except the King himself would be clearly unwise. But if the King plans to use Bute simply as a tool of despotism, how does influence differ from prerogative?

The plan, if taken literally, is next revealed as still more evidently foolish. The "reformed plan," Burke says, draws "a line which should separate court from ministry." But if Bute was "set up," if he is "the instrumental part of the project," the "reformed plan" is the unreformed plan "a little altered": both use puppet ministers in the same way. This fact accentuates Bute's meekness in resigning the "immediate and implicit submission" due him under the unreformed plan—an unwonted meekness, for Burke says later that the court system arose "not solely" (that is, partly) from Bute's ambition.[10] We cannot take this plan at face value because Burke leaves it ambiguous whether Bute is the puppet-wielder or the puppet. He seems to conclude that Bute is only a puppet, but the plan makes sense only if Bute is its projector.

Nor does the King seem to be the plotter of the court scheme. Burke declares that the scheme was "not implausible," but that it was favored by "inviting opportunities," by particular circumstances.[11] What were they? Burke lists in the next paragraph merely those opportunities favorable to the King, or to his successful and lawful rule. Then he says that though these were "singular advantages" for the King, they provided others with opportunities for power which "they could never hope to derive from natural influence or from honorable service." How are these advantages of the King transformed into opportunities for a court faction?

The cause seems not to be the malevolence of the King, for Burke explicitly excludes it: "These singular advantages inspired his Majesty only with a more ardent desire to preserve unimpaired the spirit of that national freedom to which he owed a situation so full of glory."[12] But praise of the monarch, even in a constitutional monarchy, may not mean what it says. It is usual to blame the king's ministers when it is impossible or undesirable to blame the king. Although Burke had no hopes for preferment at court in the forseeable future either for himself or for the Rockingham party, he might prudently have supposed that a change in the political situation could leave his party the least obnoxious to the King, and so Burke had a possible motive for flattery. Yet if he merely wished to keep himself "in the distinction between the virtues of the King and the vices of the Administration," like his fellow Rockingham pamphleteer William Dowdeswell,[13] it was unnecessary to contrive and elaborate the distinction between influence and prerogative. It is usual to blame the king's ministers, but not to blame a court *system*. Moreover, in Burke's report the conception and operation of the court system are not flattering to the King's understanding, and in his correspondence Burke strongly implied that the King was weak and inexperienced.[14] His true opinion of George III is shrouded in the prudence of flattery or of simple self-protection. It is probable that he regarded George III as inspired or infected with a blameable ambition, since George III must have been at least a coadjutor of the promoters of the court system. If influence is far less odious than prerogative, it may be that the influence of the king, unlike his prerogative, can menace the constitution in the absence of malevolence, or of obvious malevolence, on his part. The question of George III's participation in the court system can be left to later consideration, which will justify the possibility that Burke was sincere in praising the King's ardent desire to preserve the national freedom.

Influence has "in itself a perpetual principle of growth and renovation," because it is founded on "the interest of active men in the state." But since this "certain sort of statesmen" is in constant supply, their ambition alone would not suffice to transform the advantages of the King into opportunities for faction. The particular cause of this transformation, Burke seems to say, is a new principle, different not only from the "antiquated prejudices" of the people but also from the prevailing opinions of public men. "In order to facilitate the execution of their design, it was necessary to make many alterations in political arrangement, and *a signal change in the opinions, habits and connexions* of the greatest part of those who at that time acted in public."[15]

Next come remarks on the altered political arrangements of the new system—its attack on Mr. Pitt, and, through him, on the great Whig families. Here Burke refers to actual events, of course, but his vagueness remains; again he conceals the authors of this change by using the passive voice. In the following five pages he takes up the arguments of the cabal—arguments of "supernatural virtue" addressed to the people; "other methods" applied to "individuals," against which Burke urges the success of the previous reign; and arguments about the growth of aristocratic power, designed to alarm the people. The arguments of "supernatural virtue" have as their purpose "to reconcile the minds of the people to all these movements. . . ."

Burke then calls attention to a certain pamphlet: "In this piece first appeared the first dawning of the new system; there first appeared the idea (then only speculation) of *separating the court from the administration;* of carrying everything from national connexion to personal regards; and of forming a regular party for that purpose, under the name of *king's men.*"[16] Again he seems to confront us with a particular cause of the discontents; the "plan" now has a specific source, in this pamphlet. But it is noteworthy that Burke now identifies a speculation as the source of the new system. And the distinction between the original and the reformed plans should not be forgotten. Burke had said that the "first part of the *reformed plan* was to draw a line which should separate the court from the ministry." The separation was then part of the reformation, but this statement directly contradicts the words quoted above, in which the "first dawning of the new system" (the unreformed plan) is simultaneous with the idea of separation. This contradiction deserves attention, as it may be deliberately rhetorical rather than accidental. The later statement is part of the explanation of how the cabal is reconciling the people to its changes. The cabal's arguments would follow the institution of the plan, since they would be designed to persuade the people to accept it— unless the plan, from its commencement, required a "signal change" in the opinions of the people, as well as those of public men. If such a change were required, then we could understand how the public justification of the new system is said to be the source of the new system. The reference to this pamphlet leads the reader to expect the naming of the plotters, but the succeeding discussion of the pamphlet draws his attention to its arguments. The fact that Burke discusses the pamphlet's arguments is curious for this reason: plotters are liars, and to become entangled in answering their lies is to risk losing the opportunity for countering their deeds. Burke's entanglement with this pamphlet suggests that the arguments of the plotters are more than the ordinary effort of rascals to justify themselves publicly and nearer the center of the present menace. It suggests that these arguments constitute a problem not to be dismissed, for it is no ordinary rascality which attempts to form a "regular party" and which in consequence requires a "signal change in the opinions, habits and connexions" of the public.

Burke's meaning develops in his discussion of the pamphlet. He does not explain how it has "all the appearance of a manifesto preparatory to some considerable enterprise." He does not describe a particular plan, such as he had himself previously described, found in the pamphlet. On the contrary, far from presaging profound change, he says that it contains principles designed to appeal to the "credulous morality" of good souls. According to Burke, these principles are arguments to the vulgar; they charm everybody but a few.[17] They are plausible and familiar, not newly created. If, as Burke says, this is the "first" appearance of these arguments, their first appearance may well be merely their first recent recurrence. Since the pamphlet was written with "no small art and address," it is necessary for the few "who are not much pleased with professions of supernatural virtue" to expose it as such. But then the pamphlet cannot be the source of a plot, in the usual sense, for to advertise a new system by concealing it with plausible and familiar arguments is certainly blunted subtlety. It may be concluded that the "professions of supernatural virtue" are not merely the ordinary pieties of scheming ambition, though Burke does not mind that they appear as such.

After the arguments used for the new system, Burke discusses the nature of the new party for two pages, then speaks in the usual vague terms about its actions for another two pages. In this section, too, the "plan" as represented is incredible:

> The machinery of this system is perplexed in its movements and false in its principle. . . . The plan proceeds *expressly* on the idea of enfeebling the regular executory power. It proceeds on the idea of weakening the state in order to strengthen the court. The scheme depending entirely on distrust, on disconnexion, on mutability of principle, on systematic weakness in every particular member. . . .[18]

If avowed, these are not plausible principles: who would announce that he wishes to enfeeble the regular executory power? But Burke has said that the arguments of the cabal are plausible. He apparently follows the method we have sketched: he seems to attribute the danger to ordinary ambition, acting within a new system, because an ordinary plot is remediable within the statesman's presumption. Burke's description has a kind of counterplausibility; he makes his opponents' plausible argument implausible, but unnoticeably, by the plausibility of his own argument. Burke does not describe evil without a view to its correction. His account of the court cabal therefore describes the vague outline of a plot which is neither strictly defined nor capable of strict definition.[19]

In his treatment of Lord Bute, Burke makes clear that this effect is intended. Bute was the most prominent object of the people's blame; he was scorned and castigated in the more popular opposition newspapers and pamphlets. Hence, if the people are rarely right in their speculation on the cause of public misconduct, he should be released scot free, almost without trial. Burke claims the personal attacks on Lord Bute are petty and dangerous, asserting that "much the greater part of the topics which have been used to blacken this nobleman are either unjust or frivolous." Indeed, he says that "we should have been tried" with the court system without Bute, and will be so tried when Bute is dead.

Burke then states the cause of the present discontents, instead of providing his personal reflections upon Bute, the "supposed head" of the court faction: "It is this unnatural infusion of a *system of favouritism* into a government which in a great part of its constitution is popular, that has raised the present ferment in the nation."[20] Bute "communicates very little in a direct manner with the greater part of our men of business. . . . It is enough for him that he surrounds them with his creatures." Thus, contrary to what some historians have supposed, Burke himself did not believe (whatever others believed) that Bute managed the court cabal "in a direct manner." Bute's creatures were not his tools, but his imitators, or, at most, his advisees—men who supported the idea of administration by "insulated individuals." Burke's frequent references to the "Bute party" in his correspondence before 1770 are to those who obey Bute's principles, not those who yield him "an immediate and implicit submission."[21] It may be repeated that Burke does not wish to dispel the impression of conspiracy which he has built up with his rhetoric. But Burke's understanding of the danger to the constitution, we may note, seems to concentrate upon the idea of administration by insulated individuals.

Judgment by Appearances

Shortly after his treatment of Bute, Burke says: "They who can read the political sky will see a hurricane in a cloud no bigger than a hand at the very edge of the horizon, and will run into the first harbour."[22] A cloud no bigger than a hand is not itself dangerous; its tendency is dangerous. Yet on the next page Burke's rhetoric comes to an evident climax. "We are at present at issue upon this point. We are in the great crisis of this contention; and the part which men take, one way or the other, will serve to discriminate their characters and their principles." He had just spoken of the need for the "natural strength of the kingdom" to interpose "to rescue their prince, themselves, and their posterity." Here is the appropriate place for Burke to direct the enthusiasm he has aroused and to provide masterful inspiration, hustle in the storm—to give names and objects. But precisely here Burke offers nothing particular to aim at; he leaves an impression of fuzziness; he sloughs his point.

Burke's treatment of Wilkes follows this pattern. He seems to endow Wilkes, a particular person, with capacities and opportunities that the depth of his concern for the present discontents contradicts. He apparently supposes that the cabal, in opposing Wilkes, establishes by open intention a principle which he elsewhere fears it establishes by plausible misdirection. This principle, "that the favour of the people was not so sure a road as the favour of the court even to popular honours and popular trusts," is not plausible as a declared intention of any cabal. Burke has identified it as a precedent drawn from the treatment of Wilkes, yet he reports it as a precept, as if someone had intended to teach it openly. But if this principle is not plausible as the cabal's open intention, the people must be still under the spell of plausible precepts. If so, however, the following cannot be true: "This gentleman [Wilkes], by setting himself strongly in opposition to the court cabal, had become at once an object of their persecution, and of the popular favour."[23] If the people are fooled by the cabal, Wilkes cannot become popular for the sole reason that he opposes it. It is Burke himself, not "the contrivers of the scheme," who exposes the court system "in all its nakedness." It is he who connects the popularity of Wilkes with the court system by (apparently) reporting the hidden intention of the court party as a public precept, so that the indignation of the public regarding Wilkes can be represented as more perceptive than it truly is.[24] He makes the people believe that they were combating an implausible principle, which has in fact been made implausible by Burke's description of it.

Near the middle of the "Thoughts," while describing the effect of the court system on foreign relations, Burke narrates an actual incident involving Lord Rochford and Lord Shelburne. He does not delight us with the patient detail of honest history, but he does openly relate a particular transaction, as he does nowhere else in this pamphlet. Still, it is not a transaction that is solely particular, but rather "of this nature." "Lord Rochford, our ambassador in Paris, remonstrated against the attempt upon Corsica, in consequence of a direct authority from Lord Shelburne." But the French minister treated Rochford's remonstrance with contempt, because he knew from his ambassador that Shelburne was not supported by the rest of the administration. The French ambassador had reported the private disagreements of the British ministers—disagreements Burke assigns to the present court system—to his government. Hence these disagreements indicate the character of the present British regime, or the private character of the British constitution. Using this information, the French minister acted so as to make the private character of the constitution public: "By this transaction the condition of our court lay exposed in all its nakedness."[25]

If this nakedness is bad, why then does Burke himself expose the private character of the constitution—both in this instance and generally? In speaking of the incident involving the French minister, Burke says: "I represent this matter exactly in the light in which it has been universally received." But "the light" on this matter comes from Burke's description of how the private character of the constitution really works through the court system. To say that this is an example of authority undermined, which is how the matter would be "universally received," is much less than to show at length what Burke shows—that a court system can corrupt the entire government and cover its own deeds with specious pronouncements. Burke is uncandid, and even worse, he appears to be irresponsible by his own standard.

This difficulty is repeated at the conclusion of the sketch of the court system, where he says: "whether all this be a vision of a distracted brain, or the invention of a malicious heart, or a real faction in the country, must be judged by the appearances which things have worn for eight years past."[26] Readers are to judge by the *appearances* of things; they will get the truth from the appearances, from the apparently true. But throughout this pamphlet Burke has cast doubt on the appearances of the constitution and has exposed the plausibilities of the new court system. And in the next sentence but one, he refers to "those who compose all the exterior part of the present administration," thus revealing that their power cannot be judged by appearances. Burke's own speech makes the standard he offers for his speech seem dubious. How is it possible to judge truly by appearances?

To judge by appearances is to judge by the appearances as Burke presents them. Already the court faction has had to make itself public to some extent—for all its plausibilities—having evidently changed at least the former tenure of the ministers: "The people, without entering deeply into its principles, could plainly perceive its effects, in much violence, in a great spirit of innovation, and a general disorder in all the functions of government."[27] Burke helps to publicize the court faction by exaggerating it, but only up to a point. If the reader regards the state of the British constitution as it appears in Burke's pamphlet, he sees a new situation of extreme danger; but Burke refrains from calling it tyranny. Since so many actions of the court faction are characteristic of tyranny, the characteristic degeneration of monarchy, this omission should not go unnoticed: it means that Burke believed that the British constitution is remediable in its present form. It is not yet necessary to try merely to improve a tyranny *qua* tyranny, to make it milder without challenging its basic form. Indeed, one should say that Burke is attempting to *anticipate* tyranny. His rhetoric exaggerates the present development of the danger in order to sound an alarm, yet it minimizes the ultimate stage of the danger, in order to respect the statesman's presumption. For if the cause of the danger is a plausible new principle, then the people are at fault for their susceptibility to this principle. When Burke's chief remedy, his conception of party, is examined, it will be seen that it is justified for the same reason as is his rhetoric on the cause of the present discontents: party will also help to anticipate tyranny.

It is now possible to summarize the political understanding which guides Burke's rhetoric. In general, remedial action requires blaming particular causes. Yet in this case it requires that many people be made aware of a danger so that they will do something. Therefore the particular cause of the evil must be widespread; it seems to require more for remedy than particular punishments. Contrary to what one might suppose, Burke gives *more* evidence than is strictly necessary to show that the constitution is in danger. The wise man sees the hurricane cloud on the horizon, but those whom he must persuade do not. Thus Burke exposes the court system by exaggerating it, an action which, in the best case, may be irresponsible. But the present situation is not the best case. The statesman, or the private man acting as statesman, must intervene to protect the constitution; this he does by using a rhetoric that tends to change the character of the constitution and by exposing the private working of the constitution to the public. The statesman would not make this intervention, however, if he could not also propose a remedy—party—which counters the revealed danger by amending the public constitution. The statesman, or the best statesman, need not himself judge by appearances; but he must expect that others will.

We have seen enough to conclude that Burke's purpose in writing the "Thoughts" was not, in the narrow sense, to further the interests of the

Rockingham party.[28] There are two letters that confirm this conclusion. In one letter Burke warned Lord Rockingham that the publication of the "Thoughts" (then imminent) "must put you on Terms irreconcileably bad, with the Court and every one of its adherents" without conciliating the other opposition. The "Thoughts" would help to keep the Rockingham party out of power.[29] Since a partisan purpose, in the narrow sense, involves seeking office, Burke did not have such a purpose.

Burke also wrote that the "Thoughts" contained the "political creed of our party."[30] The manuscript was passed among members of the Rockingham party for comments, and Burke apparently made some changes, perhaps in accordance with these comments. But that the "Thoughts" was not an ordinary party document is shown by a letter to Burke from his friend Dr. Leland, kept and annotated by Burke, and now among the Fitzwilliam manuscripts at Sheffield. Dr. Leland wrote:

C. O'Hara in a conversation in Mount Gall.[agher] naturally asked if I had received and read the Thoughts etc. My answer was accompanied with a criticism I shall not repeat; qualified, however, with one remark, that in my opinion the business of a House of C. had some little effect on the style of our friend, for that in a few places the phraseology was not as elegant as usual. I was directed to ascribe this to the very extensive communication of the work, and the author's admitting some insertions from other hands: and it provoked me, I confess, that when he accepted the thoughts of other people, he should not take the trouble of giving them his own colouring.

Over the line reading "extensive communication of the work," Burke wrote: "No such thing Dr Leland! every word bad & good his own"; and over the line reading "he should not take the trouble of giving them his own colouring," he wrote: "No such thing!—E. B."[31]

This evidence confirms what first acquaintance with Burke would suggest—that he was using the Rockingham party for a statesman's purpose more than he was being used by them for their party purpose.

CHAPTER THREE

Bolingbroke's System

Burke's purpose is to oppose the menace of Bolingbroke's idea of the Patriot King by a new remedy, that of party government. In this chapter and the next, we shall try to prove that, in Burke's view, Bolingbroke's theory is the cause of the present discontents. This is not an improbable thesis, since other interpreters have in a general sense advanced it;[1] it must be proved, however, because Burke does not mention Bolingbroke in the "Thoughts," although he does mention "that political school," whose connection to Bolingbroke will be shown.

Bolingbroke is the author of "A Dissertation upon Parties," the most prominent work on parties extant at the time that Burke wrote the "Thoughts," which was almost the first work to recommend parties. Bolingbroke is also the author of the pamphlet called "The Idea of a Patriot King," which advanced an idea supposed by George III's contemporaries to have influenced him, and the "Thoughts" concerns the court system established by or through George III. Moreover, in Burke's first published work, "A Vindication of Natural Society," he parodied Bolingbroke's principles, as he said in the preface to the second edition (and there only), by demonstrating their threat to established civil society. These facts establish that Burke was thoroughly familiar with Bolingbroke's writings in general, and that he would have had them particularly in mind while composing the "Thoughts."

Our proof that Bolingbroke's theory is the cause of the present discontents has two parts: first, the common ground between Burke and Bolingbroke, that "the great parties" no longer exist, must be shown;

41

second, the arguments which follow from this common ground must be compared.

The disappearance of the great parties of the seventeenth century followed the removal of the religious issue from British politics (or its reduction to manageable importance) in the Revolution Settlement of 1688–89, secured by the last defeat of the Stuart Pretender in 1746. The removal of the religious issue from politics was prepared and facilitated by various kinds of natural religion proposed to subdue the conflict caused by revealed religion, of which Bolingbroke's deism was one. But Bolingbroke's deism was connected to a political system, the idea of the Patriot King; and we are contending that Burke referred to this system when he attacked "the professions of supernatural virtue" used to recommend the court system. The opposition between Burke and Bolingbroke can be shown only by further consideration of the importance of the religious issue for the origin of parties in Britain. This aspect of party origin has been generally slighted in favor of a feeling of relief that modern parties are not divided by a religious issue. But it is impossible to understand the success of modern parties, and therewith the issue between Burke and Bolingbroke, without considering the religious issue as it affected parties.

The Entire Dissolution of the Great Parties

The novelty of Britain's political situation in the 1760's was a commonplace of that decade. Burke also gives the reasons for this novelty without argument. The first reason is itself a commonplace: "The great parties which formerly divided and agitated the kingdom are known to be in a manner entirely dissolved."[2] This and the other reasons are the "singular advantages" of George III at his accession, advantages not possessed by any of his predecessors since 1688. According to Burke, these advantages were seized by the court faction as an opportunity for a new kind of aggrandizement; according to Burke's opponents, they were welcome as an opportunity for a new kind of reformation, the court system. Besides the dissolution of the great parties, the singular advantages were: George III's succession as the third Hanoverian king, which could attract the zealots of hereditary right; his inheritance of a war in which Britain was everywhere victorious; the absence in him of "foreign habitudes or attachments"; the utter defeat of the Pretender; an ample revenue for the civil establishment; the extended influence of the crown; and the absence of any reversionary hope for opposition.

Sir Lewis Namier has given his opinion that the political situation of the 1760's was new only for the reason last named, and hence only moderately new.[3] This last reason may be briefly explained; Burke does not do so because it is second nature to those who live under a monarchy. In a monarchy, those who oppose the reigning king seek the protection of royalty in some form, in order to avoid the suspicion and the injustice of disloyalty. Consequently, they seek the protection of the heir apparent. In Britain's constitutional monarchy, the opposition sought such protection more openly than in stricter monarchies; and after a period of disgrace, in which the leaders of the opposition unrepentantly attempted to demonstrate their indispensability to the reigning king, they sometimes forced their way back into favor and exchanged the protection of a potential king for the protection of the actual king. Thus occurs a confusion of paternal and political power. Since the king has political power, he cannot relinquish his paternal power when fathers normally do; and while the prince frets under an unusual paternal dominion, he is teased further by the prospect of his succession and by the flattery of his father's opponents.

This defect is inherent in hereditary monarchy but was exaggerated in Britain's constitutional monarchy. The residence of the Prince of Wales was actually the avowed meeting place of opposition to all the Hanoverian kings; and the Hanoverians always had especially bad family relations, even for royalty, because the weakness of the king's political power made a show of the weakness of his paternal power. The quarrels ceased in the nineteenth century, when the king lost nearly all power to extend favor and the opposition turned to the people for protection.

But in 1760 George III had succeeded his grandfather, his father having died in 1751; and there was as yet no reversionary resource against him (a defect he soon and amply supplied). According to Namier, this circumstance sufficiently explains the novelty of the political situation. As George III had no sons and had inherited his father's resentment toward his grandfather, he was free to be more impetuous than his Hanoverian predecessors. This impetuousness held no danger of tyranny; it was only an expression of normal resentment by means of an abnormal freedom. There is no need here to examine Namier's argument in detail, for he admits what was asserted by Burke and generally admitted at the time, that the "great parties" of the seventeenth century were "in a manner entirely dissolved."[4] In the context of heated party conflict, however, George III's inherited resentment would have been more dangerous than Namier believed it actually was. George III would have used the angry passions of others to gain his own satisfaction; or he would have been caught in those passions, and his normal resentment, however excusable, would have produced an explosion. The dissolution of the great parties is necessary to Namier's opinion that the absence of reversionary resource explains the novelty of the political situation in the 1760's.

We have discussed the meaning of the dissolution of the great parties, but what is meant by the *entire* dissolution of the great parties? Their conflict had been settled in 1688–89, but the Settlement was insecure for two generations. There was a Stuart Pretender, who had supporters in Britain and encouragement from Europe; there were numerous Tories, who had as much or more difficulty in forgetting that they had been losers as the Whigs had difficulty in forgetting that they had been winners; the throne passed to a new line of succession, a foreign line too; and the policy of Britain was, until 1713, deeply involved in the very Continental war from which the Pretender had most to hope. The guaranty against these uncertainties was the continuance of power in the Whig ministers, the lineal or political descendants of "those great men" (as Burke called them in the "Thoughts") who had made the Revolution and the Settlement of 1688–89.

But the need for this guaranty showed that the Settlement had not yet completely succeeded. On occasion the Whig ministers shouted up these insecurities, perhaps only to serve themselves; still, the success of their argument, sincere or not, is evidence for the danger they claimed, and they were successful as long as they could provoke a Tory snarl. The trial of Dr. Sacheverell in 1710 (of which Burke made artful use in his "Appeal from the New to the Old Whigs") was the most notorious proof that the party opinions of the seventeenth century were merely suppressed, not effaced. The *entire* dissolution of the great parties in 1760, with all their vestiges, meant the complete success of the Settlement of 1688–89. Burke's list of the singular advantages possessed by George III indicates this success, for each item refers to the removal of a trouble which had resulted from Britain's seventeenth-century conflicts. From 1760 on, the Settlement of 1688–89 could be taken for granted; it no longer had to be defended.

This event, and the common realization of it on all sides, created the novel political situation of the 1760's. On one side, it provided a new opportunity; on the other side, it brought a new danger. The supporters and students of Bolingbroke saw an opportunity to institute his non-party government, as the condition which he had long claimed to exist in reason —the entire dissolution of the great parties—had at last become manifest in fact. Their actions and their plans impressed Burke and those whom he influenced as a new danger, one more insidious than the forthright tyranny of the Stuarts and no less harmful. In Namier's view, there was no danger of tyranny in the 1760's because there was no sign of Stuart tyranny in rebirth, because "the great parties" were "known to be in a manner entirely dissolved." He failed to notice, however, that a serious conflict was possible about the meaning of the Settlement of 1688–89. In Burke's mind, it was precisely because the new enemies to the constitution recognized the Settlement that their plan was more plausible and more dangerous than the Stuart tyranny. The new enemies did not bring out the "ancient furniture" of tyranny as a signal for "retrospective wisdom and historical patriotism." They made their plot in private, but announced it to the public as a reform long overdue. The great parties formed on the religious issue having departed, a new division over the rule of gentlemen arose. It was born not as a residuary of the great parties, but by virtue of their departure.

We turn now to that part of Bolingbroke's system which is based on the dissolution of the great parties, in order to identify the issue between Bolingbroke and Burke.

Do the Parties Have Real Differences?

"A Dissertation upon Parties" first appeared in 1733–34 as a series of letters in the *Craftsman,* a periodical founded and maintained by Bolingbroke to express vehement opposition to Walpole's ministry. The letters were then published together in 1734, with a sarcastic dedication to Walpole in the form of an introductory letter. In this introduction, Bolingbroke announces that the purpose of his work is "to explode our former distinctions." Former distinctions are considered to be the cause of present distinctions, or parties; and parties are the cause of the corruption in an otherwise excellent constitution. The "Dissertation" discusses the history of the great parties of the seventeenth century, with many comparisons to present politics. Like other writings of Bolingbroke, it is so frequently pointed to differences with individuals that it must be excursive. Yet Bolingbroke is always mindful that his policies are generally applicable, since they are based on "first principles"; so he gives to his allusions appropriately lofty expression, not so much to conceal them as to dignify them. The superior tone of this introduction, typical of his political and even of his philosophical writings, foretells his political program; and if the introduction to the "Dissertation" is compared to the beginning of the "Thoughts," the issue between Bolingbroke and Burke becomes almost sensible.

Bolingbroke is a private man, like Burke, and unlike Burke a former exile; but he has none of Burke's caution in presenting his opinions to the public, that is, to those in power. Private persons "may represent such things as they judge to be of use to the public, and may support their representations by all the reasons that have determined their opinions." "Let them stand or fall in the public opinion, according to their merit."[5] Private men of ability who wish to offer free advice to "persons of weight and consequence," as Burke called them, need not be delicate. Bolingbroke believed that such an offer could be unwelcome only to a corrupt minister, one as blinded to the claims of merit as he believed Walpole to be. Bolingbroke speaks to Walpole as the minister Walpole should be and is not; obviously, he does not speak to Walpole, but to "public opinion," to the "wisdom of the nation assembled in parliament." Burke finds a semi-legal justification in the Riot Act for a private man to speak without being called upon; he first (briefly) considers the ministers' opinion of the cause of the present discontents as a "compliment due"; and he does not blame the King or the ministers for the court system, though he sharply attacks the opinions on which the court system is based. While protecting the presumption in favor of the people's feelings, Burke addresses the ministers as though they were open to persuasion, despite the private opinion in his letter to Lord Rockingham that they could not be fully persuaded. His principle seems to be that men in power *must* act on prejudice if they are to rule in accord with popular feeling, and yet they may be partly open to persuasion if approached with caution: "Nations are governed by the same methods, and on the same principles, by which an individual without authority is often able to govern those who are his equals or his superiors; by a knowledge of their temper, and by a judicious management of it."[6] It seems that the prejudices of ministers must have the same respect that ministers must have for the prejudices of the people. Respect for prejudice seems to be the distinguishing character of public speech, no matter who speaks, for all speech in public is, in the decisive sense, official or ministerial. Yet respect for prejudice is possible because prejudice can be judiciously managed when popular feeling, which is reliable, is distinguished from the crude and obsolete speculations of the people. It is clear that ministers and those who presume to advise them must not share the speculations of the people. Whether, in Burke's view, they can share in popular feeling while managing the popular speculations must be left open for the moment. Burke appears to have a complicated respect for the prejudices of the ministers and the people, with regard to their feelings and speculations. Bolingbroke implies that the "public opinion" can, in principle, adopt the most meritorious private opinion, and that in consequence, there is no excuse for a minister who does not welcome advice, and no respect due to him if he does not.[7]

These remarks on prejudice are not merely introductory, for the status of prejudice is nothing less than the theme of Bolingbroke's "Dissertation." The purpose of the "Dissertation" is to show that the seventeenth-century divisions were real and the seventeenth-century parties excusable, but that since these divisions have been resolved, there is no excuse for the eighteenth-century parties. In explaining the history of these real and apparent party divisions, Bolingbroke is faced with the following difficulty: If there were real differences in the seventeenth century, how could they have been completely resolved in the Settlement of 1688–89? Resolvable differences are, in a sense, not real differences. On the other hand, if there were no real differences in the seventeenth century and the Settlement was therefore possible, what accounts for the difference between the serious seventeenth-century parties and the frivolous eighteenth-century parties? Bolingbroke puts the difficulty in this way: Can a prejudice make a real difference? That is to say, is a prejudice real? This metaphysical or epistemological question is a matter of very practical concern for Bolingbroke, as can be seen in his explanation.[8]

"It is a certain truth," Bolingbroke says, "that our religious and civil contests have mutually, and almost alternately, raised and fomented each other."[9] The origin of the parties in Britain is neither in religion nor in Christianity simply, but in the absurd system of divine right first broached by "that anointed pedant," James I. The principles by which James I governed aroused opposite principles, more frenzied and more evil in their application, under the Commonwealth, when Parliament was thought to rule by a different divine right; but James I was the original cause of the parties, because he introduced a real difference between them. The Restoration was a reaction against the Commonwealth, and therefore did not fully reconcile the parties: the religious differences were not settled and the king's prerogative was again too high. Nevertheless Bolingbroke says that in the years 1660–80 the court and country parties were re-established.

According to Bolingbroke, the existence of the court and country parties is in a sense the normal situation under Britain's free constitution. The country party is authorized by the voice of the country, and it is formed on principles of common interest, not on particular prejudices directed to particular interests. "A party, thus constituted, is improperly called party; it is the nation, speaking and acting in the discourse and conduct of particular men."[10] This party represents the united nation and will prevail sooner or later in a free constitution. The court party is formed on the particular interests of the court, which, as Bolingbroke makes clear in "The Idea of a Patriot King," are not the true interests of the king. Since it has a false basis, the court party is only temporary; the country party is the only legitimate party, and thus is not properly called "party." Yet there is a sense in which the coexistence of the court and country parties is normal, for there are always men of ambition eager to serve themselves in a court party, and up to now there have been untaught monarchs ready to employ them. When the constitution is in a healthy condition, it is without parties; but the constitution in its present spirit has an endemic susceptibility to the formation of a court party, and the interests of the nation must be frequently called to life as the country party.

But whereas the danger from the court party is manageable, the danger from political-religious parties is extreme. These parties are based on real differences, for they divide the country party. This was done twice in the seventeenth century; for the first time the country party was divided into Cavaliers and Roundheads by the absurd notion of divine right, the second time, during the Exclusion Bill crisis, they were divided into Whigs and Tories by apprehensions of extremism. Bolingbroke says that Whigs and Tories were not really Roundheads and Cavaliers:[11] they were imagined to be so, and the country party was split by this apprehension, as if by the right to anticipate harm from a supposed enemy. But the conduct of James II was sufficient to cure the folly of party, that is, to reunite the country party. In the Revolution of 1688 "both sides purged themselves . . . of the imputations laid to their charge by their adversaries." Whigs and Tories had never been what they had accused each other of being, but "even the appearances were now rectified."[12] It would seem, then, that the Whigs and Tories existed only from 1680 to 1688. Yet Bolingbroke says that "the ghosts" of these parties (parties which were in their heyday only "appearances") "have continued to haunt and divide us so many years afterward"; and he even says, contradicting himself, that the Whigs and Tories "kept up the appearances" of their old animosity after 1688.[13] In sum, the real differences between the British seventeenth-century parties were produced by the original folly of James I in choosing the absurd system of divine right as the ground of his rule. This choice brought about the apprehensions which split the country party. These apprehensions were at first justified, but as Britain experienced the folly of divine right and the divisiveness of partisanship, the just apprehensions of divine right were laid to rest and the apprehensions of the opposite parties were exposed as unjust. Real differences between parties are based on just, or at least excusable, apprehensions of danger to a free constitution. The differences become less real—or more ghostly—as they become less excusable.

Parties became inexcusable after the Settlement of 1688, and they have since maintained an unnecessary existence. The Revolution began a new era, because in principle it reunited the country party on a permanent basis. This is a Whig basis, it should be noted, for the Whigs had always professed the principles which paved the way for the Revolution, while the Tories only *acted* on those principles in the event.[14] But if the Whig principles were (in the main) the principles of the Revolution, and if those principles were permanent, then the Whig principles must be true. Bolingbroke does not hesitate to say, "the present constitution of the British government" is "agreeable to nature and the true ends of government." "Our constitution is no longer a mystery; the power of the crown is now exactly limited, the chimera of prerogative removed, and the rights of the subject are no longer problematical, though some things necessary to the more effectual security of them may be still wanting."[15]

The British constitution can be based on true principles because these principles can become "the very genius of a people." Bolingbroke's belief is evidently in the tradition of Hobbes and Locke, who argued that civil society can be based on a general recognition (within natural law) of the right of self-preservation, which is deduced from the true nature of man. As one's natural right of self-preservation is easy to see or to claim, according to these writers, the belief that a society can be founded on truth cannot properly be called intellectualism, except by comparison to a later irrationalism. Bolingbroke did not intend by this belief to give a new freedom to intellectuals for the discussion of those beliefs which a society might adopt as truth. True principles which became available to the common understanding would be indisputable; the people would not have to tire or tease themselves with philosophy.

It does not follow, however, from the difference between a true constitution and the disputation of party intellectuals that Bolingbroke's system was an obstacle to party government as it is understood today. The widespread opinion that party government developed as men gradually appreciated the need for a loyal opposition must be re-examined. Bolingbroke was perhaps the most vehement opponent of party government in British history; he went so far as to deplore his own party administration of 1710–15.[16] Yet he held a version of a belief which made party government possible, the belief that a society can be founded on true principles, or "first principles." But it is necessary to know what Bolingbroke thought these principles were in order to see how party government developed from them.

First Principles

Bolingbroke's discussion of first principles is presented posthumous-
ly in his four *Essays on Human Knowledge* and in his *Fragments or Min-
utes of Essays*, both of which were "thrown upon paper in Mr. Pope's
lifetime, and at his desire," during the years from 1727 to 1733. First principles are laws of nature which constitute an obligation on men insofar as
they desire to preserve themselves and to be happy; and men do desire
their preservation and happiness so strongly that they can be said to be
determined by the desire for them. Men have natures that make them
men; there is such a thing as human nature. But this nature is a law according to which men have been made, for men are creatures. Natural
law is the same as the order of Creation and was given at the time and in
the process of Creation. Natural law is therefore the same as natural religion. To understand natural law is to have an awareness of the order of
Creation, of the "system of nature," of the reasons why things and beings
have been made. To understand natural law is to know God, as much as
men can know Him. Men have an incomplete knowledge of God, because
they cannot know the entire system of the universe; there probably exist
beings on other planets who have a greater, if still incomplete, knowledge
of God. But men have been dignified above other creatures known to men
by the gift of that reason which allows them an awareness of natural law,
or natural religion. It would be clearly false and presumptuous to suppose
that men are God's favorites, for other animals have reason. But only men
have the power of generalizing ideas, and consequently may have a reasoned awareness of their obligation as God's creatures.

The assertion that natural law and natural religion are identical is the
essence of Bolingbroke's deism.[17] When men examine nature, "the aggregate of things which are" or "the immense aggregate of systems," they become convinced that it was made by an infinite power and wisdom. "A
multitude of things, which might be made in manners and placed in positions almost infinite, are so made, so placed, so contrived that they are
visibly appropriated to the particular uses to which they serve, and to no
other."[18] The works of God give us the ideas of *infinite* power and wisdom
because they surpass all the bounds of human conceptions. Every new
discovery of natural philosophy (or science) confirms this infiniteness by
surprising us with the previously unknown relations of things. Bolingbroke believes that men are able in this way to see further than they can
conceive.[19]

"Right reason consists in a conformity with truth, and truth in a conformity of nature."[20] But right reason discovers a kind of determinateness in nature, in which a multitude of things that might be anywhere are, by their relations with each other, placed where they have a single, visible use. It does not find a kind of inherent reasonableness, in which heterogeneous parts show their place in the whole by exhibiting the differences among them. Right reason finds a pattern, an arrangement of pieces—the evidence of a unified, rational will—rather than an anatomy of organically related parts. Because the system of nature is mechanical and contrived, understanding nature is like understanding a machine. To learn the purpose of the artificer one attempts to remake the artifice—to experiment; one does not merely admire an eternal whole which consists of unmade, or self-generating—and therefore immutable—parts. That is why men discover the Lawgiver in the laws of nature.[21] They see the result of a systematic will, systematic so that it can be completely or infinitely wilful; the infinite wisdom of God is a consequence of His infinite power. They do not see an inherent reasonableness which is striking precisely because it could not have been made. It follows also from the infinite power of God that He must be one; and Bolingbroke's deism is accordingly monotheism.

Natural religion is for Bolingbroke a *deduction* from Locke's theory of ideas.[22] Bolingbroke records his general agreement with Locke's theory in his first essay on human knowledge. There are no immutable essences—no perceptible species for theoretical understanding, no moral essences for practical purposes. To Locke, human knowledge consists of complex ideas collected from simple ideas and made by the human mind. Bolingbroke asserts, against Locke, that complex ideas are real (not fantastical) when they are copies or archetypes of things existing in nature, and he means moral ideas especially. Locke had said that complex ideas, except those of substance, were not copies of anything.[23] Bolingbroke agrees with Locke that moral knowledge is as capable of real certainty as mathematics, but the reason is not the necessity that moral and mathematical truths (being archetypes of the mind's own making) represent themselves accurately. The reason is that both the moralist and the mathematician have copied their abstractions from prior observations, that murder is wrong and that a circle is round, made before they turned moralist and mathematician.

Bolingbroke is willing to say that archetypes of complex ideas exist in nature because he is willing to argue that nature has been made systematically by God. True natural religion is so obviously distinguishable from Christian scholasticism that it is not necessary to fear that archetypes will be mistaken for visible species. Bolingbroke argues as follows: There is no "nature" in the Aristotelian or scholastic sense of immutable essences; yet there is order in nature. Therefore, order has been created. The creator of this order is too marvelous in power to be human; hence God is the first (efficient) cause of the system of things. The second order of causes, which is composed of actually visible causes, originates with God.

Locke had not deduced a natural religion from his theory of ideas; he wrote an essay, *The Reasonableness of Christianity,* to show which parts of Christianity appear most reasonable in the light of natural law. Bolingbroke, however, makes a flat distinction between those parts of Christianity which are true, and consequently natural theology, and those parts which are mere "artificial theology." Artificial theology, according to Bolingbroke, was invented by ancient philosopher-legislators who became priests because they wished to add "the sanction of revelation to the dictates of right reason." They adopted "the distinction of a public and a secret doctrine"; the public doctrine of systematized superstitions was used to reform the manners of half-savage peoples and the secret doctrine of true monotheism was reserved for the few initiates.[24] This distinction had its excuse in early times, but the public mysteries have since supplied the interests of priests. Their authority has been placed beyond public accounting, becoming an *imperium in imperio.*[25] Christian priests, from St. Paul, have followed the teaching of pagan philosophers and imposed mysterious inventions, such as the doctrine of the Trinity and the "trite ceremony of baptism," on the simplicity of true Christianity.[26] Scripture, or perhaps only the gospel, contains the word of God. But even Christ had to speak with some reserve for political motives, and the darker passages leave the authority of Scripture merely probable, when compared to the "certain" and "obvious" law of nature.[27] Inspired by the clear visibility of natural religion, Bolingbroke felt obliged to criticize the complications of artificial theology. He blamed the modern philosophers who had made wonderful discoveries in corporeal nature for not broadcasting the discrepancies between their discoveries and biblical history.[28] In particular he blamed Locke for supposing that morality must be supported by the impressive untruths of artificial theology.[29] All men are capable of attaining a sufficient knowledge of natural theology and religion, that is, sufficient for what seems most important to each.[30] Contrary to Locke's *Reasonableness of Christianity,* Bolingbroke asserts that artificial theology hinders, not helps, reason in its struggle with the passions.[31]

It follows that Bolingbroke delivers "the whole truth of things as it appears to me"; for no distinction between public and private doctrine is necessary when a society can be founded on truth. Metaphysics has been exposed as jargon in modern times, Bolingbroke says; but modern philosophers, having begun by exposing metaphysics, have too often ended with it. With natural religion, as with political parties, there is no excuse for error; so error is greater when it has been created by some philosopher or scientist. Natural law lies open to all. There is no need for "Locke, that cautious philosopher" to seek the reasonableness of Christianity, because a man does not have to be a careful student in order to know the law of nature, as Locke had thought.[32] The plain man is a better philosopher than the supposed philosophers, for he does not push his inquiries beyond the "phenomena" of "corporeal nature." The great modern philosophers, from Bacon and Descartes, were needed to counter the jargon of the scholastics, but the findings of these modern philosophers have, in a sense, emancipated the ordinary man from the need of philosophy other than natural philosophy, or science. It must be said that Bolingbroke speaks in the spirit of this new freedom, very confidently and very loosely. The society founded on true first principles dispenses with both artificial theology and its parent, philosophy. Since the foundations of natural theology are found in natural philosophy, society cannot dispense with scientists, for only from modern science can men learn that "phenomena" and "corporeal nature" exist and that the sky is not the ceiling of the world. What Bolingbroke sometimes calls "common sense" and praises as "right reason" would be more accurately called elementary modern science.[33]

Men can know the works of God, not the nature of God; they can reason a posteriori from the works of God to the will of God, not a priori from His nature. God has made the universe for the sake of the universe, Bolingbroke says, not only for men. God is not immediately present in the operations of nature, but has left the things of nature mutable by men according to the systems of nature. There is then a general providence of God for the universe, not a particular providence for a favored species or for favorite members of that species. As the universe is not made especially for men, they cannot justly complain of what seems injustice to them.[34] The general providence for men provides for men in societies, not for individuals, because in Bolingbroke's opinion, as we shall see, men are social creatures. God has given men the means of attaining happiness through government; and when men fail to found government on first principles, they suffer unhappiness, which is the general and necessarily indiscriminate sanction of the law of nature. In this respect Bolingbroke distinguishes moral from technological progress: they do not vary inversely, but their manner of advance is opposite. Technological progress proceeds from the individual inventor to mankind, whereas moral progress requires government and proceeds from the society to the individual. The sociability of men, their need for government, seems to be a result of the generality of God's providence. Apparently Bolingbroke reasoned a posteriori from the sociability of men to the generality of providence, since it seemed clear to him that men can survive and be happy only in a mass and on the whole. Nature's god has allowed men to appreciate this essential fact of their situation and so elevated them above the merely instinctual species. But what men have to appreciate is that this god cares nothing for individual men but provides only for the species, not exactly in the same way as for the other creatures, but in societies.

The natural sociability of man is the most interesting feature of Bolingbroke's first principles. It is his greatest difference, as he sees it, from Hobbes and Locke; and his confidence in natural religion, which was not fully shared by Hobbes and Locke, is derived from his belief in the sociability of man. According to Bolingbroke, men have never been "savage individuals" or "solitary vagabonds" in a state of nature such as Hobbes and Locke suppose. Society is coeval with man in the form of families, however men began:

> If there was a first man and a first woman, they and their children (for these could not nurse and educate themselves) must have constituted a first society. If numbers of men and women sprang out of the earth at once, there might be some contests among the men about these primitive ladies, and some violence might be employed, and some confusion might arise in the immediate hurry of copulation. But after that the same instinct which had caused variance would have formed societies.[35]

The instinct of self-love, as one sees in this elegant presentation, was manifested at first as the desire for pleasure. Though reason was present in men from the first, since intelligence cannot spring from non-intelligence, the instinct of "self-love begat sociability."[36] Families kept men out of the state of individuality which Hobbes and Locke thought of as their state of nature. Bolingbroke agrees that the natural state of men is prepolitical: natural society or government is to be distinguished from civil society or government, because civil society is formed by consent and is therefore artificial. Locke sometimes acknowledged that paternal government had preceded civil, Bolingbroke says; but Locke reasoned about the institution of civil government as if consent had been taken from individual men.[37]

In fact, consent was taken from individual *families,* for individuality is the consequence of sociability, Bolingbroke believes, not the ground of sociability. Men are individuals only in the sense that they are collected into societies—familial or civil—which are individuals to one another. Civil societies were born when families were united with each other and the consent of the family government accepted for the consent of the family members. A state of war is not the cause of forming distinct societies—again, either familial or civil—but the effect of forming them; and a state of war among families is apparently the cause of civil society, in Bolingbroke's view. Nature instituted the family through instinct and directed men to civil society through reason. Men are not by nature political, but they are directed to civil society by nature. Bolingbroke quotes with approval the statement in Aristotle's *Politics* that says the first governments were kingly because they grew out of families. By analogy to Aristotle, Bolingbroke says that "man is a religious as well as a social creature,"[38] and for him man was a religious creature *because* he was a social creature. Natural religion could not be convincing to men if it did not apply to men, if the law of nature did not manifest the providence of nature's god over men. But since nature directs men to government, the necessary means of survival and happiness, God's providence is sufficiently attested. The reader of Bolingbroke can sense his satisfaction that he has made every concession to modern political philosophy in respect to nature's inhospitality to man but has concluded that nature (and hence God) nevertheless provides the remedies for the evils it has imposed.

The purpose of nature is sufficiently revealed in nature, Bolingbroke believes. In summary, his reasoning is that nature is beneficent because it is intelligible to men; but there is no intelligible nature in the sense of the old exploded immutable essences. Then somebody, who can only be God, means well to men. Bolingbroke places himself in the middle, between the ancient and medieval philosophers, who supposed that nature is beneficent and intelligible, and the modern philosophers, who say that nature is inhospitable and recalcitrant. He says that philosophers

are carried . . . some to set the principles of morality out of our sight and their own too, whilst they assume them to be derived from eternal natures, independent on the will of God; some, to lay these principles as much too low, as low as the level of human policy, whilst they assume them to be nominal natures, dependent on the will of man. . . .[39]

Bolingbroke argues that all legitimate government is by consent and that the right of consent is undeniably God-given, since all can see by right reason the benefits of society. He argues that the most important knowledge is from revelation, not from philosophy; yet revelation is available to unassisted human perception and reason, as the term "revelation" means a full revealing, though not a necessary intelligibility. Bolingbroke conceived that divine law, or revelation, and natural law were identical. By lifting or blowing this natural sovereignty to the heavens, he was able to deny what Hobbes somewhat differently affirmed of the earthly sovereign, that its will was coextensive with natural law.[40]

The difficulties of Bolingbroke's deism are found in his conceptions of natural religion and of the natural sociability of men. Bolingbroke discovers the possibility of natural religion by denying the intelligibility of nature in immutable essences: if there were such essences, nature would have its own meaning independent of any Creator. Yet he admits that nature gives hints to human perception in the form of archetypes of real, complex ideas.[41] Although nature is not intelligible in itself, nature leads men to the understanding of God. But nature leads men to an understanding of the natural god, who explains the system of nature as far as men can understand it. Either God is part of the system of nature, however, and nature is after all intelligible; or God is above nature, and an understanding of mere nature is impossible and cannot produce any conclusions about nature's god. Bolingbroke's natural religion is a forced mating of philosophy and revelation that is made plausible by Locke's theory of ideas. The thesis of that theory is that men can have knowledge about the knowledge they cannot have, and Bolingbroke converted this refined ignorance into a cold and abstract piety for a Creator reasoned to a posteriori.

If the vital evidence for natural religion is found in the natural sociability of men, we must question Bolingbroke's view of the prepolitical state of nature. Since men are naturally sociable and the family constitutes a society, why is civil society necessary? What makes it necessary to pass from the natural and instinctive family to artificial civil society? Since nature directs men to civil society, there must be some natural need which drives men out of natural society; there must be some inescapable defect in the family. Indeed, Bolingbroke says that men become unsociable after they have satisfied their sociability. Their societies become individuals to one another. Then the result is a state of war.

Societies become in all respects individuals, that is, they have no regard to others except relatively to themselves; and self-love that promoted union among men, promotes discord among them. Like the philosopher of Malmesbury's wild men, they act as if they had a right to all they can acquire by fraud or force: and a state of war, so far from being the cause, has been the effect of forming distinct societies, though by the general plan of nature the propagation of mankind makes it necessary to form them.[42]

The "distinct societies" in this passage are certainly civil societies in an international state of war and seem also to be families in a prepolitical state of war. But Bolingbroke needs to distinguish between those societies (families) which can unite to avoid a state of war, and those which cannot and need not unite but must forever remain in a state of war. Hobbes made this distinction with his doctrine of sovereignty: individuals can unite by transferring their own natural sovereignty to an artificial sovereign, but the artificial sovereigns cannot unite because the sovereignty they have is for the safety of the people and not theirs to transfer. Bolingbroke agrees that "there must be an absolute power in every civil society placed somewhere."[43] Presumably the existence of absolute power is what distinguishes civil society from the family. Then the family must be defective for not having absolute power; "natural government" must be imperfect government. Then, to say that men are naturally sociable is to say only that they are led by nature to form societies so imperfect that their formation is the beginning of a state of war.

It may be suggested that family government, or paternal power, is imperfect because fathers have either too little or too much control over their grown sons, who are also fathers. They have too little control if their paternal power does not extend to all affairs of their sons, including their grandsons, but they have too much power if their paternal power destroys the paternal power of their sons. Thus the family tends to dissolve into warring individuals unless this "grandfather problem" is resolved by some power outside and above the family—political power or legislative power.[44] The problem of the heir apparent, to which Namier refers, is a special case of the grandfather problem, the case in which political power is passed within the family. Nature raises the grandfather problem by driving men into families, but does nature solve it? Bolingbroke can answer this question affirmatively, and thus conclude that nature is beneficent to man and that natural religion is possible, only if he agrees with Aristotle that man is by nature *political,* not merely social.

By way of illustrating the difference between natural religion and Christianity, Bolingbroke says that polygamy is in accord with natural law and the prohibition of it is absurd. Polygamy is natural because it is the best means of increasing the population, which improves the strength and wealth of every state. In this reasoning it is clear that Bolingbroke has proceeded beyond the elementary instinct of nature, which may be a desire for reproduction or merely for pleasure, to a reasoned improvement of the chances of survival, accomplished by increasing the number of those who must survive. The particular form of matrimony favored by natural law, polygamy, is justified for an end which the family by itself can neither envisage nor achieve. For reproduction neither requires nor assures an increase of population. Polygamy would then have to be established by civil law in preference to monogamy or polyandry, which are sufficient for reproduction merely. While reproduction requires only a family, increase of population is assured only by the state, which needs it.[45] Natural law would seem to be specifically political, then, rather than vaguely social. But Bolingbroke does not draw this conclusion; he seems to deny the substance of modern natural law, self-preservation, as elaborated by Hobbes and Locke. To Bolingbroke, the natural sociability of men quite naturally produces insociability, a state of war, from which men must extricate themselves by artificial covenant. Therefore, it is misleading in this context to say that nature directs men to civil society when it does so by demonstrating to them the dreadful inadequacy of its own arrangements. In this sense Hobbes and Locke also thought that men were naturally sociable. Bolingbroke wished to make certain modifications in the political implications of modern natural law, to do which he seemingly rearranged the fundamentals of modern natural law. Under examination he would have to choose the lesser modifications or the fundamental changes; he could not have both. One may suppose that Bolingbroke dared to say that men were naturally sociable only because Hobbes and Locke had successfully rebelled against the dominant Aristotelian political science. A belief in the natural sociability of men consequently no longer signified allegiance either to what Bolingbroke called "the kingdom of darkness" or to the "whimsical republic" of Plato.[46]

The practical importance of these lesser modifications for British politics, however, was not small: they are certainly topics for this study. The one which became the central issue between Bolingbroke and Burke, as we shall see, was Bolingbroke's program for giving rank to "men of ability." His opinion that men were sociable in a state of nature permitted him to distinguish between personal and social equality. Personal equality exists in man the least of all creatures, but social equality is a true consequence of the individuality of human societies (families) in the state of nature.[47] Bolingbroke thus secures an implication more favorable to an aristocracy of talents than could be had from Hobbes's flat insistence on the equality of men in the state of nature. This complicated issue will be considered in a later discussion.

Two of Bolingbroke's modifications of modern natural law were also attempted by Burke, in his way: a belief in the primacy of duties over rights and a new reliance on history. The first of these can be seen most readily in the policy Bolingbroke recommends for the Patriot King, which Burke opposed in the "Thoughts." If natural rights are given with the assurance of fulfilment or with the means of fulfilment, Bolingbroke believes that they may be said to be God-given. If God-given, they are duties: men march as they must to claim what was given to them. Yet because the rights are given mediately through government they must be claimed in a spirit of patriotism. Patriotism is *the* political theme of Bolingbroke, but it figures hardly at all in Hobbes and Locke. Patriotism springs from something other than an abstract regard to the state of nature. To understand it, we must take up Bolingbroke's new reliance on history.

Bolingbroke asserts that men can plainly discern natural law in the works of God, in the general providence of God. This means that men can see natural law in operation in civil society; they do not have to see it in operation before civil society was formed, when it was uncontaminated by and also unsupported by civil law. The beneficent providence of God sufficiently reveals the first principles of duties to God, that is, to oneself and to other men, so that men do not have to consult the intention of God, at the beginning, before civil society arose and His providence became evident. As there is no original sin in Bolingbroke's natural religion, so is there almost no state of nature in his natural law. Bolingbroke says, in contradiction to Hobbes: "Now for those who never experienced the evils that men are exposed to out of society, it is enough to say that they feel, and must feel, without the help of this contrast, unless they are idiots, the benefits of society. . . ."[48] Accordingly, Bolingbroke gives his thoughts on the state of nature only in his theoretical works; in his three most practical political writings—"A Dissertation upon Parties," "A Letter on the Spirit of Patriotism," and "The Idea of a Patriot King"—he mentions the state of nature only once. Natural law is obvious in the works of God, because men can feel the benefits of society without contrasting it with the state of nature. Hobbes and Locke, who make the state of nature the center of their political teachings, thought quite the contrary: they believed that men will never accept the legitimate restraints of civil society unless they appreciate the rigors, or at least the inadequacy, of natural law as it operates outside society. In their view, men can easily see the benefits of natural liberty but not the need for a restrained civil liberty.[49] Therefore they did what they could to keep the state of nature in the thoughts, if not in the experience, of ordinary citizens.

Bolingbroke's deism is almost a substitute for the idea of the state of nature. This state, in which man finds his unchanging human nature and from which he flees in anxious disgust into civilization, almost fades from sight in Bolingbroke's system. It becomes the general providence of nature's god, by which man, instead of having a nature, is revealed to be a creature. Bolingbroke does not go so far as to challenge the very concept of human nature, as Rousseau does in his *Discourse on the Origin of Inequality* (1759). He believes, as we have noted, that human intelligence could not have emerged from non-intelligence; indeed this is his reason for supposing a divine intelligence to be the first cause of the universe. But he finds the first principles of natural law in history, from which he reasons a posteriori; in addition, he uses history to illustrate principles known non-historically. It is not only that the social contract which concludes the state of nature has become the "original contract," as it did in Hume's theory. The terms of entry into society can be reasoned by a comparison of the "experience of other men and other ages with our own." This is the "great use of history"; this is what Bolingbroke means in his well-known saying, borrowed "from somewhere or other in Dionysius Halicarnassius," that "history is philosophy teaching by examples."[50] Bolingbroke believes that every civil society began by consent (that is, through families), as no force would be impressive enough, and no fraud clever enough, to prevail against the plain principles of natural law. Therefore, the first uniting of civil society had to be according to natural law.[51] But it is probable, according to Bolingbroke, that most actual societies did begin by the force and fraud of those who held the power of a pre-existing civil society. Civil society formed by conquest is formed by imperialism. Thus the conception of the state of nature does not provide an obvious and relevant practical guide to an existing civil society.

There is an ambiguity in the term "first principles" between first in nature and first in origin, and true first principles "for us" (which Bolingbroke takes to be first in nature) may not be the true original principles. It is easier and safer to consult the history of any society by drawing a contrast between the happiness that is apparent when that society is conducted according to natural law and the misery when it is not, than to take one's bearing from the original need to escape the state of nature. The general providence of God is a clearer guide than the earliest entry into civil society. For Britain, Bolingbroke adopts the view, reasoning a posteriori from later history, that the British constitution began as a free Gothic constitution.[52] This view would be criticized today as unhistorical, and Bolingbroke admits that there is little evidence about the origins of Britain or of any other society. But he believes that the Gothic constitution serves as a historical substitute for the state of nature. It is the beginning that Britain *must* have made, considering its later history. Bolingbroke reasons *to* the Gothic constitution instead of reasoning *from* the state of nature. Thus the true and sufficient guide for the British people is found in the history of the British constitution, not from its beginning, but in its operation. Bolingbroke states this opinion in the "Dissertation upon Parties" and illustrates it with the short history he gives there.[53]

The issue between the religious parties, which Bolingbroke intended to foreclose with his deism, has now been settled, if not quite concluded, on terms more advanced than his. The compromise between modern liberalism and Judeo-Christian revelation by which we live has made ever fewer concessions to revelation. From our perspective Bolingbroke's deism must therefore appear timorous or ridiculously cautious. But we forget not only the public strength of Christianity in those days, represented by the doughty champions of orthodoxy and neo-orthodoxy against whom Bolingbroke argued in about half the bulk of his writings, but also the problem of revelation itself, which has been in no way resolved, but only suppressed, by secularism in modern times. Bolingbroke himself did not give this problem its due; he intended its removal from public discussion by presenting it as solved, unnecessary to discuss. But he himself had an awareness of it, as well as an understanding of the "first philosophy" of modern science, which is rare today among those without his practical preoccupations. That men necessarily occupy themselves with things which are above men and that this occupation is reflected in politics are truths still to be found in Bolingbroke's natural religion.

The purpose of deism was to present a broad front against divine right, which was, in different ways, the principle of the chief religious parties of the seventeenth century. To make this broad front, Bolingbroke extended natural religion to make possible an alliance with atheism; for, as he explains, the atheist is only somewhat less bound to natural law by interest than the theist is by duty. While the theist reasons from natural law to a divine lawgiver, the atheist "would laugh very justly at the man who should tell him, that he was not obliged to pass over the bridge, though he might be drowned in the torrent, because there was no act of Parliament for it."[54] Spinozists and Hobbists, though guilty of many absurdities, are not men of depraved morals merely because they are atheists.[55] At the same time, in Bolingbroke's view, natural religion condemns or fails to sustain many Christian dogmas. Yet he announces that the "first principles of good policy" in religion are "a test and a toleration"—a test oath, because a government needs the support of a national religion; toleration because the fatal effects of theological disputes and ecclesiastical quarrels, that is, religious parties, must be prevented.[56]

The discrepancy between natural religion and the national religion (which in Britain would include Christian dogmas not recommended by natural religion) can be explained by the difference between general and particular providence. General providence, as we have seen, needs to be particularized by civil society, for God's providence lacks the purchase of a natural conscience and takes effect on particular men only through the sanctions of civil law. The Church of England is, in turn, the chosen establishment of the civil magistrate, and serves as sanction for its laws. Natural religion needs civil society, which needs a national religion. Does Bolingbroke then return to the opinion of Hobbes and Locke that morality requires an "artificial theology," that is, some dogmas which cannot be sustained (though they may not be contradicted) by natural religion? Bolingbroke does not say, but he seems to believe that the national religion can be refined to natural religion in time. There is no permanent need for artificial theology, because Christianity can be stripped of its false dogmas and remain Christian through the authenticity of the gospels. Bolingbroke, in presenting the case for natural religion, argues as much for a reasonable Christianity as did Locke; but in his view, reasonable Christianity is true because it corresponds to natural religion. His support of the religious test, which in Britain included taking an oath to dogmas said to be false by him, was not mere hypocrisy, for one may allow a decent interval for the spread of true religion when false religion has been made harmless by the institution of toleration.

This fact is the clue to the connection between the history of party and the history of religion in Britain. Hobbes had constructed his doctrine of absolute sovereignty partly in order to remove the divisiveness of religion from civil society, to destroy the religious or political-religious parties. When a church claims authority equal or superior to that of the sovereign, the result is an *imperium in imperio,* which brings civil disorder and war. Accordingly, Hobbes defined the church as a meeting of professed Christians; if lawful, this meeting is called at the command of the sovereign; the true or lawful church is the same as the commonwealth.[57]

Bolingbroke accepted the subordination of religion to the sovereign, but having discovered the identity of natural religion and natural law, he concluded that the sovereign did not have to be identified with the church. The sovereign should give preference to the national religion, but he should permit other churches to exist, as their common ground in natural religion makes them amenable to proper control and thereby harmless to public peace. Natural religion is true religion, and a society based on natural religion, in which the natural is the national religion, is based on truth. For Hobbes, because society is based on true natural law, the sovereign cannot tolerate many churches. For Bolingbroke, because society is based on true natural law, the sovereign *can* tolerate many churches. The opinion that society can be based on truth justifies both the worst intolerance, because myths can be dispensed with, and the broadest tolerance, because myths, if they can be dispensed with, can be made harmless. It is not merely that the dark precedes the dawn: the success of the religious intolerance in the doctrine of absolute sovereignty prepares for the abandonment of intolerance. The genesis of tolerance is in intolerance. If dogma can be defeated, why bother to destroy it?

From about 1660 to 1770, parties in Britain were generally considered to be unrespectable, disturbers of the peace, because they had been parties of religious doctrine with conflicting political claims. Bolingbroke not only proved the possibility of religious toleration, as did Locke (and others), but he was able to point to the success of toleration in Britain since the Settlement of 1688–89. He was able to show convincingly that seventeenth-century party conflict had been removed. Bolingbroke therefore concluded that parties no longer had a reason for existence; but Burke, contrary to Bolingbroke, concluded that party conflict could be transformed into tolerable party competition. The relation between religious toleration and the respectability of party can appear first as a parallel, expressed in terms of a proportion: Hobbes is to Bolingbroke in respect to religion as Bolingbroke is to Burke in respect to party. But the relation between these concepts is actually more than a parallel, because the settlement of religious conflict was a *prerequisite* for the toleration of party competition.

The premise of this settlement is that society can be based on truth. Bolingbroke said that truth can become "the very genius of a people."

> The authority of a sect, and much more of a state, is able to inspire, and habit to confirm, the most absurd opinions. Passion, or interest, can create zeal. But nothing can give stability and durable uniformity to error . . . such opinions, like human bodies, tend to dissolution from their birth. They will be soon rejected in theory, where men can think, and in practice, where men can act with freedom.[58]

Erroneous opinions are ephemeral. Thus, nobody has a truly partisan interest, derived from his opinion. There are never any *real* differences between parties; there are only false apprehensions, which can produce actions that are actual enough, but which need not exist and "tend to dissolution from their birth." Because it is possible to have society based on truth, Bolingbroke believes that it is possible to have society without parties. His effort to find real differences in the English parties is embarrassed by this premise. He wishes to say that the parties of the Civil War were derived from false apprehensions of truly harmonious interests and yet preserved the obvious differences between seventeenth- and eighteenth-century parties. Consequently, he must say that the eighteenth-century parties are ghosts of apprehensions.

One may briefly compare the political science of Bolingbroke with that of Plato and Aristotle on this point. For Plato and Aristotle, the politics of a country is determined by its regime (*politeia*). The character of the regime—which may be democratic, aristocratic, or monarchical, one of their defective counterparts, or some mixture—is reflected in the dominant, or public, opinion of that country. Public opinion is never truth but always opinion or myth, that is to say, a partial truth which claims to be the whole truth. One can see the partiality of public opinion by comparing the contradictory public opinions of various regimes. But it is not easy to to make a careful comparison, for the truth is hidden in contradictory assertions. Those who are able and willing to make an inquiry into the truth, not to say a successful inquiry, are too few to support a society and so busy that they have to be supported by society. Since every regime advances a partial truth, it follows that every regime is partisan with respect to the whole truth; for example, a democratic regime sustains as the public opinion what would be the opinion of the democratic party, a partial truth. Every regime is perforce a ruling party, because the truth of contradictory opinions cannot be resolved on a social level, even if it can be resolved among friends, and one opinion must be chosen. Not all opinions are equally worthy of choice, but all are inevitably partial; thus every regime is necessarily intolerant, though in different degrees and of different things. At the same time, Plato and Aristotle teach an awareness of the necessity of intolerance and the extent of necessary intolerance—which mitigates its ill effects among educated men and those whom they influence. Bolingbroke's premise, the premise of modern natural law that society can be based on truth, inspires an extraordinary intolerance by its ambition and a corresponding tolerance either by its initial confidence or by its later disillusionment. If society can be based on truth, the political organization of society can be non-partisan; and if politics can be made non-partisan, parties can be made harmless or even beneficent. Experience may have shown that contrary to expectation, politics cannot be made non-partisan; but experience has shown, at least, that parties in Britain can become harmless.

Burke seems to follow Plato and Aristotle in his famous praise of prejudice:

> You see, Sir, that in this enlightened age I am bold enough to confess, that we are generally men of untaught feelings; that instead of casting away all our old prejudices, we cherish them to a very considerable degree, and, to take more shame to ourselves, we cherish them because they are prejudices; and the longer they have lasted, and the more generally they have prevailed, the more we cherish them.[59]

In fact, what he praises is not good or sound prejudices, but the wisdom of prejudice as such. Prejudice is inevitable, but it is harmless and even reasonable. Prejudice becomes reasonable by means of Burke's theory of prescription, which will be discussed. That theory is an advanced product of the shift (which Bolingbroke helped initiate) from a reliance on the state of nature to a reliance on history as the source of "first principles." Burke does not really abandon the belief that society can be founded on truth; he attacks the belief that it can be founded on *abstract* truth, since he believes that moral and political truth is not abstract. Prejudice can be tolerated, even encouraged, for precisely the reason that Bolingbroke thought it can and must be abolished. To develop this issue between Burke and Bolingbroke, the issue which appears in Burke's "Thoughts," one must understand Bolingbroke's program for the abolition of prejudice and its derivative, party.

CHAPTER FOUR

Bolingbroke's Program

Writing in 1733, Bolingbroke said that the current difference between the parties was about the justification of corruption. Whigs and Tories were obsolete, he thought; but the court and country parties have reappeared with an avowed difference of principles. This is not a difference of *national* principle, however, and the country party is not divided, as it was in the seventeenth century. The practitioners of corruption have impudently defended their conduct with a justification of corruption, which makes the present difference. To rally the country party against this danger, "more silent and less observed,"[1] Bolingbroke conceived a program against corruption, which he advanced in two pamphlets, "A Letter on the Spirit of Patriotism" and "The Idea of a Patriot King." A study of his program confirms that what he advocated is what Burke attacked in the "Thoughts" as "supernatural virtue." It also suggests some reflections on the nature of a party whose sole purpose is to abolish parties. For Bolingbroke not only opposed parties but thought that they could be dispensed with; beyond this, he argued that a free state could cure itself of corruption solely and sufficiently by adopting a policy of dispensing with parties. This superpartisan filled pamphlets with denunciations of partisanship, to the surfeit and disgust of readers today, whose experience with party professions will make them ready to acknowledge, and then to dismiss, a vintage humbugger like Bolingbroke. But Bolingbroke did not merely collect commonplace slogans in order to make his way into office. His professed antipartisanship was seriously meant and competently argued. To do him justice, one must understand his program; for Bolingbroke's antipartisanship is the soul of the earliest open partisanship in Britain.

Patriotism without Prejudice

In his "Letter on the Spirit of Patriotism," written in 1736 and published in 1749, Bolingbroke shows that his program is in genesis a program for an opposition. The danger to be opposed is the corruption of the court party, led by Walpole and supported by the false impression, which Bolingbroke attempted to dispel in his "Dissertation upon Parties," that the Whigs had to remain in office to protect the Settlement of 1688–89 against the Tories. In eighteenth-century British politics, "corruption" had a technical meaning, besides its usual meaning. "Corruption" (also called "management" by those who defended it) was similar to modern American "patronage": it was the employment of lesser officials, especially by the crown, to secure their loyalty and the loyalty of their patrons; and thus it meant choosing officials whose convenience was not confined to their abilities, and sometimes did not include abilities. But corruption, or the "influence of the crown," was practiced for a different purpose than patronage—to get a majority for the crown's measures in Parliament. This did not imply fixed partisanship, but a loyalty to the crown or to the ministers who shared the influence of the crown, which was suitably rewarded.

Like patronage, the practice of corruption produced an amiable ease of relations among the givers and receivers and a corresponding disdain for ideological fervor. Its amiableness was not a product of the tolerant superiority of a professional manager of votes and an expert minister to the needs of the people. Rather, it came from the amateurishness of the surviving tradition of classical statesmanship, by which political wisdom was thought to consist of a general understanding of politics combined with the ability to make a particular determination as the occasion demanded. One could be *prepared* for making a particular determination, but one could not be *trained* to make it, for politics was understood, by the British governing class, to deal with all departments of human concerns and to require an attention to the opinions or prejudices of the governed. An act of statesmanship could not be cut into aspects in a bureaucratic manner; politics was thought of as a whole, because it was concerned with the whole, the common good. Nor was it believed that society could be made (at least in principle) so free of prejudices, that a ruler could change the methods of his rule as easily as a mathematician could correct a mistake. For both reasons, statesmen attempted to practice politics intelligently, not as a profession, and their amiableness was the tolerant superiority of statesmen who understood the men with whom they had to deal. Patronage, as Lincoln Steffens has shown, is the work of professional politicians and is a consequence of professionalism in politics; corruption was the work of amateurs, and a necessary (nobody thought it wholesome) consequence of aristocratic rule.[2] By attacking corruption, Bolingbroke advanced the cause of professionalism and bureaucracy in politics, and so prepared (as Burke perceived) for the rise of patronage, the characteristic disease of professionalism. Professionalism in politics is now taken for granted, as it cannot be escaped. But at one time it was possible to be eagerly hopeful about the good effects of professionalism, and such eagerness first took the form of Bolingbroke's attack on corruption.

Bolingbroke's expression for this eagerness is "the spirit of patriotism," and we must examine both terms. "Spirit" in Bolingbroke's language (whatever his conduct) does not imply the warlike ardor of a partisan spoiling for a fight. "Spirit" means "constant application," "animation," "exertion," "industry"—all as complements to "genius."[3] Nature has supplied sufficient genius to the opponents of the court party, but genius must be applied to spirit. "Patriotism" is a real duty, Bolingbroke says, as provable as any other moral duty. It binds those superior few who are "designed to be the tutors and the guardians of human kind"[4] as well as those who must have spirit to supply their lack of genius. All are bound by this duty strictly, since for Bolingbroke patriotism is a strictly provable duty. The general providence of God over men is through societies, to which men are directed by God's created nature; the civil law is the instrument of providence. The obligation to submit to civil law is "a principal paragraph in the natural law," Bolingbroke says in "The Idea of a Patriot King." This law is not revealed to men by God in the ordinary sense, but is "discoverable by so clear and simple an use of our intellectual faculties, that it may be said properly enough to be revealed to us by God. . . . It follows, therefore, that he who breaks the laws of his country resists the ordinance of God, that is, the law of his nature."[5] But only good laws are laws of this obligation, for only good government can be the divine intention. Patriotism means love of one's country when, and only when, one's country acts in accordance with natural law.

The belief that a society need not be founded on prejudice yields patriotism without prejudice.[6] This is a startling conclusion. Bolingbroke puts the "intellectual joys" of the real patriot above those of Descartes and Newton, because the formation of a political scheme "to one great and good design" is as lofty and as absorbing as their projects, and vastly more important. If the patriot carries his scheme to successful execution, he becomes the Lawgiver's lawgiver and enjoys a "pleasure like to that which is attributed to the Supreme Being, on a survey of his works."[7] Bolingbroke is by no means able to prevent the man who imitates God from becoming almost divine. Such a man has a true divine right if he has made good laws. But since true or good laws are discoverable by a clear use of intellectual faculties, the patriot has a clear divine right to oppose bad laws. Patriotism without prejudice makes available a clear right, indeed a duty, of opposition without reservations. Because he knows that a society without prejudice is viable, a patriot does not hesitate to oppose a prejudice held dear by his country; and he does not have to wait for a "long train of abuses" from an erring government before he opposes it.[8] It is paradoxical, but on reflection reasonable, that the strictest patriotism is convertible to the boldest opposition, and that this philosopher of patriotism was the first philosopher to sustain a right of open opposition.

The moral duty of the patriot is in fact an intellectual virtue, and yet an attainable virtue. Patriotism is as cold as philosophy, but as accessible as prosperity. Virtue is "seated . . . on an eminence," but "not placed on a rugged mountain of difficult and dangerous access."[9] While the lawgiver has at least a difficult task, the British patriot, protected by all that laws can provide, needs no lawgiver. "Even able knaves would preserve liberty in such circumstances as ours. . . ." What the British patriot needs is not difficult and dangerous virtue, but spirit. To act with spirit is to act by a system, which is to be virtuous in Bolingbroke's sight. "Every administration is a system of conduct: opposition, therefore, should be a system of conduct likewise; an opposite, but not a dependent system."[10] If an opposing party is systematic in its conduct, it will find sufficient genius and virtue to give it direction without the need for recourse to able knaves.

The spirit of patriotism is thus reducible to the duty to be systematic, when administering the laws, in the way that the laws imply. Britain's free constitution has been maladministered by the use of corruption, which has circumvented the ends of that constitution. New laws will not effect a reform, because laws are general and must be administered. Bolingbroke agreed with Machiavelli that new laws cannot master corrupted men, but will only serve their corrupt intent. The laws must be administered by a system directed to the same ends as the laws; if they are not, an opposing party must act on such a system in order to achieve a proper administration. It must not act in a "dependent" system, as if to counsel the ministers, but independently, like an opposing army. In recognizing the limits of laws,

Bolingbroke broadened the scope of statesmanship. But if statesmanship can be systematized, then it can be appropriated by an opposition. Because an opposing party can be patriotic without reservations, it can become its country's statesmen in deed, as well as in principle. The distinction between public officials and private men, which Burke developed so skilfully at the beginning of the "Thoughts," tends to disappear, and therewith the delicacy which this distinction imposed on a prudent opposition.

A Program against Prejudice

"The Idea of a Patriot King" was written in 1738 and published in 1749 to forestall the publication of an incorrect version. Although Bolingbroke had intended this pamphlet for publication, he had meant to publish it on an occasion of his choosing, to catch a political opportunity, or else after his death, when the policies he had promoted would be less damaged by the antagonisms against himself.[11] The "Patriot King" was apparently shown to Prince Frederick, the Prince of Wales and heir apparent, whose death in 1751 permitted his son George III to take the throne in 1760 without any "reversionary resource" for opposition against him. (We shall discuss later the evidence which suggests that George III was the first to apply the idea of a Patriot King.) It seems reasonable that Prince Frederick was at some time a significant addressee of Bolingbroke's pamphlet, and doubtless Bolingbroke would have accepted an honest offer of high office under a Patriot King. Whether this pamphlet was a piece of jobbing flattery elegantly turned for a polite but stupid audience is a question best answered after examining it.

It becomes clear in the "Patriot King" that the "system of conduct" recommended to the opposition in the "Letter on the Spirit of Patriotism" resembles a modern "program." The duties of citizens under a free constitution, which are chiefly to oppose corruption, are elaborated in the duties of a Patriot King, who must take particular measures to clean out and prevent corruption. These "particular measures" are "general doctrines," or "first principles," applied "to the present state of Great Britain."[12] These general truths about the nature of men are applied to a particular time and location, and their application can be systematic because these generalities are true of all men. Bolingbroke's program does not begin with assertions about the British, but about all men, and then about those in the situation of the British. Therefore its conclusions cannot be challenged, except in case of faulty deduction; its premises or its "philosophy" must be challenged. Bolingbroke's purpose is to make argument over each "particular measure" impossible, since each measure has a place in the system, and so to make argument *unnecessary*. In this way politics is not bothered with the uncertainty of individual judgment on individual matters. By using the system men may also propose new laws or new measures, not merely with the confidence of men who possess the truth about political things, but with that of men who know that popular prejudices can be displaced by this truth. The perfect program is a novel constitution, or at least a rearrangement of the government, which includes or implies the displacement of popular prejudices by popularized truths. Few programs have been as perfect as this early one of Bolingbroke's; it reveals the nature of programs, which party programs today are unable to attain but are unable to stop trying to attain—the systematizing of politics.

The religious parties of the seventeenth century did not have programs in this sense, because their manifestos (for example, the "Grand Remonstrance" of 1641) were argued not as deductions from human nature but as interpretations of Scripture and religious tradition. As Scripture is not unambiguous in the light of human reason, such interpretations are not fully systematic, or "ideological," to use a word of later origin. They convey God's commands in social and political matters; but they are not contrived by men sovereign in the affairs of men or completed in accordance with the necessities of men. They are based on revealed knowledge, not on natural knowledge, and they seek to spread faith, not confidence. However revolutionary they may be, they seek to make politics serve God, and only consequentially the needs of men. They do not apply "first principles"; they apply the word of God; and they are systematic only to interpret revelation, not to order men's affairs as men can see them. Political programs as we have them today are no longer advanced with the confident belief that truth (that is, truth accessible to men on their own) can become public opinion; yet this confidence is the basis of a program in its perfect sense. General truths are not myths or prejudices which need to be corrected in the cockpit by expert statesmen; they are simple truths which can be publicized without becoming ambiguities, and simple truths are guides to action against myths or prejudices. The program is in origin and nature an instrument of enlightenment.

Bolingbroke begins the "Patriot King" with a summary of "first principles" for all governments, but especially for monarchies. The virtue of monarchy might seem to be its freedom from the restrictions of programs: when Bolingbroke's admirer, Thomas Jefferson, came to draw up his party's program, he directed it against the "monarchical" character of the Federalist administration. Bolingbroke is eager to demonstrate that, by true first principles, monarchy is not "arbitrary rule," even of the best man, but is best suited for instituting a program against corruption.

The first kings were elevated to majesty as a reward for pre-eminent merit, and then awarded divinity. But the second reward gave an advantage to priests over the simplicity of early mankind, and unmeriting men began to keep and to obtain kingly rank because of mere proximity in blood to the last king. This pretended divine right contrasts with true divine right, the right of every king who reigns where the civil laws have ordained monarchy to govern well. Bolingbroke says that a hereditary monarchy is absurd in theory, but in practice is preferable to the periodic commotions of an elective monarchy. Limited monarchy is in a sense an imitation of God, for God did not rule arbitrarily, but made Himself a rule; and a king cannot claim a more absolute rule. When monarchy is the essential form, it has the advantage, noticed by Burke in Bolingbroke's writings, of being more easily tempered with aristocracy and democracy than either of these can be tempered with it.[13] One must distinguish legislative and monarchical power: the former is the absolute, unlimited, and uncontrollable power which must be lodged somewhere in every government, but not properly in one man; in Britain the latter is the executive power and a veto as a share in the legislative power. The British constitution has been brought so close to perfection that no king can rule securely unless he is a Patriot King; and yet such a king has as much power as the most absolute monarch and more securely and agreeably than he. "Patriotism must be founded in great principles, and supported by great virtues."[14] Yet the principles are more important than the virtues, because the virtues alone will not produce good government; and the education of princes should concentrate on the principles, not on the virtues. Bolingbroke has an answer for those who suppose that it is impracticable to advise a king to limit his power; he recommends the opinion of Machiavelli, who he says will have authority with these objectors, that the sure way for a prince to gain fame and security is to revive a corrupted free constitution, rather than to establish a tyranny.[15] This is not the motive that a good prince would have for governing by true principles, which would be duty. But Bolingbroke gives no reason why citizens should hope for this higher motive and proposes no deeds that a good prince could accomplish only by having this higher motive. True principles are enough without great virtues. "A prince, who does not know the true principles, cannot propose to himself the true ends of government; and he who does not propose them will never direct his conduct steadily to them."[16]

How is the Patriot King to re-establish Britain's free constitution? Bolingbroke adopts Machiavelli's distinction of the orders and spirit of a constitution. The orders are the different classes and assemblies of men, with their forms, powers, and privileges—what political scientists today call "institutions." The spirit is the character of the people. Only free states truly have a constitution, and they can suffer degeneration both in orders and in spirit. To preserve its freedom, a free state corrupt in spirit needs new orders suited to its corruption; but such new orders are difficult to achieve, either gently or violently. Bolingbroke quotes Machiavelli: "If this possibly can be done, it must be done by drawing the constitution to the monarchical form of government." This is the other advantage of a limited monarchy:

> To preserve liberty by new laws and new schemes of government, whilst the corruption of a people continues and grows, is absolutely impossible: but to restore and preserve it under old laws, and an old constitution, by reinfusing into the minds of men the spirit of this constitution, is not only possible, but is, in a particular manner, easy to a king.[17]

How does the Patriot King awaken the spirit of the constitution? He simply ceases to use corruption as an expedient of government. When he does so, which is as soon as he is raised to the throne, "the panacea is applied." The Patriot King is so far from being a skilful statesman that the advantage of monarchy is the ease with which the statesman's discretion may be replaced by a program against corruption.

The five particular measures of this progam are given in a short formula before they are explained: "Under [a Patriot King, men] will not only cease to do evil, but learn to do well; for, by rendering public virtue and real capacity the sole means of acquiring any degree of power or profit in the state, he will set the passions of their hearts on the side of liberty and good government."[18] The program of the Patriot King is this candid appeal to the heartfelt passions of men of "public virtue and real capacity." What is public virtue? Evidently it is that virtue which is required to serve the public, not all private virtue. In fact, it is devotion to the first principles of government as Bolingbroke has given them, a devotion which can be as stern as duty and as cold as interest. Bolingbroke not only depreciates "great virtues" compared to first principles, but he identifies "public virtue" with devotion to these principles.

Taking a distinction from Bacon, Bolingbroke says that "real capacity" is wisdom, rather than cunning. Wisdom includes cunning, however, and the difference is one of degree, not kind, for they often have the same objects and means. The wise man sees further than the cunning man; he sees into remote relations and indirect tendencies; he sees "that scheme of the reason of state" which "contains all the great principles of government, and all the great interests of his country." The wise man has farsighted cunning; he thinks of fame rather than applause, and his principles are tempered with dissimulation rather than outright simulation.[19] "Public virtue" really adds nothing to "real capacity," as the principles of patriotism are the maxims of farsighted cunning. In formula Bolingbroke's program is the promotion of "men of ability," as they came to be called by his followers in the 1760's; it creates an aristocracy of talents.

Aristocracy of Talents

The idea of an aristocracy of talents had its early development in the political philosophy of Hobbes and Locke and was carried further by Bolingbroke. It may be explained briefly as a conclusion reached from the belief in natural equality. If men are by nature equal, they are by nature free, or unsociable, since society requires rank. Men who are by nature free are not by nature political; they must be *civilized*. Far from justifying a general democracy, the idea of natural equality in Hobbes and Locke supports an artificial civilized aristocracy. For, according to these authors, if equality is the natural state of man, this "state of nature" is war or at least inconvenience. The prepolitical state of nature was as necessary for deriving the inequalities of men as for showing the fundamental equality of men. Civilization advances as it overcomes and because it overcomes the fundamental equality of men in the fear of death, and permits the less fundamental inequalities to develop. These inequalities are not differences in virtue, as the ancients called it, or in private virtue, as Bolingbroke said. Virtue requires some resistance to the fear of death or desire for life, for the sake of the good life. But the good life has several representations, and as a result, inspires several parties; when the good life is allied to religion, as it has been formerly, in its popular representations at least, the parties will be passionate and may become fanatical and cruel. And even if virtue in its severality does not bring civil war, it distracts men from the sober pursuit of prosperity, which is needed for almost any practice of virtue that they may set for themselves. That is why inequality must be built artificially upon natural equality: when men ponder how they are by nature equal, they recall their natural rapacity or penury and chase the illusions of virtue from their minds. Natural equality is more fundamental than natural inequality because it is the basis of the end for which men construct civilization, self-preservation. For the sake of this end, those inequalities which are productive, the inequalities of talents or abilities, must be selected from those which are distracting, the inequalities of virtue. A social hierarchy thought to be in some sense natural is replaced by a new aristocracy of talents, prized because it is civilized, or unnatural.

Bolingbroke adopts this conclusion of Hobbes and Locke with his characteristic sovereignty: "I have sometimes represented to myself the vulgar, who are accidentally distinguished by the titles of king and subject, of lord and vassal, of nobleman and peasant; and the few, who are distinguished by nature so essentially from the herd of mankind."[20] As we have seen, Bolingbroke's belief in the natural sociability of men enables him to distinguish between social and personal equality, and apparently allows him to support an elite of talents more solidly than Hobbes and Locke. But his acceptance of their fundamental principles is unquestionable. We have remarked that in Britain liberalism made its early progress not against the aristocracy but within it. If later democratic liberalism moved more slowly than early liberalism, it fought an enemy disarmed and in its similar way convinced. Compared to the seventeenth-century gentleman, the eighteenth-century gentleman was literally disarmed: he carried a cane instead of a sword. He also led the opinions and habits of the British public from a problematic concern with honor and religion to an absorption in commerce, liberty, and religious indifference. Bolingbroke's statement quoted above is not democratic, but it is revolutionary with respect to every existing society: a society without prejudices requires a society without privileges. It is Plato's "vision of virtue"[21] become practicable, so that there is no longer any excuse for not establishing it or any reason for hiding it in a noble lie. With its greater practicability, however, Bolingbroke's program implied much less difference, if any, between the few and the vulgar; and we in the liberal democracies now wonder why he went so far and stopped so short.

The first particular measure in the program of the Patriot King is that "he must begin to govern as soon as he begins to reign,"[22] a phrase that became a catchword at the accession of George III in 1760. Since his aim is fully practicable, he must from the first execute it. That is, he must "purge his court" to assure himself of men that will serve the same principles on which he intends to govern. If the preceding reign has been bad, the men in power will have been busy and bold adventurers, thrusting into party intrigues, "often without true ability, always without true ambition, or even the appearances of virtue." Since clemency is a virtue with limits, some of these men will be abandoned by the Patriot King to national justice (though not to party fury). The purge is to culminate in impeachments for those who have committed "enormous crimes," Bolingbroke says with solemnity. All the rest must be cast out, "together and at once."

The program begins with a purge intended to secure men of true principles. It is not enough to find men of ability; the Patriot King must be served by men of ability who believe, contrary to some able men, that ability should be decisive. There is no shortage of ability, for nature has "done her part";[23] the problem is finding men who accept the *principle* of ability. Since true first principles can be found and applied and since they can harmonize the conflicting interests of men, there is no excuse for opinions. It is worth repeating that Bolingbroke not only believes his principles to be true (it is easy to believe this without supposing that people generally are capable of living by them) but he also believes that his principles are *applicable* and may be reasonably applied with a purge. As the purge is today a practice of both democratic and totalitarian parties, it is revealing that, in this early appearance, a purge is intended to cleanse the government not merely of incompetents but also of able and loyal men who will not govern on the basis of the principles which are asserted to be true. Ability is, in practice, subordinate to the *principle* of ability.

The term "purge" had a religious origin as did so many features of parties; but its modern political practice is unlike the religious conception of a purge. In the latter, men must cast out all but the saintly characters from a group of people, just as they purged their souls of sin. "Colonel Pride's purge" of the Long Parliament in 1648 was acted upon this conception. But the purge Bolingbroke proposed was directed against this conception, which he thought cruelly strained human nature to promote the interest of a few rulers. Bolingbroke's purge was intended not to cleanse the state of sin, but to cleanse it of those prejudices which disturb a secure liberty; and in this purpose his purge was to engage in its service passions considered sinful, such as ambition and greed. The middle position between suppressing the passions and co-operating with them is ruling them by reason; and this middle position raises doubts about whether a man should rule other men quite as he rules his own passions. But Bolingbroke considered that, according to the natural law of human character, passions could be swayed only by other passions. It is interesting that a policy to engage the passions could be as hard-hearted as a policy to suppress them.

Next, the Patriot King must replace those purged. He does not have to make new laws; he brings a new spirit, makes a new people. But to do this, he must appeal to a new class of men. In the "Spirit of Patriotism" Bolingbroke says: "I turn my eyes from the generation that is going off, to the generation that is coming on the stage." First principles are especially attractive to the younger generation: the "Patriot King" is written not only for Prince Frederick but for heirs apparent in general. There is more than a hint of Machiavelli in this:

> Absolute stability is not to be expected in any thing human. . . . The best instituted governments . . . carry in them the seeds of their destruction. . . . Every hour that they live is an hour the less that they have to live. All that can be done, therefore, to prolong the duration of a good government is to draw it back, on every favorable occasion, to the first good principles on which it was founded.[24]

Since "absolute stability" cannot be expected, it should not be attempted. Since the supposed wisdom of the older generation depends on stability, the younger generation must be encouraged to recall the first principles and found the government anew "on every favorable occasion." This refounding is not an exploit but a task; it can be inspired by a careful, well-taught Patriot King and carried out by men of steady competence. It does not require boldness from the prince or turmoil and violent purgation in the aristocracy, as Machiavelli believed. Since Bolingbroke's first principles are the best parts of natural law, the founder of a state was necessarily the most moral man alive, rather than a major criminal, as Machiavelli asserted.[25] The recall of first principles can be accomplished within the British constitution, and by a king with the assistance of the titled; yet the effect is nevertheless antiaristocratic. The recall attempts to stifle the claims of men of great virtue to the honor of public office and to substitute the claims of men of abilities who will serve the public, not by deeds that bring glory in this world or the next, but by the steady administration of laws that secure liberty. The constitution, settled in 1688, has been administered by an "oligarchy,"[26] which must be so termed not because it is Whig but because it has disturbed the Whig Settlement of 1688–89.

"To espouse no party, but to govern like the common father of his people" is the third measure of the Patriot King; this is contrary to the teaching of Machiavelli. Bolingbroke is so confident of the efficacy of his first principles that he thinks they can be established without partisanship and improved by the younger generation under the leadership of a "common father": "The true image of a free people, governed by a Patriot King, is that of a patriarchal family, where the head and all the members are united by one common interest, and animated by one common spirit. . . ."[27] It is not that the Patriot King has a biblical authority; rather, he rules over a community, like the family, which has quarrels but which has no incurable differences of opinion over the ends of association. The Patriot King has so little need to govern by party, Bolingbroke says, that he is not even exposed to the *temptation*. "Party is a political evil, and faction is the worst of all parties." Parties are groups of men associated for purposes which are not, or are not allowed by others to be, those of the community; and parties become factions when personal or private interest becomes predominant in them. After these definitions, Bolingbroke proceeds to a proof that the Patriot King will never, under any circumstances, have to espouse a party. We shall speculate later why he should give this proof, which is at least very unusual: most thinkers who oppose party do not find it necessary or helpful to argue that every possible party is unjustified. But first it is necessary to know the argument.

When the Patriot King ascends the throne, there may be parties either when the people are united in submission to him or when they are not so united. When the people are united in submission to the king, they may be divided on general principles or on particular measures. If they are divided on general principles, the Patriot King should adopt the rule of the constitution, whatever that may be, render all proceedings more orderly and deliberate, and defeat party by defending the constitution. He should lead men from acting with a party spirit to acting with a national spirit. If the people are divided on particular measures under his administration, he should, if necessary, admit his mistakes and not impute just complaints to a spirit of party. When opposition to his particular measures is unjustified, he need only use the instruments of the crown and appeal to the people, by whom he will be supported. "Groundless opposition, in a well regulated monarchy, can never be strong and durable. To be convinced of the truth of this proposition, one needs only to reflect how many well grounded attacks have been defeated, and how few have succeeded, against the most wicked and the weakest administration."[28] It seems that the Patriot King can count not so much on the justice of the people as on their desire for repose and their awe of monarchy. In all these instances, the Patriot King may temporarily favor one party, but he will neither espouse nor proscribe a party.

When the people are not united in submission to the Patriot King, he should still not despair of reconciling them, even though he may be obliged, like Henry IV of France, to conquer some of his own subjects. He should remember peace in the midst of war and give the rebels what Locke might have to call a civil knock on the head.[29] If the factions are not in arms, the Patriot King has only to withhold his authority and purse from the faction in power and to "mark out" the opposing faction to the people—since the factions "break in but little on the body of his people." Even the most implacable partisans, such as the Jacobites, can be made harmless; they can be coaxed into "quiet submission and patient expectation." On the whole, then, there is no light "in which these divisions will appear incurable." The great instance of parties subdued is found in the reign of Queen Elizabeth, who united the people and kept intrigue within the court. Bolingbroke's argument that parties are never incurable seems to suppose that there are two sorts of men: the unambitious people and the ambitious, political men, whose heartfelt passions the Patriot King may enlist when he has convinced them that the unambitious people will prefer peace and non-partisan union.[30]

Encouraging commerce is the fourth measure of the Patriot King. This policy is not the freely chosen specialty of Britain; it is strictly implied by the first principles. "The wealth and power of all nations depending so much on their trade and commerce . . . a good government . . . will be directed constantly to make the most of every advantage that nature has given, or art can procure, towards the improvement of trade and commerce."[31] France and Holland may be more or less fit by situation and government for commerce, but they are nevertheless bound in reason to encourage it. Commerce is the only activity which promotes "all the ends of good government," listed by Bolingbroke as "private security, public tranquillity, wealth, power and fame."[32] Since it promotes all these ends, it is a non-partisan policy; and it can promote all these ends because they are non-partisan ends. Everyone desires these ends, not because they constitute the highest happiness, but because they furnish means to happiness. When the ends of government are not happiness but the means to happiness, the policy of that government can become non-partisan. Bolingbroke participated in the sovereign intention of modern political philosophy to change the ends of government from happiness to means to happiness, whose practical implication is commerce. To serve this intention, military policy must vary according to the needs of commerce. Bolingbroke condemns Pericles' dreams of military glory, which distracted the Athenians from honest industry and made them hunger for the fruits of conquest; and he condemns the "Continental policy," as it was called in the 1760's, of sending British troops to fight the French in Europe—a policy begun by William III and Marlborough, but regarded as Whig. Marlborough's glory is too bright to be sustained, and its memory will incite and afterwards dismay whomever it captures, unless it is supplanted by a more calculated desire for empire.[33]

The bearing of the Patriot King constitutes the fifth measure of his program—his decorum, decency, and grace. The Patriot King, unlike the great men of the past, must not give himself over to private pleasures or private vices, because great passions set a bad example to the people. He should be like Caesar's wife, not like Caesar. To achieve "popularity,"[34] "the sole true foundation" of monarchical authority in England, the Patriot King must set aside the self-conceit of kings who imagine that their ability and their authority have a source independent of the natural rights of the people. He must modestly forsake the traditional honor and dignity of kings, sanctioned by the claims of divine right, and accept the mitigated dignity of a trustee of the people, set off with a cold "legal reverence." This mitigation is stylishly effected by "certain finishing strokes, a last hand as we commonly say, to be given to all works of art."[35] Virtue must have a polish of amiableness, a handsome disguise, and a set of manners. Here Bolingbroke shares the tendency of Locke (and in lesser degree Shaftesbury, not to speak of the later aesthetic movement), to make virtue descend to nice manners.

Supernatural Virtue

It is now necessary to return to Burke's "Thoughts," to discover the connection between the idea of a Patriot King and the cause of the present discontents. The inquiry begins with the passage in the "Thoughts" on "supernatural virtue," which we take to be a reference to Bolingbroke's theory.

> To recommend this system to the people, a perspective view of the court, gorgeously painted, and finely illuminated from within, was exhibited to the gaping multitude. Party was to be totally done away, with all its evil works. Corruption was to be cast down from court, as *Ate* was from heaven. Power was thenceforward to be the chosen residence of public spirit; and no one was to be supposed under any sinister influence, except those who had the misfortune to be in disgrace at court, which was to stand in lieu of all vices and all corruptions. A scheme of perfection to be realized in a monarchy far beyond the visionary republic of Plato. The whole scenery was exactly disposed to captivate those good souls, whose credulous morality is so invaluable a treasure to crafty politicians. Indeed there was wherewithal to charm everybody, except those few who are not much pleased with professions of supernatural virtue, who know of what stuff such professions are made, for what purposes they are designed, and in what they are sure constantly to end.[36]

This passage has been quoted at length because we propose to adopt, for the purpose of this inquiry, the assumption that Burke wrote it carefully. Whether it will stand the weight of the interpretation to follow cannot be told without a test, that is, without adopting the assumption. Anyone who wished to say that because Burke wrote the "Thoughts" with speed,[37] he wrote with heat and with haste, or because he was Irish and imaginative he wrote with passion and irrationality, would have to make the same test and the same assumption.

This "scheme of perfection" far beyond the visionary republic of Plato consists of "professions of supernatural virtue." Plato's visionary republic unites virtue and power in the philosopher-kings; Bolingbroke's theory unites public spirit and power in the Patriot King. Yet this scheme is far beyond Plato; it requires that the king have supernatural virtue. Supernatural virtue would be the virtue of God; this scheme makes the king into God. All disgrace is defined as sin, as disobedience to the king, or God. The court, which is likened to heaven, is "finely illuminated from within"—rather than from outside; the king, like God, presents himself to the world by his own power, instead of accepting himself as he appears to others. "Supernatural virtue" is not traditional Christian divine right, as Burke reports it in this passage. According to Christian divine right, the king is appointed by God because he possesses, and in order to propagate, human, or *natural* virtue. The best king has that virtue which is available to men, although perhaps not to the extent of a saint. His virtue has divine sanction, but this does not make it supernatural. Supernatural virtue is not founded on the "antiquated prejudices" of divine right that formed the basis for misuse of the king's prerogative, although it may have the effect of misusing the prerogative; it is likely to be in combination with the "interest of active men," the new basis for the misuse of influence.

One should also note the balance of public spirit, on the one hand, against all vices and corruptions, on the other. The opposite of vice is not virtue but public spirit; public spirit has replaced virtue. In addition, party seems to be the single source of corruption, according to the "professions of supernatural virtue"; hence the scheme of perfection consists simply in the abolition of party, which is thought to be fully and perhaps easily possible.

Burke's criticism of the "professions of supernatural virtue" describes the method of their operation.

> Many innocent gentlemen, who had been talking prose all their lives without knowing anything of the matter, began at last to open their eyes upon their own merits, and to attribute their not having been lords of the treasury and lords of trade many years before, merely to the prevalence of party, and to the ministerial power, which had frustrated the good intentions of the court in favor of their abilities.

These professions unlock previously existing restraints on ambition by locating public spirit in the court; it now seems quite justified to serve the court by giving free rein to one's ambition. "Innocent gentlemen" who previously restrained their ambition with a certain innocent virtue will lose their sobriety, their habit of speaking prose; they will treat the effacement of party as a promise to remedy their own insignificance. The next sentence, "Now was the time to unlock the sealed fountain of royal bounty . . . ," shows that their ambition will be joined with avarice.

What were the effects of these views on the one who is said to have "supernatural virtue," the king? One must arrive at them by interpretation, since Burke did not announce them. The professions would encourage the king to believe that he has supernatural virtue. The idea that perfection is attainable by abolishing party flatters him as it does other "innocent gentlemen"; it loosens the restraints on his pretensions. In the traditional view, such flattery might seem to indicate the presence of tyranny (as "supernatural virtue" might seem to be traditional divine right), for it is well known that tyrants love flattery. But there is an important difference in the size of the pretensions of the traditional tyrant and those of the king under the influence of "professions of supernatural virtue." Aristotle says that the tyrant claims to be the only free man in the regime, to have a monopoly on spirit and self-sufficiency—a claim that brings conflict between him and the notables.[38] But in Burke's discussion, the abolition of party is the only aim mentioned; and the king does not have a monopoly of virtue, but only, with other members of the court, a monopoly of public spirit.

Lastly, these professions seem to be insincere; they offer "a perspective view." They come from the crafty politicians of the court, and they are exactly disposed to captivate good souls of "credulous morality." The credulous good souls include "many innocent gentlemen" whose distinguishing quality is "their abilities." Gentlemen with abilities who are not remarkable for birth or wealth are the most credulous of this scheme of perfection. They are also the most dangerous, because if their ambition is encouraged, they tend to serve or even to become "crafty politicians." Thus credulous goodness is not sufficient goodness; by "professions of supernatural virtue," it may be made to serve craftiness. Credulous men must be assisted by the understanding few, who are not much pleased with these professions, to resist the temptation to ambition. Burke himself must show these professions to be mere professions, a task that he can best perform, as we have seen, by exaggerating the plot behind them.

How do the "professions of supernatural virtue" correspond to Bolingbroke's program? The Patriot King is a "panacea"; he can "easily" restore a free constitution; the measures he must take are "extremely easy." Yet he has never yet appeared; he is utterly unknown to history.

A Patriot King is the most powerful of all reformers; for he is himself a sort of standing miracle, so rarely seen and so little understood, that the sure effects of his appearance will be admiration and love in every honest breast, confusion and terrour to every guilty conscience, but submission and resignation in all. A new people will seem to arise with a new king.[39]

The Patriot King is an easy and complete remedy, but one which has never been applied. This curious conjuncture in Bolingbroke's remedy precisely fits the untried and novel "scheme of perfection" that is found in Burke's description of "supernatural virtue." The essential symptoms of constitutional degeneration in Bolingbroke's analysis, party and corruption, correspond exactly to Burke's words in that description. But is the virtue of the Patriot King "supernatural virtue," as Burke has described it?

Bolingbroke's idea of the Patriot King is designed explicitly to replace traditional divine right, just as is Burke's "supernatural virtue." To make the task of the Patriot King easy, Bolingbroke has made it simpler and less taxing. He has replaced the traditional virtue of the king, whose greatness over popular virtues secured for him analogies with or even the attribution of divinity, with public spirit, or patriotism. He is a *Patriot* King, which is less than a noble or good king. Patriotism has the advantage of being a potential common denominator of the people. The reader will have noted that Bolingbroke's hostility to parties was expressed in the assertion that they were associations for certain purposes "which are not, or which are not allowed to be, those of the community by others." But the pretended divine right of kings, which must be believed implicitly, "as few will do,"[40] is just such a purpose, suited to divisive partisanship, because it is incapable of gaining common assent.

The Patriot King, then, is part of a "scheme of perfection," which has been created by reducing the standard of perfection. He can easily perform his task, unifying the nation, because that task is easy. He needs only patriotism or public spirit, not great virtue. He holds himself with decorum, not pride, and receives a legal reverence, not a humble deference. He can abolish parties because he does without the purposes that occasion parties. Many commentators have regarded Bolingbroke's theory as unseaworthy, because it requires a foolish faith in the goodness of men or in the possibility of making them good. Macaulay supposed that Bolingbroke's program was meant to put cupidity to sleep with "a few fine sentences about virtue and union."[41] But although Bolingbroke's writing certainly leaves an impression of pomposity, studied virtuousness, and naïve exactness, his theory is coolly politic. A literal interpretation of its executor is the clue to its working: the Patriot King is merely patriotic, although in a generalized sense. When lamenting the inconvenience of elective monarchy, Bolingbroke asserts that "Stoical morals and Platonic politics are nothing better than amusements for those who have had little experience in the world." He blames Cato for "the natural roughness of his temper" and for refusing to employ "those seeming compliances that are reconcilable to the greatest steadiness."[42] Bolingbroke's patriotism, based on realistic first principles, contains these "seeming" compliances.

Burke strongly implied that the "professions of supernatural virtue" were insincere, that they raised the pretensions of the king and encouraged the ambition of gentlemen of abilities. One may reasonably suppose that this could be his view of Bolingbroke's principles. The contrast between Bolingbroke's florid rhetoric and his lowered requirements suggests that he may have wished to impose upon his readers. The corresponding contrast between the decorum he recommends to the Patriot King and the many kinds of intemperance which he recommends by the example of his own life points to the same conclusion. The effect of his rhetoric may well have been what Burke criticized, for his rhetoric emphasizes the policies that the king must assert, not those he must abandon according to the theory, and the pretensions that gentlemen should advance, not those they should withdraw. The danger might be that the king learns the assertiveness, but not the discipline, of the Patriot King. Walpole speaks of "advice bequeathed by Lord Bolingbroke, who had, and with truth, assured the Late Prince of Wales that the Tories would be the heartiest in support of prerogative."[43] Thus the practical effect of Bolingbroke's rhetoric, despite the apparent intention of his theory, might be simply to encourage the abuse of prerogative—an effect which Bolingbroke might easily have foreseen.[44] We cannot decide here the truth of this criticism, but it seems to be a criticism that Burke might reasonably have made. If so, then the correspondence between Burke's sarcastic description of "supernatural virtue" and Bolingbroke's theory is complete.

The issue between Burke and Bolingbroke, as Burke saw it, was the dangerous advantage the court received from the operation of the program of "supernatural virtue" on "men of ability." Bolingbroke argued, on the other hand, that corruption in its special meaning was the sole cause of general corruption. To say that corruption was necessary to maintain a majority in Parliament does not answer his argument, for the mechanics of making a majority cannot settle the character of the constitution. One must defend those ministers for whom the majority was maintained and for whom corruption was practiced. Accordingly, in the "Thoughts" Burke does not justify the practice of corruption in the influence of the crown (so far as he does) without also justifying the privileged eligibility of the great Whig families as ministers. Bolingbroke did not attack corruption without also attacking this privilege; he attacked corruption for the purpose of replacing the rule of the great families with the rule of men of ability, led by the king. Burke defended the rule of great families and tried to modify it with the respectability of party, both to secure the greatest part of the influence of the crown for the great families and to make the operation of corruption serve party principles.

CHAPTER FIVE

The Bolingbroke Party

Burke and Bolingbroke did not confront one another directly, but contended indirectly through Burke's attempts to counteract the influence of Bolingbroke. Although that influence was not located in a single person or group, those who were affected by it had a single intent: to be a party against parties. There exists some evidence of Bolingbroke's influence on George III, which will be given later in outline. But Burke did not present the malevolence of George III as the cause of tyranny, for two reasons. Clearly, he could see dangers in a direct attack on the king as a tyrant. But, in addition, he asserts that the "furniture of ancient tyranny" is mostly worn out or unused; a new tyranny will not be the same as a Stuart tyranny.

In our study of Bolingbroke it was noted that the assertiveness of the Patriot King resembled the Stuart notions of prerogative, but was not the same. A cardinal difference is the *idea* of the Patriot King: it is necessary to spread this new idea and to oppose the traditional views of the end of the state, especially the mistaken respect for honor and the false piety in the breasts of the people, to which the Stuart kings appealed. Hence the influence of Bolingbroke might appear not only, and not chiefly, in the education of George III but also in the education of the public to the idea of the Patriot King. Such influence could be seen not so much in collected manuscripts of private transactions as in pamphlets offered at large.

In the "Thoughts," Burke mentions a single pamphlet, which he calls *Sentiments of an Honest Man,* and the political writings of Dr. Brown, both of which belong to a "political school." The task of this "political school," Burke says, is to recommend the court system to the public. Our present purpose is to investigate this "political school" as the source of danger to the constitution. Having found that Burke's attack on "supernatural virtue" probably refers to Bolingbroke, we may now ask whether this "political school" has any connection with Bolingbroke. It must also be asked whether the "political school" referred to in the "Thoughts" has any connection with "a certain political school," one of whose emanations Burke discussed in his "Observations on a late Publication Intituled The Present State of the Nation," published in 1769. The "political school" was a school of writers supporting the court; "a certain political school" was a school sharing opposition with Burke's party. If those schools are the same, we shall be led to inquire how Bolingbroke's doctrine, so hostile to faction, is available for the use of an opposition group.

John Douglas and Dr. Brown

John Douglas and Dr. Brown are the only members of the "political school" to whom Burke specifically refers. Both are more openly (but not more profoundly) antiaristocratic than Bolingbroke; chiefly, they denounce "great men" and the idea of honor held by the "great men." In studying these writers, we shall inquire into Burke's reply to their attacks, which we find surprisingly concessive. Honor is an aristocratic virtue; thus Burke's conception of honor is linked with his view of the British constitution, of the danger to it from Bolingbroke's theory, and of the remedy for that danger.

Burke's discussion of the *Sentiments of an Honest Man* (as he calls it) is in the section which includes the phrase "supernatural virtue," from which we have already supposed that the "Thoughts" was written to oppose Bolingbroke. But since Burke identifies this pamphlet in a footnote (one of only four footnotes in the "Thoughts"), our attention is directed to the original. Whereas Burke refers to actual incidents of the first decade of George III's reign with vague, evocative allusions and describes these incidents with the exaggeration necessary to incitement, he names the pamphlet that praises supernatural virtue and seduces "innocent gentlemen." Besides the professions of "supernatural virtue," he says that it contains "the first dawning of the new system": "There first appeared the idea (then only in speculation) of *separating the court from the administration;* of carrying everything from national connexion to personal regards; and of forming a regular party for that purpose, under the name of *king's men.*"[1] What do we find to fit this description in the pamphlet to which Burke directs us?

The first difficulty is that there is no pamphlet with this name. It is usually assumed that Burke meant to refer to *Seasonable Hints from an Honest Man,* published anonymously and written by John Douglas under the patronage of and at the instigation of Lord Bath.[2] Burke or his printer apparently mistook the name. The false reference serves a purpose like that of the vagueness with which Burke surrounds the incidents he narrates. Burke's vagueness both suggests and obscures the particular cause of the present discontents by borrowing generality from obscurity and plausibility from allusion. Nevertheless, the presence of a reference seems to require a comparison of Burke's description with the original pamphlet.

The suggestion that power is to be "the chosen residence of public spirit" certainly appears in the *Seasonable Hints;* Douglas avers that the new king must show his resolution to break all factious connections of "great men" from the beginning of his reign. A weak king has "the means of liberty, but wants spirit to assert it"; hence a new king can be strong, that is, free of clogging faction, by means of this spirited assertiveness. A strong king can be a good king because he will be popular; the people, composed of honest men (country gentlemen of independent fortunes and loyal principles), will sufficiently support him against parties of "great men." Thus when the king does wrong, no party will be strong enough to support him against the people; when he does right, none will be strong enough to oppose him.[3]

The great men seem to have independent power because a misplaced sense of honor binds their factions; but their consequence comes only from their distribution of the king's influence. The great men have bought dependents with the king's influence and then insolently argued their own indispensability to the king from the number of their dependents. To assert himself against these men, the king can test the loyalty of their dependents by offering them employment separate from their honored masters. In this way he can show the weakness of their sense of honor as compared to their interest in office; the dependents have only to stoop to their interest to reach their virtue. Hence, as Burke said, disgrace at court "stands in lieu of all vices," for disgrace at the court of such a king signifies an unnatural, studied factiousness which is contrary to both right and interest.[4]

"Great men" were able to borrow the king's influence in the previous reign only because they had a plausible pretense, the danger of Jacobitism. They used this to force themselves on George II as a party, an importunate confederacy designed to limit the King's choice of ministers to themselves; and they ensured a complaisant Parliament by means of electoral corruption, buying seats for their dependents and excluding the natural representatives of the people, the honest country gentlemen. But this pretense has worn thin and party distinctions no longer have any meaning, since this is "a nation of Whigs." The great men have "long basked themselves in the warm sunshine of a court."[5] They must make way for honest men, and they will make way if their pretense is discovered and their indulgence withdrawn.

Fortunately the present King has taken the reins. He has moved to separate the great men from their dependents: "If I may be allowed to credit *some* facts, which every one of my readers must have heard,—it should seem that the long-wished for time is come, when subjects may expect to receive favors from the crown, without owing the obligation to all-directing ministers."[6] To secure an honest parliament, it remains to hold an election unsullied by corruption.

Douglas anticipates that some will call this program "eutopian," but it seems to correspond more precisely to Burke's description of a plan professing "supernatural virtue." The hint quoted above sustains the impression that it is dedicated to "innocent gentlemen who had been talking prose all their lives." But there is a difference between Burke's description of the plan and Douglas' actual program. As one might have expected by now, Douglas is silent on the idea that Burke attributes to *Sentiments of an Honest Man,* the idea that a regular party of king's men should be formed for the purpose of separating the court from the administration. Douglas does not advocate that, nor does he propose any party activity for that purpose. The phrase "King's Men or Members" does occur in *Seasonable Hints,* but these men are praised only by implication, as enemies of the great men;[7] those whose conduct *is* held up as an example for all are the independent members, the honest country gentlemen. Burke regards the attack on "ministerial tyranny" as tending to separate the court from the administration, by teaching the king to rely on men of talent, whose importance he has created, rather than on men of great property and illustrious family who have an independent source of importance. But Burke's accusation that a cabal had been formed with the avowed purpose of effecting this is, as we have argued, less serious and more rhetorical than his perception of a dangerous tendency in this direction.[8]

Burke's reference to Douglas' pamphlet secures this conclusion, for Burke can have meant no other pamphlet. No pamphlet published at the beginning of George III's reign (or from 1755 to 1770) matches the scheme of "supernatural virtue" so well as Douglas' *Seasonable Hints*, though others contain elements of it. If Burke meant this pamphlet, it is past belief that he *accidentally* included things that were not in it in his description of its contents. If he did, he carelessly left the best clue to the detection of his carelessness—the footnote—which is at the same time a record of the ease with which he could have corrected it. This footnote refutes Burke's description of the pamphlet's contents—insofar as his description claims that an unstated intention is an avowed purpose. By including the consequences of the pamphlet as part of its purpose, he makes the pamphlet speak the whole truth; he makes it franker. The "sentiments" of an honest man are franker than his "seasonable hints"— if indeed an honest man ever hints. Burke's description of the pamphlet reveals that Douglas is deficient in frankness.

John Douglas is not a singular menace, as Burke shortly explains; he belongs to a political school, one of whose principal topics is "an effectual terror of the growth of an aristocratic power, prejudicial to the rights of the crown, and the balance of the constitution."[9] Burke says in a footnote to "political school": "See the political writings of the late Dr. Brown, and many others." Dr. John Brown had published in 1765, the year before his death, a political work called *Thoughts on Civil Liberty;* he was best known for his *Estimate of the Manners and Principles of Our Times*, which was chiefly a moral treatise.[10] Both works include antiaristocratic topics, which have been derived from a conclusion about morals; Dr. Brown disbelieves in the worth and efficacy of honor.

A summary of his views must suffice. Dr. Brown makes the beginning typical of modern political philosophy: the natural liberty of men in a brutal state of nature.[11] Civil liberty is possible from the salutary restraint of equal laws; but laws, because they rely solely on fear, are not enough. They must be based upon virtuous principles and manners; the principles are religion, honor, and natural conscience, and they serve to confirm civil liberty by the idea of duty. Religion supplies that idea by implanting a more awesome fear of God and adding the hope of divine rewards; honor furnishes an incentive to public spirit by encouraging a love of fame, a relish for the applause of men. Both are separate from, but contributory to, natural conscience. Natural conscience receives the implanted religion and honor and issues particular dictates of self-approbation or disapprobation. These principles, and other manners, must be infused in the conscience through education, so as to "form the habits of a youthful heart to a coincidence with the general welfare." Natural desires are too strong and harmful to be left as private vices that may procure the general welfare. Hence they must be ruled by the "highest passion," which is public spirit, the result of an educated conscience. The common good is simply the strength of the state, because a single-minded concentration on the state's strength is necessary to overcome the strength of licentiousness, the expression of natural liberty found in civil society.[12] Britain, according to Dr. Brown, is presently suffering from a crisis of moral corruption, which has brought external and internal weakness; this crisis has two causes: false honor and wealth. The corruption shows itself chiefly in the highest ranks among "those who lead the people,"[13] because they are particularly susceptible to the temptations of false honor.

Now the association of honor with the highest ranks can be found in Aristotle. A brief explanation of his conception of honor will help us to understand Dr. Brown's meaning and to indicate the character of Burke's criticism of Dr. Brown, for Burke, as well as Dr. Brown, was very far from agreeing with Aristotle. According to Aristotle, honor is an external good, perhaps the greatest of external goods, and the due reward of virtue. Because virtue is unequally distributed, honors are unequal. They also reflect, among virtuous men, inequalities of opportunity for the great deeds which attract honor, for great deeds require great occasions, and these are few.[14]

Moreover, a good man cannot be good without being conscious of it. The enjoyment of this consciousness is an internal good, but also, like honor, the reward of virtue. A good man knows he is better than others and feels disdain for them. Honor then signalizes not only superiority but disdain; it essentially requires preferences and distinctions among men. But men seek assurances of their goodness, that is, the reinforcement of their consciousness of goodness from those they believe able to perceive it. Good men are thus led to seek the association of their equals, or near-equals, in virtue, who would best perceive their virtue. Honors from *them* would be most valuable as they would come from those most qualified to bestow honor, even if they were not the actual givers of honor. Thus, although a man's honor seems to be diminished when shared, honored men by preference seek to associate with those few others who have or are worthy of honor.

It is only natural in a society that rewards virtue to have gradations of rank, with small groups at the highest levels. On the other hand, since popular government is the rule of the people, it must claim that men are equal in the ability to rule, and it therefore is hostile to honor. Popular government tries to make the people the sole fountain of honor, and emphasizes the giver of honor, not the receiver—that is, the reward more than the virtuous action that earned it. It calls its honored men "public servants," as if they served the public instead of seeking out great and difficult deeds which might also benefit the public.

Of course in actual societies, honor is often not properly bestowed; presumption is rewarded rather than merit. Following the partly erroneous view that good comes from good, men may seek to associate with a few others of equal birth, instead of those of equal virtues. Gradations may become stratifications, as the families of men who were honored replace or merge into the groups based on shared honor simply. In practice, the regime of honor, or the regime of virtue rewarded, degenerates into something less than its intention. We should expect those who attack the "aristocratical power" to oppose, in some way, the idea of honor and to castigate and ridicule the errors likely in a regime of honor.

Honor, according to Dr. Brown, has a military origin in a "spirit of defense"; this spirit is perhaps appropriate to the state of nature, but is useful to society only when it is directed to national defense.[15] In Aristotle, honor (in its ordinary meaning) finds its culmination in military activity, in facing danger for great causes. This does not mean that war is simply preferable to peace, but only that it is preferable to some kinds of peace, and war is always for the sake of the other kinds of peace. If greater good can be had by war, then the great-souled man will forsake the peace of mere security.[16] But Dr. Brown, as we have seen, believes that *the* purpose of civil society is to avoid the war which is characteristic of the state of nature. Thus the natural origin of honor immediately makes it suspect; if untamed, it may provoke an atavistic return to brutal nature. There are, then, two methods by which honor may be tamed. One is Christian religion, which cleanses honor of its spirit of conquest and softens its preference for war.[17]

But Dr. Brown recognizes the strength of desires for honor; if they cannot be successfully opposed by Christian religion, they must be transformed. In civil society he sees honor as a principle of the soul, one constituent of conscience. It is the "pride of virtue," the "love of fame"; it is something internal, not an external good. The good man contemplates his honor—which is the "applause of men"—not his goodness; honor accordingly becomes an incentive to do good, instead of a reward for having done good.[18] But as constituent of conscience, honor helps to supply the idea of duty, a standard with which to discipline desires. Honor is both an incentive and a standard; if it is the "applause of men," then honor is popularity, what the people approve. In this way, the gradations characteristic of the "regime of honor" are leveled. That is, Dr. Brown is not merely hostile to honor in the manner of a traditional supporter of popular government; he has transformed it. He has in a manner abandoned the distinction between virtuous activity and its external reward, which was stressed by Aristotle and which remains even in the stratified and degenerate "regime of virtue." For even the falsely haughty noble is haughty because he thinks his goodness (though he mistakes it) superior to the recognition of it by others. To find their own goodness, Dr. Brown's honorable men look hopefully, even timidly, to the people, who confer honor.

But if honor is "the applause of men," what is false honor? Dr. Brown criticizes the aristocracy, the "great men," for its attachment to "ties of false honor," for placing private interest above public spirit. The great men, who are placed where high offices are tempting, are open to flattery from their friends; thus the naturally keen ambitions for office are turned into debilitating squabbles. Such squabbles necessarily injure the state, since the common good is identical with the strength of the state, and strength requires a minimum of, or the abolition of, faction.[19] Honest men accordingly put national strength first and are ready to join a "rational and salutary union" to secure and support it. But ties of "friendship, gratitude and blood" impede this union by affording plausible grounds for flattering those who pretend to be above the public and for rousing party-rage, which is an effeminate survival of honor's military origin, harmful to the true national defense.[20] On the other hand, the poor, or the populace, are not free of personal interest and are also liable to dependence upon the great men. Therefore those who covet true honor should seek the applause of honest men, men in the middle state: landed gentry, the country clergy, the more considerable merchants, and tradesmen, the substantial and industrious freeholders and yeomen.[21]

There is another cause of the present moral corruption, however. Great wealth has destroyed the habit of industry in the highest ranks, since the increased trade has brought an unearned increment to the largest landed men. Their tastes have become luxurious and effeminate, a condition to which Sir Robert Walpole yielded in instituting widespread use of corruption in offices and favors, but which he has now exacerbated by teaching them to expect corruption. These men now expect and claim the great and lucrative offices not only because of ambition but also because of avarice.

Thus the real danger to the constitution now comes from the aristocratic branch; its monopolizing of offices, as evidenced by the increasing influence of the Lords in the House of Commons, may destroy honest ambition in the younger gentry and incite them to use the political power of their greater property violently and illegally against the Lords. The remedy is to remove incapable men from public office, and so far as measures are concerned, to obey the united voice of the people, which is the surest test of truth.[22] In particular, Britain needs a great minister who will regard the interests of the prince and people as inseparable. Having thus abolished all ministerial influence in Parliament, "he will endeavor to destroy Party Distinctions; and to unite all men, in the support of the common and national welfare."[23] We may guess the identity of this great minister to be William Pitt, since Dr. Brown had someone definite in mind and wrote this advisory panegyric in 1758.

Dr. Brown thus declares two causes of the dangerous growth of aristocratic power, false honor and wealth, though he seems uncertain about the relation between them. Yet, returning to Burke's discussion of the "political school" of which Dr. Brown is a member (the only one named), we find mention of only the *latter* of his arguments. Aristotle's views on honor were summarized not only to bring out Dr. Brown's meaning, but also to show the direction in which Burke might have criticized Dr. Brown, had he wished to defend the traditional idea of honor. It cannot plausibly be argued that Burke overlooked Dr. Brown's depreciation of honor, since it is very prominent in Brown's writings, and also, as we shall see, in the writings of the "many others" in his political school.

Burke makes scarcely a move in this direction. On the contrary, in a discussion of only two pages he offers one generalization, of the few disclosed throughout his writings:

> I am no friend to aristocracy, in the sense at least in which that word is usually understood. If it were not a bad habit to moot cases on the supposed ruin of the constitution, I should be free to declare, that if it must perish, I would rather by far see it resolved into any other form, than lost in that austere and insolent domination.[24]

Burke is no friend to aristocracy in the usual sense. Literally, "aristocracy" means the "rule of the best"; and in the usual sense, it refers to the rule of the great families, those called the aristocracy in Britain. An aristocracy of this sort is "austere and insolent domination"; Burke seems to regard it as the worst kind of oligarchy. What he defends is "aristocratic power," the great *influence* of the peers in the kingdom—that is, their place in a balanced constitution. This influence comes from their property; they are "men of property." If the constitution were merely a reflection of the powerful forces in a society, it would be hard to keep men of property from public concerns, because property is power. But since, in addition, the British constitution aims at liberty, it is not desirable to restrain such men, for the great influence of wealth seems to be a natural consequence of liberty.

Such is Burke's exiguous defense, in the "Thoughts," of the great influence of peers in general. As to the charge that particular peers have monopolized offices in the past, he replies that their "uniform, upright and constitutional conduct," their public and private virtues, have procured for them "influence in the country." Their influence thus *depends* on popular favor; it must be influence with the people; indeed, the importance of these peers is the "effect and pledge" of the people's importance. It is not that the peers are great by their virtues, then popular by the reputation of those virtues; they are influential with the people because of their virtues and great only because the people are great. They do not perform great deeds; they are noted only for their "uniform, upright and constitutional conduct." Yet only they can perform the political activity which earns influence, because only they are placed high enough, by their wealth, to do so. But their wealth is only the consequence of liberty, which is spread among the people; for liberty seems to be most secure when men use it to get wealth, and men are unequal in their ability to get wealth. Wealth gives its possessor a high perch only as a consequence of that widespread, more valuable possession—liberty— and serves as a pledge of its security. Activity which earns public reputation and which is done *for* the public—"upright conduct"—is secondary to the activity of the public, which shows most fully "the spirit of liberty" and in which peers share as the opulent members of the public. The peers' "state of independent greatness," as Burke describes it here, must then be independent of the king or court, not of the people. Their "proper dignity" must be conferred on their wealth only as a support to liberty, which is popular. Their "spirit" must mean spirit in defense of their power, in the service of the people's importance, for Burke also interjects a censure of those peers "who are always in the train of a court."

One consequence of this dependence of the aristocracy on the people, as seen by Burke, is a considerable depreciation of groups of friends among the peers. If the importance of the peers is caused by the people's importance and not by the importance of their deeds, they should seek reassurance of that importance by securing the trust of the people, instead of by seeking the friendship of a partner, or potential partner, in great deeds. Peers who seek each other's company for virtue thereby attainable would gather as fellow public servants, to promote activities done for the sake of more important activities, not those done for their own sake, like great deeds. A good peer can best support his own consciousness of his goodness not with his "peers," but before the people, by showing them that he is trustworthy.

In the course of this short defense of aristocracy Burke does not mention the "ties of false honor" which Dr. Brown had assailed, but he greatly deplores the attempt of the court party "to alarm the people with a phantom of the tyranny of the nobles." The latter is a dangerous attempt on that relationship most relevant to the virtuous peer's consciousness of his goodness, and thus to his goodness itself, his relation to the people. The former ties of honor are merely associations of men who are engaged in activities together to secure more important activities; the importance or degree of goodness of these associations cannot be decided without reference to the more important activity. Burke later shows that friendship among peers associated in parties protects popular liberty.

Clearly Burke's position is far removed from that of Aristotle. According to Aristotle, aristocracy is one of the good forms of constitution; in the strict sense of the rule of the best, it might mean rule by philosophers. In the absence of philosophers, Aristotle prefers the rule of gentlemen, who ought to be well off. To set riches as a qualification for rule is to admit an element of oligarchy, which is the rule of the rich for their private good, the characteristic corruption of aristocracy. But the gentlemen should be rich so that they will have leisure for moral and political cultivation and can thereby appreciate the rule of the wise. Wealth is for political virtue; it is not, as it was for Burke, a necessary consequence of liberty, whose possessors can be made to serve liberty. For Burke, popularity rather than honor is the reward of virtue; greatness among the aristocracy is subordinate to popular trust of that class. If we take seriously his denunciation of aristocracy in the usual sense as "austere and insolent domination," it must mean that the usual aristocracy, claiming supremacy because of its political virtue, is simply oligarchy. He defends the aristocratic power on the grounds of wealth, and therefore liberty, not honor. Burke's peerage seems to be composed, not of doers or rulers, but of *leaders*. The tentative and surprising conclusion then is that Burke partly accepts the criticism of aristocracy made by "that political school."

"Many others . . ."

We turn now to the "many others" in "that political school" mentioned in the same footnote in which Burke names Dr. Brown. These many others are of course represented in the very extensive pamphlet literature of the 1760's. If one attempts to characterize that literature as a whole, one must mark its special virtue as attention to argument. Almost all the authors follow a reasoned path, leaving a trail easy to see; and unburdened by doubt of the objectivity of value judgments, they feel free to prove that their recommended course is better than others, instead of relaxing after a simple assertion. Nor were there fixed party tenets at hand, convenient to indolent reasoners; "Whig" and "Tory" provided matter for constitutional reflections or personal denunciations, but not for party programs. Bolingbroke's program was at hand, but its application was not fixed, nor were its issues hackneyed. On the other hand, the seriousness of purpose of these authors is sometimes in question. They speak for "the public," and most of the pamphlets are accordingly anonymous;[25] but many authors were supported by patrons, though they were not usually hired to write a particular pamphlet. As a result, they try to peek at each other's name and source of support, and they trade charges of interestedness, spoiling the natural attraction of the hidden with labored innuendo. It was not a manly vocation.

Since the views of the "many others" do not differ markedly from the views of the two whom Burke singled out—Douglas and Brown—we may be content to show those resemblances briefly, in order to establish the existence of a "political school." And since it still remains to connect this school with Bolingbroke, the two tasks can be done at the same time. First, one must connect Brown and Douglas, although the reader may already have done so. They are alike in their preference for a free, and therefore a strong, state, a state maintained by honest men against the falsely honorable "great men." They are more openly antiaristocratic than Bolingbroke; the ambition of "innocent gentlemen" is more to the fore in their writings; but this is what Burke, in a way, had predicted. They both distinguish faction as *the* basic political evil, the culmination of all corruption. They differ chiefly in the agent to whom they assign the task of abolishing party distinction by an assertiveness to which honest men can rally: Douglas wants the King; Brown wants a "Great Minister," no doubt Pitt. But this is a small difference. It is no more than plain justice to assign these two men to the same political school, now composed of two. The connection of these two to Bolingbroke is no less plain. It is especially vivid in the *Seasonable Hints* of John Douglas, whose patron was Lord Bath, a former associate of Bolingbroke. Douglas' appeal for a spirited king amounts to Bolingbroke's for a Patriot King in all but name. Dr. Brown's relation to Bolingbroke is only slightly less clear. Dr. Brown, though praising Bolingbroke in other respects, attacked his irreligion and in the *Estimate* pronounced Montesquieu to be his favorite author. But in that same treatise he quoted with approval Bolingbroke's intolerance of faction; and in the *Thoughts on Civil Liberty,* he contradicted Montesquieu's claim that a free society must tolerate faction. Montesquieu did not disclose the bleakly Hobbesian view of the state of nature which Dr. Brown adopts. Dr. Brown seems to be predominantly a disciple of Bolingbroke.

These difficulties with Dr. Brown illustrate the problem in ascribing influence to Bolingbroke. There is first the difficulty in proving that one political philosopher has affected a host of vulgarizing writers. Unlike premodern political philsophers, Bolingbroke intended, as a direct consequence of his philosophical conclusions, a wholesale reformation of political society, brought about chiefly by the spread of his doctrine. He therefore *wanted* his doctrine to be vulgarized; he wanted it to be seized upon, made simpler to suit uncomplicated minds, and fitted to less harmful prejudices in an alliance against the worst prejudices. Indeed, it seems that he started on this task himself in "The Idea of a Patriot King." We would therefore expect to find his doctrine impure, alloyed with incompatible ideas, tainted by inadequate comprehension of the full doctrine. The hallmarks to look for are a few simple political ideas, which may be caught in slogans: first, the idea of the Patriot King, then the absolute intolerance (as opposed to the traditional disapproval) of faction, the depreciation of honor, and the attack on the great families.

But it is also hard to single out Bolingbroke's ideas from those of others when he is not named. As we have seen, Bolingbroke took his basic principles from Hobbes and Locke, who were also "Enlightenment philosophers" in the manner just defined. They sought popular disciples and they (Locke especially) gained them. Their ideas have been diffused along with those of Bolingbroke,[26] frequently by Bolingbroke himself. In fact, it is in some respects contrary to Bolingbroke's intention, to separate his influence from Locke's. If one were to define strictly Bolingbroke's precise contribution to modern political philosophy, one might have to narrow the search for his influence to the idea of the Patriot King alone. But then Bolingbroke intended to propagate other ideas associated with this one; so his influence (what he meant to popularize) is larger than his contribution (what was his alone). For example, since he wanted men to hold the view that civil society is artificial, he adopted as his intended influence, the extension of Locke's influence. We cannot suppose that the fragments of Bolingbroke's thought found scattered in political pamphlets of the 1760's indicate an exclusive and profound attention to his principles; but the spread of his influence did not require, and was not intended to require, that kind of attention from pamphlet writers. When we see in political pamphlets the program of the Patriot King, supported by those principles of modern political philosophy that Bolingbroke shared, we may reasonably conclude that Bolingbroke's influence is decisive. When we see ideas advocated whose manifest tendency is to further that program, we can suspect such influence to be present.

Perhaps influence is most surely present when the author names his mentor. But he may not name it correctly, as we suspect in reference to Dr. Brown. In Bolingbroke's case, his open doubts about the truth of Christian revelation and his political association with the Pretender—no less dubious but certainly inglorious for its flighty nature—gave his name an odium that no patriotic or prudent man would lightly choose to share. This odium is perhaps sufficient cause of the scattering of his influence, for an influence which cannot be avowed can hardly be gathered. Yet it is astonishing that Bolingbroke's views should be quoted and praised as often as they were, which was more often than the views of the great Whig lords whom Burke celebrated in the "Thoughts."

These Whig lords were, in a way, the founders of the present realm. It is true that they were not celebrated as such, because this would have implied a discontinuity between the Stuarts and William III unfavorable to the claims of legitimacy of the Hanoverian kings and harmful to the habit of obeying them. But if the Whigs could not pose in popular opinion as founders, they were surely very prominent ushers; and they were highly successful ushers, identified with the current, well-established regime. Further, the reputation of these ushers was available, by family tie and by political connection, for appropriation by Bolingbroke's political opponents during his lifetime and after. Hence Bolingbroke and his principles must have had powerful charm to overcome the influence of the great Whig lords, the partisan inheritance of his opponents—especially when manifest dishonor and thorough failure, both always so impressive to the people, told against him. It would certainly be no surprise to find Bolingbroke's influence unavowed; or to find, as is frequent, his political principles accepted without acknowledgment, and his religious views attacked.

One last difficulty has already been dealt with indirectly: the objection that Bolingbroke's principles are mere verbiage, in no way distinctive, and therefore are inconsequential. We have, in the analysis of Bolingbroke, shown the innocent appearance of Bolingbroke's rhetoric to be deceptive and have indicated the Aristotelian views, with different consequences, themselves closer to traditional platitudes, against which Bolingbroke contended.

We turn to those writers that most clearly show the influence of Bolingbroke. Owen Ruffhead is a prime example. In *Reasons Why the Approaching Treaty of Peace Should Be Debated in Parliament* (1760), he argues that Parliament should consider the terms of the peace treaty, because Parliament is now uncorrupt and untouched by faction—an event for which he gives the credit to Pitt. But in *Ministerial Usurpation,* published later in the same year, he notices an "undue Ministerial influence," caused by pretensions of rank. Rank gives the Duke of Newcastle, for example, pre-eminence only as a subject, not as a statesman; that is, rank should not affect the King's choice of his ministers. Even if Newcastle and the other great lords are good men, they offer no security of government: ". . . how dangerous and miserable must the condition of that kingdom be, which depends for its security, on the personal virtue of its governors, who cannot ensure their own existence for a moment!" Security is then the great aim of a state, and faction its worst enemy. But these ministers, by means of their rank and opulence, lure their followers into their factious schemes: "Men of little knowledge and less reflection cherish a groundless confidence; They are more attached to names and persons, than to material and essential properties. Under a Patriot King and a virtuous Administration, they can form no idea of a future tyrant or traitor."

Ruffhead here shows himself to be not only an advocate of Bolingbroke (although he does attack him for the Treaty of Utrecht) but a careful student of his ideas; he produces the Patriot King as an *innocent* idea, not as an edifying one; he presents it as an idea incapable of bringing political evil, which is defined in terms of insecurity, not of vice. By 1763, in his *Considerations on the Present Dangerous Crisis,* Ruffhead has become disillusioned with Pitt; he praises him for his attempt to destroy parties, but blames his vanity for his resignation, which encouraged faction and gave the administration to the incompetent Lord Bute. Ruffhead, like Dr. Brown, here disagrees with Montesquieu's belief that faction is a necessary and tolerable result of a free society; he asks the king to discountenance both parties by choosing non-party men for offices: ". . . there are some honest independent, moderate *neuters* among us, who have never walked in the trammels of party." Ruffhead ends with the same appeal to "innocent gentlemen" that Burke noticed in Douglas' *Seasonable Hints.*[27]

Sir John Marriot, a former dependent of Newcastle, addressed his *Political Considerations* (1762) to his former patron in an attempt to persuade him to stay in retirement. This is never an amiable theme, and Marriot did little to sweeten it. We have a new system of government now, he said: free from the "miserable spectacle of faction." This is fortunate, for ". . . the permanency of every blessing we enjoy under Providence depends upon our unanimity. . . ." Britain now needs men "to direct public opinion, and to combat prejudices, old and new"; and who can better do so than an Honest Man, "a more illustrious title than the Greatest Monarchs can bestow." Marriot outlines the program of the Patriot King, without calling him such:

> . . . if it is possible to put the reins of government at any time into the hands of virtue, it is possible to do it with the greatest hope of success at the beginning of a reign, when the prince declares himself the enemy of corruption and requires nothing of his people but to be free; when the reasons pleaded for encouraging venality no longer subsist in the firm establishment of the throne, once in danger from a foreign pretender, but now filled by a Sovereign born in this country. . . .
> How happy an opportunity is there then offered, under these circumstances, of destroying . . . all ancient distinctions so fatal to the common good.[28]

Tobias Smollett, the novelist, was the editor of a weekly paper, *The Briton,* in 1762 and 1763; this was the publication that inspired the name of John Wilkes's famous *North Briton.* The present administration, Smollett declares, because it "defies the censure of prying envy and unwearied faction" and because it has been chosen by a sovereign who rules "without distinction of party," is "a phenomenon which, I believe, never appeared in England before." Bolingbroke stressed the newness of the idea of the Patriot King, and Smollett seems to have picked up that theme. At the same time, it is possible for the idea of the Patriot King in vulgarized form to inspire aggressiveness in the service of the crown's "ancient lustre," as it did in George III—in place of the true, more realistic goals of the Patriot King; and Smollett begins *The Briton* with a (for him) fulsome puff of the "exalted virtue" of the young King. Smollett continues, arguing that British success in the war is due to Britain's "universal spirit of union . . . sprung from a national conviction of party-inconvenience"—thus pointing out that it is the task of the people to make a strong, uncorrupt government possible. The people are not "the vulgar of England"; they are the King's loyal subjects, and as such, should enjoy "equal liberties and privileges." Even if they have great property and family, they can "have no natural pretension to be minister." The King's choice is personal; he should choose the person *he* knows best.[29]

Concurrently with *The Briton, The Auditor* appeared, edited by Arthur Murphy, a playwright and actor. Its purpose was to extinguish national prejudices and "to refute or laugh out of countenance all party distinctions." Murphy says, "I shall not have recourse to Bolingbroke, for I do not want to captivate the imagination with a glow of lavish ornament. . . ." But that Murphy's literary distaste does not extend to the substance of the idea can be seen in No. 29 of *The Auditor*, which he begins by quoting Bolingbroke on the origin of Whiggism. After the Hanoverians came, Murphy continues, Whigs and Tories "retained only the nominal existence of former divisions; their essence underwent a total change"; they became court and country parties. This again is Bolingbroke's observation, repeated by Sir Lewis Namier. But even this difference is now at an end:

> By the accession of a king *born and bred in these kingdoms*, who glories *in the name of Briton*, a revolution in parties has been brought about, which men of gloomy imaginations despaired of, and from which all sanguine lovers of their country may promise themselves the most solid advantages; a revolution which renders a court-party unnecessary, for the crown has nothing distinct from the public welfare to ask; a revolution, which makes even the cares and wishes of the well-intentioned supererogatory, for the king takes the lead himself in a general plan of sound national policy.

We note the reference to revolution, an easy revolution based on consulting only what the King would do in his own interest (because his own interest is not distinct from the public welfare), and not dependent on the "cares and wishes of the well-intentioned"—perhaps as opposed to their *interest*.

In this same number Murphy triumphantly asks why parties should be revived when there is no danger of tyranny. It is necessary to quote him at length, because his rhetorical questions suggest Burke's difficulty in rousing opposition to the "cabal" in the absence of the "furniture of ancient tyranny":

> And is this a season in which any honest man can with decency call for a revival of parties long since extinguished? Has the crown made any strides towards an unconstitutional power? Have any designs to strain the prerogative, or to entrench upon the rights of the subject been discovered? Has any popish lord been sworn of the privy council? Why then are the old principles of resistance, exclusion, abdication and deposition to embitter our minds again? Have the tories renewed the old exploded doctrines of divine right, passive obedience, and non-resistance, so as to require a check to bring them back to a more temperate system of government? If this were the case, it would be an honest, it would be a patriot work to set up a *whiggish union* to controul a dangerous faction. But we boast a king upon the throne who has studied, and respects our excellent gothic constitution, and requires no kind of passive obedience or non-resistance from

his subjects, but that which they owe to the laws; and in discharge of this duty he himself holds up to his people an illustrious example; an example which all good men admire, and which only a few turbulent persons amongst us are not willing to imitate.

"There is a species of men in this country," Murphy states, "who consider themselves possessed of an hereditary right to the favors of the crown." Under their "ministerial system," talents do not advance; but the present king encourages "virtuous ability." Murphy quotes the advice of the "judicious Machiavel," that the prince should avoid the minister who courts popularity and hence independence. The minister will regard only the honor of the prince if he owes his honors to the prince. Thus, the best ministers are men of talent who owe their rise to the king, those whose honor rewards their interest. If the king follows this policy he will strip the parties of their adherents, since they will "shortly find their patron, strenuous as he has been in mischief, able to draw but a scanty number into the vortex of his giddy politicks. . . ."[30]

Thomas Pownall, who was the governor of Massachusetts in 1757, wrote the *Principles of Polity*, a dialogue stating "the grounds and reasons of civil empire," in 1752. In 1764, he wrote a pamphlet called *The Administration of the Colonies*, which was dedicated to George Grenville, though it differed somewhat from Grenville's policies. Pownall's *Principles of Polity* is a theoretical work whose design is to cure a practical consequence of Locke's principles.

The theory of the social contract, according to Pownall, has recently been misrepresented as a mere coalition between the king and the people, as if there were two conflicting parties in the state of nature. The "noble author of the *Dissertation on Parties*" has shown the error of this; he has argued that such a coalition is no true union, but makes a government which must be carried on by parties and oppositions.

Indeed, this specious coalition contract now gives a handle to parties, who base their activity on a false understanding or a false claim of natural liberty. Against this view of the social contract, Pownall justly quotes Locke, that not the people and the king, but the people with each other, are the first contractors. The community, Pownall says, at first composed of equals, is a natural communion with a single interest, not an artificial grouping; though equal as contractors, its members have rank according to their property. Property, understood as a part of the community secured by the contract, places its possessor in society just as surely as its matter fixes the station of any part of the universe; therefore influence in government should be proportionate to property, because this "real and manifest" rule opens no quarrels. In short, Pownall makes some modifications of Locke's doctrine without challenging its fundamentals, and he does this in response to Bolingbroke's opinion on the intolerableness of faction.[31]

Charles Lloyd, a Member of Parliament and political agent for Lord Grenville, wrote several pamphlets that show traces of Bolingbroke's influence. This influence is most prominent in *The Anatomy of a Late Negotiation,* which begins with a quotation from Bolingbroke: "The Spirit of Liberty is a jealous spirit; and Faction is equally the object of its jealousy, whether the views of Faction be directed in favour of the Crown or against it." The true spirit of liberty does not try to divide the strength of the kingdom; only party rage is designed to deceive and betray. The present discussion is caused not by just one man, Wilkes, but by the nobility—in this case Newcastle and Devonshire—who have tried to force Pitt on the King. Luckily the royal breast is firm.[32]

John Almon, a publisher and a prolific (because repetitious) pamphleteer, praised Bolingbroke as "the best political writer that ever appeared in England." Using Bolingbroke's distinction between the Tories as the country party and the Whigs as the courtiers' party, he traced the bad effects of ministerial influence in George II's reign and concluded that George II had lived to see the spirit of party extinguished by Pitt. Pitt is the man who changed the face of affairs in Britain; his entrance into the Ministry was forced by "the general voice of an abused people" against the great families. The aristocratic part of the constitution is too heavy, and it is now possible to find true virtue only among "the middle rank of mankind."[33]

In *The History of the Late Minority,* appearing in 1766, Almon, still a partisan of Pitt, claims that if Bute were not in existence, not one of the recent evils would have occurred.[34] Bute took his ideas of government from a "silly paper" delivered some years ago by the chiefs of the Tory opposition, which, after promising to destroy faction, listed some measures against corruption to be taken by Prince Frederick at his accession. But Almon did not consider the aim of destroying faction to be silly, for he praises Pitt as an enemy of parties and attacks Newcastle as a party man, a creator of obsequious dependents. And he chiefly attacks the Rockingham group because they co-operated with Bute. Ever since his resignation, Bute has carried on a clandestine administration; when the Grenville administration tried to expel Bute's friends, the King dismissed it for this reason alone. If at that time the Rockingham group, the "Late Minority," had refused to take office, the Favorite would have been beaten. But it accepted office, and Bute's influence is as strong as ever. Almon's writings are hostile to the King and in the interest of the "Patriot Minister" Pitt, but his antiaristocratic attack on party is Bolingbroke's.

John Douglas' patron, Lord Bath, wrote a pamphlet in 1763 welcoming "the warm and zealous affection of all ranks to our patriot king." This virtuous King has introduced "an uncorrupt and strenuous administration"; and as a result, "our parties and prejudices have now most happily ceased." "The mean arts of corruption" have been "nobly discountenanced by the highest authority and all honest men have been invited from the throne to cooperate with their sovereign in advancing the prosperity of the nation."[35]

The author of *A Letter from a Gentleman in Town,* writing in 1763, exclaims: "A patriot king, and a patriot minister have been described in the writings of the learned, and held up as objects of admiration and desire: I fear this country has beheld them both [George III and Bute, in this case] and has not known them."[36]

Another author, in *The Conduct of the Administration in the Prosecution of Mr. Wilkes* (1764), notes the same fact and suggests a reason:

His majesty, therefore, seems to have formed himself, I mean with regard to the government of his kingdoms, upon the Idea of a Patriot King. Yet, unhappily, while we acknowledge all the virtues, necessary to form that most exalted of all human characters, because most capable of doing good, still we must suppose a patriot people too, to be the objects of those virtues, that they may produce their natural and desirable effects.

Wilkes is animated by the spirit of party, and in appealing to the mob (as distinguished from the people), he only follows the example of the "gentlemen": "Already have they [the gentlemen] alarmed us with the terrors of an aristocracy, by assuming a kind of hereditary right to all the great employments of government. Already have they exposed us to popular riots and confusion, by appealing to the decisions of the populace."[37] The gentlemen are thus in alliance with the rabble, whose poverty makes them dependent, against the Patriot King, who seeks the support of a patriot people.

Burke's Observations

We have been able to construct a "political school" based on the ideas and recommending the policies to which Burke alludes in the "Thoughts," and which are characteristic of or directly attributed to Bolingbroke. There is other material to be considered for this connection. In 1769, Burke wrote a pamphlet, "Observations on a Late Publication, Intituled, 'The Present State of the Nation.'" He begins this pamphlet as he begins the "Thoughts," with a discussion of the intervention of a private man in politics. First he says that party divisions are inseparable from free government; then he asks what a good citizen should do when he is confronted by this circumstance. Private citizens should be neutral and innocent; public men must act, or desert the post entrusted to them by the laws and institutions of their country. But they must act with moderation; and that is why "a very respectable party" has quietly borne repeated attacks "for these two years past, from one and the same quarter of politics." Moreover, this party has suffered these attacks from another opposition group in the knowledge that there was a plan, long and successfully pursued, to "break the strength of this kingdom by frittering down the bodies which compose it, by fomenting bitter and sanguinary animosities, and by dissolving every tie of social affection and public trust"—a plan to which they could not wish to contribute. Finally a pamphlet has appeared, however, that offers such indignities to the country that it is no virtue to ignore it: "This piece is called *The present State of the Nation*. It may be considered as a sort of digest of the avowed maxims of a certain political school, the effects of whose doctrines and practices this country will feel long and severely."[38]

Having observed the phrase "political school" in the "Thoughts," our question must be: Is this the same political school? First, we can see that the reference in the "Observations" is more restricted than that in the "Thoughts." Here Burke speaks of "two years past"—i.e., since the end of the Rockingham administration; and the "political school" refers only to apparent fellow opponents of "the plan." *The Present State of the Nation* was written by George Grenville and William Knox; the other pamphlets which Burke names in a footnote are *History of the Minority*, written by John Almon; *History of the Repeal of the Stamp Act*, probably by Charles Lloyd, an agent of Grenville;[39] *Considerations on Trade and Finance*, written by Thomas Whately, a dependent of Grenville; and the *Political Register*, which was printed by Almon. Now Almon was an adherent of Pitt and Lord Temple (at that time separated in politics from his brother George Grenville), and he heavily criticized Grenville's administration, especially in its handling of Wilkes. Thus, although *The Present State* came out of the Grenville party and another reference to the author's "faction" could only mean the Grenville party,[40] Burke seems to refer to opposition groups generally, except for the "very respectable party"; but he includes "a set of men who pretended to be actuated by motives similar to theirs." If we judge by the pamphlets mentioned, we conclude that the "certain political school" of the "Observations" is smaller than "that political school" of the "Thoughts."

The content of the pamphlet Burke attacks must also be considered. Burke's "Observations" on that pamphlet consists of four parts: the Introduction already described, an analysis of *The Present State*, a defense of the Rockingham ministry, and a proposed remedy for the canker Burke sees in the constitution[41] (this will be compared later with the remedy offered in the "Thoughts"). Burke's analysis of *The Present State* begins with this remark about its tone:

> As to the composition, it bears a striking and whimsical resemblance to a funeral sermon, not only in the pathetic prayer with which it concludes, but in the style and tenor of the whole performance. It is piteously doleful, nodding every now and then towards dulness; well stored with pious frauds, and, like most discourses of the sort, much better calculated for the private advantage of the preacher than the edification of the hearers.[42]

This passage quickly recalls the "professions of supernatural virtue" so useful to "crafty politicians," which we have examined in the "Thoughts." Those professions are also pious frauds, have the same end in view, and use the same means—a specious concern for the edification of "innocent gentlemen."

Burke's analysis of *The Present State* comes in clear, summary form immediately after his remark on the tone of that pamphlet:

> The apparent intention of this author [of *The Present State*] is to draw the most aggravated, hideous, and deformed picture of the state of this country which his querulous eloquence, aided by the arbitrary dominion he assumes over fact, is capable of exhibiting. . . . But far the greater and much the worst part of the state which he exhibits, is owing, according to his representation, not to its radical weakness and constitutional distempers. All this however is not without purpose. The author hopes, that, when we are fallen into a fanatical terror for the national salvation, we shall then be ready to throw ourselves—in a sort of precipitate trust, some strange disposition of the mind jumbled up of presumption and despair—into the hands of the most pretending and forward undertaker.

The Present State draws a picture of utter constitutional distress, then attempts "the reformation of a corrupt world" by remedies "ridiculously disproportionate to the evil" it represents.[43] Burke first proves, by quotation and by implication from the text of the pamphlet, how intolerable Britain's situation would be, if it were as represented; then he shows how inadequate the proposed remedies would be. Next, he denies that Britain's situation is truly represented in the pamphlet. Without following the detail of Burke's analysis, we can see that its outline is the same as that of

Bolingbroke's system. Bolingbroke's system also rested on a judgment that the constitution was entirely corrupt and in its present state illegitimate and intolerable; and his system also emerged with a solution to such radical disruption, which, though unprecedented, was surprisingly easy to execute—"perhaps in the course of the present Parliament," *The Present State* asserts.[44]

The cause of the present difficulties, according to *The Present State*, is the last war, which though it "ended happily" for Britain, was very costly. It only ended happily because England "had a prince on the throne who preferred the future welfare of his own people to the glory of making conquests upon his enemies; and was willing to forego the honours of new triumphs, to secure to them the blessing of peace." The glory and honors of the war are the king's alone; they do not pertain to the people, who must have the blessings of peace, that is, commerce and industry. Burke notices how this opinion lessens the achievements of British valor; and we must remark that it is consistent with Bolingbroke's depreciation of military glory. "The unfortunate expenses of the late war" were a constant topic of the Grenville connection, who always made a show of their scruples and spoke primly of thrift, to spite the great deeds of the war.[45]

Lastly, *The Present State* includes a disapproving reference to the "great men of the nation," implying that their influence, though diminished, is still pernicious. After listing a number of measures favored by the Grenville connection as cures for Britain's corruption, the authors recommend that the administration be committed to "men of virtue and ability." It has already been suggested that this is a catch phrase of those, under Bolingbroke's influence, who wished to purge the state of its aristocratic elements; and it is noteworthy that Burke adverts to the use of this phrase in *The Present State*. He shows that, after the general condemnation of all classes and of all recent administrations but that of Grenville, the phrase makes sense only as a particular assertion of the Grenville ambition; in itself, as a description of a proper administation, it "conveys no definite idea at all." Those who, by the condemnation of the authors of *The Present State*, are not among the ranks of "men of virtue and ability," according to Burke, are "many of them of the first families"—and Burke presents a defense of their importance, which will be considered later. Here we remark that Burke again turns his attention to, and comments severely upon, an aspect of *The Present State* that is characteristic of Bolingbroke's influence.[46]

It may then be concluded, first, that *The Present State* advocates Bolingbroke's policies in all its chief arguments—that Britain suffers from the desire for military glory (no matter whose desire), that its consequent difficulties require a reformation which is surprisingly easy, and that this reformation must be accomplished by "men of virtue and ability." *The Present State* contains no mention of Bolingbroke, however, though there is a quotation from Locke. Secondly, Burke saw these policies as the chief arguments in *The Present State* and opposed them, though he did this also without mentioning Bolingbroke. Thirdly, the chief arguments in *The Present State*, as reported in Burke's "Observations," are those which he attacked in the "Thoughts" as typical of a "political school,"—with one exception. We may recall that in his analysis of Douglas' pamphlet (the chief product of the "political school") in the "Thoughts," he said that "power was thenceforward to be the chosen residence of public spirit." The association of power and public spirit naturally does not appear in his analysis of *The Present State*, an opposition pamphlet; and this is the chief difference between the "political school" mentioned in the "Thoughts" and the "certain political school" mentioned in the "Observations."

There were, then, no strict party lines which delineated Bolingbroke's influence in the 1760's; so far, we have encountered one cluster of influence around George Grenville. A second cluster was around William Pitt, the favorite "patriot minister" of John Almon and Dr. Brown; and Pitt, to speak briefly, constantly opposed the idea of a monarchy limited by ruling through aristocratic connection, and always preferred a non-party administration of able men, led by himself, the most illustrious example of risen merit in England in the eighteenth century. The third cluster was around the King. In 1769, when Burke published his "Observations," the three groups were in separate camps: Pitt had just retired, because of his gout, from a ministry roundly censured in *The Present State;* he had the cool respect of the King, who remembered both his great deeds during the Seven Years' War and his desertion of Leicester House, before George III's accession, that made those deeds possible. Grenville, who differed with Pitt on American policy, was detested by the King, who in 1765 preferred even Rockingham to him. But it had not always been so. The "Boy Patriots," as Walpole called them, had been prominent in the opposition during the 1735 Parliament; they included William Murray (later Lord Mansfield), George Lyttleton, Richard Grenville (later Lord Temple), George Grenville, and William Pitt.[47] They had previously been political students of Bolingbroke, at this time in France, and had listened to his conversation at Leicester House and attended his speeches; and now they served under the Prince of Wales, who was resentfully opposing his father's minister, Walpole—that is, Frederick, prince of Wales, father of

George III, friend of Bolingbroke and follower of his principles, whose court, according to Burke's "Thoughts," was the reputed source of the new project carried into execution by the court cabal under George III. The three clusters of Bolingbroke's influence were, at this time, intimately associated, except for George III himself, who seems to have been tutored by students of Bolingbroke.

George III's subpreceptor was the mathematician George Lewis Scott, appointed on the recommendation of Bolingbroke; his subgovernor was Andrew Stone, a close friend of William Murray; and the first preceptor he had was Dr. Francis Ayscough, who was related to and recommended by Lord Lyttleton. In the absence of research into George III's education, it is hard to know how much weight to give to this evidence of association. An influence ill taught or ill learned is certainly curtailed, but the influence of Bolingbroke on George III seems to have been strong. There is ample evidence of Bolingbroke in the letters of George III, although they are somewhat vague and confused. In 1762, George III wrote that he plans a complete and utterly new reformation, "a path unknown," which is to be accomplished by acting through his advisers rather than his ministers. This is an easy reformation, "which probably this session will quite effect"; and it consists of the frustration of "the wicked machinations of faction." George III even understood correctly why the reformation can be so easy. If society can be founded on truth, all hostility is impermanent and irrational, and ambitious men can be trusted to abandon their "wicked machinations" for the sake of their ambition: "When men see no other resource they will even aid in that [reformation in government] rather than be driven out: if on perseverence this should not be effected by the venality of the age. . . ."[48]

Last and most important in this summary, George III's policy, so far as it was his and not decided by events and by greater men than he, was at least in part the Bolingbroke program. He tried for five months to rule without secret-service funds, which were one much decried source of corruption; and in 1762, after the resignation of the Duke of Devonshire, he and Lord Bute carried out a general dismissal of the dependents of the Duke of Newcastle, in what was intended and regarded as a purge of the agents of aristocratic domination. Bute was a man of birth and wealth but, as Burke said, "little known or considered in the kingdom"; he was raised to his importance, with some pertinacity, by George III. Bute agreed that the nation was menaced by a "most factious combination of *soi disant* great men." Bute was a man who, said Dr. Johnson in 1775, "though a very honorable man . . . was a theoretical statesman,—a book minister—and thought this country could be governed by the influence of the Crown alone."[49] But which theory and what book? Boswell did not ask. Regarding the "king's men," those willing competents whom Bute and George III attempted to gather, it is not misleading to call them civil servants in genesis if one remembers that Bolingbroke intended the entire government under the Patriot King to be a kind of non-partisan civil service. Without making the detailed study of the origins of Bolingbroke's influence that ought to be made, we can offer a highly probable conclusion: Burke meant Bolingbroke's school when he said "a certain political school."

Burke attacked Bolingbroke indirectly, through those whom he influenced in the 1760's. Why did he do so? Apparently Burke *intended* to avoid delineating party lines on the question of Bolingbroke's influence. He might have thought that if Bolingbroke's influence was bad, mentioning him would increase it, or that Bolingbroke was partly right and that an attack on him by name could not discriminate the good to be saved from the bad to be denounced, or that both reasons were sound. If one supposes that Burke thought that Bolingbroke's influence was evil, as is at least largely true, then it is easy to see that Burke might fear that mentioning Bolingbroke would augment his influence. We shall consider the second possibility later.

Burke had said: "A certain political school, the effects of whose doctrines and practices this country will feel long and severely." The influence is powerful, and we saw from the beginning that its doctrines are plausible: Who is opposed to a union of harmony and strength, to the abolition of corruption, to the employment of men of virtue and ability, to the destruction of aristocratic faction? To mention Bolingbroke might send his readers to peruse those seductive doctrines or excite Bolingbroke's followers to defend and explain them more widely. Burke's first published work, "A Vindication of Natural Society," was a satire on Bolingbroke; but his famous estimate of Bolingbroke, in the "Reflections on the Revolution in France," indicates that he did not wish the general public to repeat his readings: "Who now reads Bolingbroke? Who ever read him through?"[50] It might be supposed that Bolingbroke's political failures would have cast obloquy on his doctrines and that Burke could have easily shown treason to be the consequence of the ideas of a traitor, or near-traitor. But this is to reckon without the charm of the man and of his doctrines. The fact is that the influence of Bolingbroke's writings survived his political failures, just as his personal influence revived after every twist of his career. Bolingbroke was astonishingly durable.

Party and Opposition

If Bolingbroke's influence extended to the opposition to George III, we must face an objection. How can an opposition be founded on intolerance of faction? How is Bolingbroke's influence available to those who wish to oppose the administration? Bolingbroke himself engaged in opposition, but in doing so, did he not teach British statesmen the practices of constitutional opposition?[51] Thus, contrary to his intention, did he not prepare the way for Burke's praise of party, which was only a justification of an existing condition? There are three answers to this objection, and three kinds of opposition which must be distinguished.

First, it is true that Bolingbroke was most often in opposition, and first set forth his program for a systematic opposition in "A Letter on the Spirit of Patriotism." But these facts are not inconsistent with a desire to destroy faction. We are entitled to say that Bolingbroke had a program and that he advocated the adoption of it by a party, the "country party." Bolingbroke was the first political philosopher to make the natural rights of men, however modified or disguised as the natural duties of men, the basis of an explicitly party program. He uses the term "party" usually to mean something bad, but occasionally to mean the "country party."[52] This party, it may be remembered, is not properly called a "party" because in principle it represents the country. Until the disaffected and the falsely ambitious subside to their true interests, however, Bolingbroke with reason calls the country a party. In this use of the term, Bolingbroke may seem to adopt what has been called the traditional view of party: a generally hostile attitude to party with the exception of its use in bad circumstances by wise statesmen.

The traditional view of party can be connected to the partisanship of the regime, according to Plato and Aristotle. The traditional view of party was a popular or unphilosophic view, unaware of the partiality of the regime. The Spartan did not consider himself unduly specialized and "laconic," but properly disciplined as a man. Public opinion was traditionally hostile to parties for the sake of its conception of the common good, which from a philosophic standpoint was itself partial. The traditional view deplored what it could recognize as party in the name of what it could not recognize as party; that is, it was hostile to internal divisions in order to maintain the harmony and integrity of the regime, whose partiality it could neither understand nor avoid even if it had understood.

Now Bolingbroke combines the traditional view of party with the philosophic view which is critical of it. He is not, as he seems, a simple believer in the traditional view of party. According to him, the regime is founded on true first principles, so that it is not partial. First principles are not the highest truths to which men can aspire; on the contrary, they are the lowest truths from which men can aspire. They are indisputable, and first principles are therefore neither partial nor partisan. It follows that Bolingbroke's attitude to parties is more hostile than the traditional view: he allows only one exception, a party against parties, which must establish a regime in which parties are impossible, at least during the reign of the Patriot King, whose successor can easily be educated. Holders of the traditional view of parties could never claim to have eliminated all future need for party on the occasion of one use of party, because injustice might return.

Bolingbroke advocated an antiparty party, but his party was essentially different from the parties he meant to abolish with it. It was based on principles which were essentially non-partisan; his party was to be the last party. The first modern party was the party which regarded itself as *the last* party. Jefferson, the founder of party in America, who, unlike Bolingbroke, was able to carry through a party program to organization and victory, also believed that the success of "republican principles" would conclude the possibilities of legitimate partisanship. The respectability, the praise—nay, even the incitement of partisanship—which we hear and see today in all its ludicrous postures and determined measures, in its languid unconcern and febrile vehemence, had its origin in the belief that parties can and should be abolished. When Bolingbroke's party was conceived and formed in its separate divisions, the basis for the respectability of party was laid. Bolingbroke's party attacked the traditional view, however, not for its general hostility to parties, but for its exceptions to this hostility. When the new absolute hostility to parties had succeeded so far that the traditional hostility to parties was obsolete, the foundations for the respectability of party were complete. Burke never tried to refute the traditional view of parties with respect to the "great parties" of the seventeenth century. Instead he argued for the possibility of reasonable and tolerable parties on the grounds that the "great parties" were gone beyond recall. If these parties *were* gone beyond recall, the reason was the success of the belief, propagated by Bolingbroke and others, that a society can and must be organized in a non-partisan way. The modern respectability of party has resulted from a heightened hostility to party in the sense of the "great parties."

In the second place, it is true that many pamphlets in the 1760's, including some that show Bolingbroke's influence, also praise the virtues of opposition. But one ought to consider what they say.

The author of *The Conduct of the Administration* says: "That an opposition, founded on public virtue, supported by abilities, and conducted with temper, will be for ever serviceable to the interests of liberty, no friend of liberty should deny." But there is a qualification:

> Abilities and integrity can alone entitle it [opposition] to the reverence and esteem of the public. When the contending parties in a state are nearly equal, the contest becomes dangerous to the public welfare. It is then equally the duty of an opposition, zealous for the publick good, to support administration in every scheme of national advantage, as to oppose it in every dangerous or oppressive measure.

Sir John Marriot expressed the view that an opposition to measures, not men, is necessary in some cases, for "the good of the whole results frequently from the collision of the parts." Owen Ruffhead instructed the King that he must never admit men of any cabal into the ministry; but he hoped that their cabaling opposition, founded on interest, would be superseded by an opposition founded on sentiment. "This will produce a noble competition, who shall best advise for the public welfare. *Measures*, not *men*, will then be the subjects of debate."[53]

These authors, and the several others who repeat their thoughts, attempt to justify a "constitutional" opposition only, as opposed to a factious unconstitutional opposition. They do not attempt to uphold every opposition as constitutional, but they consistently attack faction and praise opposition. The recommended opposition involves a competition of able men, together if they are like-minded, apart if they are not. This would not be a "formed opposition," based on steady and systematic discipline that involved more than the mere registration of agreement on measures; such a discipline would taint the advice offered by potential ministers with the suspicion of ambition.

But ambition, in Bolingbroke's scheme, can serve the public good, and it does so here when it is completely personal. A man in opposition can show his own worth best when alone, like Pitt; but if he associates with others in opposition, he must do so only on the basis of shared opinions, not for the sake of respect, deference, or any feeling of friendship that extends further than shared opinions. And these opinions must be the particular opinions relevant to the immediate political situation: for if they are fundamental opinions, then the regime would be falsely grounded, according to Bolingbroke's theory; and opposition to it will be opposition to factiousness itself—the first case, mentioned above. If the shared opinions arise from a lifetime of acquaintance and trust, both public and private, such as characterized the "political families," and as are familiar to readers of Trollope, the opposition would be collective, or "formed," with a group ambition, and hence improper.

The Duke of Newcastle's ambition was never for himself alone; it was for his "friends" or his dependents, men whom he knew or hoped to be faithful, as well as (or even instead of) competent. But such a group ambition makes it difficult or impossible for the king to choose those ministers who, regardless of their ties, are most able. He is forced to take some bad with the good; or, even if the dependents forced on him are themselves unexceptionable, he is required to dilute the principle of choosing by "abilities and integrity alone." The opposition of which these authors approve, however, can easily be picked apart; it is only an individual competition, even when the individuals act together. It is like a second team of individuals who seek posts on the varsity; each is ambitious and all are in a competition whose result is the general good. This kind of opposition no more approaches the modern practice of party government than does the opposition to a factious system. It is not the formed, disciplined, systematic opposition of party government; indeed, it is opposed to formed opposition, as well as to party discipline and to the idea of the "alternative government."

For party government, with party administration and opposition, is not the progressive consequence of a gradual enlightenment, in the course of which men came to think more and more highly of the virtue of opposition—first believing it tolerable, then seeing it as desirable. The idea is by itself absurd. Such a gradual appreciation of the virtue of opposition could be caused only by growing ignorance, which tries to justify an increasingly obstinate complacency. It requires that we know we know less and therefore know that we need opposition. This implication has a ring of gravity and philosophy.

But the ground and source of philosophy is the knowledge that we know nothing, from which it follows that we know we need reflection. It does not follow that we know we need somebody to oppose our actions; we could only wish to hold our actions in suspense so far as possible. From the knowledge that our actions are based on a principle which is possibly false we cannot deduce that our actions should be opposed by the actions of others, which are based on other principles, also possibly false. Aside from the fact that our principle is possibly true, it also may be true that to act on a single (possibly false) principle is better than to be acted upon by two or more conflicting principles, one of which is certainly false. It is not certain that the conflict of two or more wrong opinions is better than the harmony of one wrong opinion: it depends on the opinions. And what can be said of the incontinence of the party that knows it acts wrongly, because it finds opposition to itself desirable, yet continues to act wrongly! Does it justify opposition for the reason that it refuses to learn from opposition?

The toleration of opposition, or a belief in the desirability of opposition, must be a consequence not of gradual appreciation of the virtues of party government but of a gradual disillusionment with those virtues. Party government, in Bolingbroke's conception, begins as an attempt to reform society by the application of first principles. At first, it may claim for itself a right to oppose the government that keeps society corrupt. After it succeeds in reforming society, it may tolerate opposition of a competitive character. When it fails to reform society, it may be forced to tolerate opposition, for opposition will seem desirable to those observers who find the party's principles distasteful. This third kind of tolerated opposition is then designed for the frustration of a known evil, not for the achievement of some hoped-for good; and the conclusion that opposition is desirable is made by the knowing observer, who is, to the extent he knows it, *non*-partisan—not by the hopeful partisan. Open, formed opposition is not a prerequisite for the *growth* of party government; on the contrary, it is evidence of its *decline*. The only prerequisite for the growth of party government, given the desire to reform explained above, is a free society, or an inefficient, repressive one. Historians who believe that a tolerated opposition heralds the beginning of party government have already missed the heyday of party ambition; or, as in the case of the pamphlets under discussion, they will mistake the luminous condescension of a party after its imagined victory for the first glimmerings of a real party government.

When these distinctions are made, Bolingbroke's attack on faction becomes understandable. Bolingbroke approved of opposition of the first type—that is, opposition to aristocratic factiousness. Bolingbroke could have recommended, as his political school did recommend, opposition of the second type—that is, a competitive opposition of talents, after the system of factions had been destroyed. He disapproved of the third type of opposition—that is, open, formed opposition of parties whose original aims would have prompted them to become opposition of the first type, but whose prolonged inability to achieve those aims has led them to be content with party competition such as we have now. Burke could not expect a welcome for his opposition to Bolingbroke and his followers by hoping for consistency from his opponents, who themselves had been in the opposition. For Bolingbroke was consistent in denying that a belief in the toleration of opposition was a proper implication either of his theory or of his practice.

The "Political School" as Party

If one is searching for the most important similarity between the recommendations in these political pamphlets and party government, he should look elsewhere than to their recommendation of opposition. One should consider the possibility that the "political school" attempts to apply first principles to particular political problems as a substitute for statesmanship; Burke's central criticism of *The Present State* makes this point. Mentioning the two chief remedies proposed by that pamphlet for the rooted evils it uncovers, he remarks:

> I pass over here all considerations how far such a system will be an improvement of our constitution according to any sound theory. Not that I mean to condemn such speculative inquiries concerning this great object of the national attention. They may tend to clear doubtful points, and possibly may lead, as they have often done, to real improvements. What I object to, is their introduction into a discourse relating to the immediate state of our affairs, and recommending plans of practical government. In this view, I see nothing in them but what is usual with the author; an attempt to raise discontent in the people of England, to balance those discontents the measures of his friends had already raised in America.[54]

It has been remarked that Burke's argument against *The Present State* reveals the ridiculous disproportion between the evils that pamphlet discovers and the remedies it finds. Here Burke rightly suggests that speculation hastily expressed in public destroys more easily than it improves, since it spreads general discontent with a present good, the British constitution, by arousing the hope of improvement in particular aspects; thus it opens the way to frustration more than to ill-planned improvement.[55]

This criticism does not appear in the "Thoughts"; there Burke refers to Douglas' pamphlet (the first mentioned of "the political school") as the first appearance of the idea, "(then only in speculation)," of separating the court from the administration. In the "Thoughts" Burke does not mention the idea of the Patriot King, just as in his *Seasonable Hints* Douglas does not propose a party of the king's friends or advocate the separation of the court from the administration. Burke would not, in any case, directly oppose the idea of the Patriot King; and in the "Observations" he attacked the general idea of introducing speculative inquiries "into a discourse relating to the immediate state of our affairs" in his discussion of two less plausible remedies than the Patriot King. In the "Thoughts" he did not find it necessary to revive this criticism, though it would have fit, because the idea of the Patriot King is there repelled with the more traditional accusation of cabal. We have already shown Burke's need to fight the plausibility of the idea of the Patriot King by identifying it with a recognizable piece of the ancient furniture of tyranny. Let us consider whether the use of Bolingbroke's principles by the political school amounts to the substitution of party for statesmanship. The idea of the Patriot King does not depend upon the virtue of the king, but only upon his willingness and the willingness of the people to abide by certain principles which are easy to follow: the advancement of men of ability over men of family, the abandonment of corruption, a preference for peace over glory, and the fostering of commerce. These principles constitute the Bolingbroke program, using the word in its modern sense; for they are particular instructions to rulers, which are aimed at reformation of society by means of a lessened reliance upon the virtue or statesmanship of rulers. Bolingbroke's principles are not merely particular instructions to rulers, however, toward which they may apply their abilities. His principles are a substitute for abilities. They constitute a modern party program because they make politics into a system of new and easy truths.

The political school also sought issues in the same way as a modern party, to show the efficacy of its principles. For example, Douglas proposed to test the strength of deference to aristocratic honor by separating it from interest, by forcing the dependents of the great families to choose between loyalty and retaining their offices. He intended this not only as a private proposal to the King, but as a public test of principle, in which the dependents should show their virtue by following their interest. At the end of the "Observations," Burke met this issue on Douglas' terms, both as regarded himself and his party, when he stated that "the example of a large body of men, steadily sacrificing ambition to principle, can never be without use."[56]

The essence of Bolingbroke's party (and perhaps of Burke's partisanship) is the use of principles instead of virtue or statesmanship. The shift from a reliance on statesmanship to principles is not obvious, because it would not suit Bolingbroke's rhetoric to deny that the Patriot King has virtue; it is safer to reinterpret "virtue" or give it lip service. But the shift is nonetheless unmistakable. Bolingbroke's principles have a theoretical source in natural law and a simple application which demands only faithful administration; if the Patriot King had to be a great statesman, patriotism would be inadequate and the principles (as Bolingbroke construes them) would be pointless. Statesmanship today is so identified with political principles, even with party principles, that it is hard to recapture the realism in the shift from statesmanship to principles. Bolingbroke distinguished principles from interests, which might seem unrealistic today; but he based his principles on easily educated interests.

A sign of this shift is Bolingbroke's advocacy of opposition (of the first kind), and from this standpoint the advocacy of opposition does constitute a step toward party government. As we observed above, open advocacy of opposition is possible for Bolingbroke because he does not regard opposition as a problem. Opposition is unproblematic when patriotism is based on true and applicable first principles. A true patriot cannot avoid being loyal to his country when he supports those principles, no matter how little his country believes in them and acts upon them. Since the rulers have no excuse for not making the policy of the country conform to true first principles, the patriot can stand in opposition, or even step into exile, as long and as publicly as is necessary to bring the country to its senses. There is no compunction to hold back the protest of the patriot, and no reason to rein in the enthusiasm of opposition. To speak more generally, one could say that in political matters, at least, Bolingbroke has abolished the discrepancy between the good and one's own good. Since the good is practicable, it can be made one's own, not merely by an individual, but by a whole society. Hence, the failure to make it one's own is not a tragedy, but inexcusable stupidity or corruption. The open advocacy of systematic opposition is based on a simplified patriotism, for the wise statesman, believing in the need to respect the prejudices of his own country, could never suppose that simple opposition to those prejudices would cure or tame them. His patriotism would seek to bring his own country to the common good by the management of prejudice, for which open opposition is often an unlikely instrument. Opposition is problematic when a statesman fears to hurt his own country by reforming it; he cannot know for certain when to urge his country to its best aspirations and when to leave it in its typical moods. The advocacy (not just tolerance) of opposition is a sign and a consequence of the shift from statesmanship to principles.

Now what is the relation between the political school and the court cabal whose activities have been discussed? We suggest that they are in a manner the same. In one place Burke refers to the cabal as the preacher of the doctrine (discovered to be a hallmark of the political school), that "all political connexions are in their nature factious." Again, he says that "our court moralists" have frowned on the "partiality which becomes a well-chosen friendship."[57] But if the cabal preaches, and in this aspect is identical to the political school, it also represents, of course, the practice of the doctrines it preaches. But Burke presents that practice in a peculiar light. He presents it as if the dangerous consequences of the doctrines of the political school had come about and were visible but no longer were protected by the plausibility of those doctrines. The missing element in Bolingbroke's political school is a central organization uniting the members of the school and directing them to action. Burke supplies this missing element in his vague, allusive, exaggerated, yet on the whole persuasive account of the court cabal, which some historians tell us never existed.

But he deprives the cabal of its most plausible claims; for example, he never mentions the idea of the Patriot King; he never gives a complete summary of the cabal's program, so as to deal it an adequate refutation. So the court cabal appears as treason or near-treason, which has been ineffectively (because guiltily) veiled, but now is exposed for all to see and act against. It appears to be a conspiracy of flatterers, albeit a systematic conspiracy, around a susceptible King—an old problem, comprehensible in traditional terms, a scene staged with the "ancient furniture of tyranny." But Burke regards the doctrines of the "political school" as false, though they are plausible and publicly unrefuted by him. To report false doctrines is misleading, even if they are reported in company with their refutation, when one knows that the refutation may not be persuasive, and when other means to combat them are available.[58] Hence Burke's account of the court cabal is not truly misleading to those who read it as a literal report; while its vagueness should be enough to plant a suspicion of the truth in the skeptical. The court cabal is the supposed consequence of the political school, and to say that the cabal and the school are the same, in the way Burke said it, is not misleading.

We conclude that the "political school" was a party very like a modern party. If this is so, then the 1760's in England were the heyday of party ambition—that early period in the history of any modern party outside a totalitarian state, when the party wants to achieve its program rather than justify opposition to it. In America, owing to circumstances and to the genius of Jefferson, the heyday of party ambition coincided with the period of obvious party predominance in the government; Jefferson was both the founder and the organizer of party government. There was no such coincidence in England, and consequently it is difficult to estimate the general importance of the political school in the 1760's.

John Douglas, Dr. Brown, Lord Bath, Owen Ruffhead, Sir John Marriot, Tobias Smollett, Arthur Murphy, Thomas Pownall, William Knox, Charles Lloyd, John Almon, and perhaps two anonymous authors are those writers whom we have identified as members of the political school. But there are some others who show traces of Bolingbroke's influence, although less than the substance of his political views: Oliver Goldsmith and Dr. Johnson, among literary figures; Nathaniel Forster, Charles Jenkinson, Josiah Tucker, Catharine Macaulay, Joseph Priestley, Andrew Henderson, Dr. Robert Wallace, John Dalrymple, and anonymous others, among political writers.[59] There were writers who opposed the antiaristocratic conclusions of these writers, such as John Butler, William Dowdeswell, and Sir William Meredith, all in the Rockingham connection; and a great many pamphleteers who reasoned on narrow grounds, but who did not make their basic views clear.

But if one considers those pamphlets which contain substantial judgments on the constitution and if Burke is left out of the balance, then Bolingbroke's political school would hold sway. Its writers were abler in argument, more insistent in tone, more profound in reflection than its opponents, Burke excepted. The more important pamphlets and newspapers, those which stated a view that others commented upon or attacked, were usually those of the political school—Douglas' *A Letter to Two Great Men* and *Seasonable Hints,* Dr. Brown's *Estimate of the Manners . . . ,* Smollett's *The Briton,* Murphy's *The Auditor,* and Knox's *The Present State.* And when we add William Pitt and the Grenvilles among the statesmen, as well as George III, the sum of Bolingbroke's influence, though disunited, is very great. Bolingbroke himself sought for adherents to the idea of the Patriot King not from the Whigs, who might have had encouragement from Locke's political writings, but from the Tories, who were more numerous than Whigs and who chafed under the imputation of disloyalty and the proscription from high office. But as Bolingbroke accepted the fundamental principles of Locke, his "new Toryism" can be said, by its influence on George III, the Pitts, the Grenvilles, and then all their followers, to have spread these principles to men who took their political inheritance, by descent or by resentment, from the Royalist side of the Civil War. Bolingbroke helped to resolve the seventeenth-century differences on the Whig basis, but he did so in a manner which rendered them obsolete—less the Whig reasoning of 1680 than Locke's reasoning and the Whig reasoning of 1688. Despite the failure of the idea of the Patriot King, he thus in great measure achieved his intention.

Without the study still due the subject, one can yet say that the influence of Bolingbroke upon the politics of the 1760's was greater than that of any other source. It is then wrong to say that there was no party government in the 1760's. There was a strong party flourishing then, whose basis was mostly modern, though it was without the organization of the modern party. Historians overlook it because they suppose that open, formed opposition marks the growth, instead of the decline, of party government. What is more to our present concern is that Burke's "Thoughts" can be understood only in the light of this fact. His argument in defense of party was a riposte to the party already existing; he preferred party competition, similar to modern party government, to the triumph of that party he opposed. Thus in England the first open argument for the respectability of party was defensive, against an attacking party which was not called a party or was called "the country party," while in America party first appeared on the attack. This is an important difference, but it is founded on a more important similarity in the character of the attackers. Bolingbroke's "first principles" and Jefferson's "republican principles" were simplified truths designed to replace the old, oppressive prejudices by substituting party government for statesmanship.

CHAPTER SIX

The British Constitution: Popular Government

Burke's analysis of the danger of tyranny in the 1760's was presented in a deceptive form, but, after inspection, his description of the vague court plan discloses a deeper awareness of Bolingbroke's influence than was first apparent, thus correcting and justifying the deception. It is now possible to reach a conclusion about Burke's analysis of the danger by examining his remedies for it, which are two: popular control of the House of Commons and party government. These remedies seek to redress an imbalance in the entire constitution; therefore one must first have a view of the constitution as Burke sees it. This chapter begins the consideration of the first remedy, in order to develop Burke's view of the British constitution; the next chapter considers both remedies together. It will be shown, first, that Burke considers the British constitution to represent popular government similar to that of *The Federalist*, and, second, that Burke thinks it possible for the people to rule themselves only by means of the rule of gentlemen. To Burke, party is an establishment for the rule of gentlemen in the context of popular government. Thus one must understand what Burke means by popular government in order to understand his introduction of party into the public constitution.

At the beginning of the "Thoughts," Burke implies that the British constitution is now "fully formed and mature."[1] It is not perfect; it would be better, for example, if it were rid of government corruption in elections. But it does not require any major changes or any further development to ripen its potentialities, much less to correct its deficiencies. Burke does not propose any major change in the constitution; or, to be properly cautious, Burke does not make any proposal that *results* in a major change to the constitution, although a major remedy may be necessary to counteract a major danger. Then, in Burke's view of the constitution, one does not have to make allowance for major changes in the future, though there may be cause for fear; the British constitution, strengthened by these remedies, is as good as it can be. One does not have to look beyond Burke's description of present practice and the implications of his description to find his view of the constitution as a whole.

This description is found in Burke's opposition to Bolingbroke's influence and can be most easily observed if we match Bolingbroke against Burke. Burke has remedies for Bolingbroke's influence. The question must be that which confronts every proposed remedy, once it is supposed possible: Does it compromise with the disease, or will it effect a cure or even an improvement? But if the constitution is now fully matured, improvement is ruled out; the issue is between compromise and cure.

The Monarchy and the Monarchical Principle

In the "Thoughts," Burke distinguishes three political elements of the British constitution—monarchy, controls, and the people. Thus an inquiry might seem to require three parts, in order to find the sovereign element which permits us to characterize and to name Britain or the British constitution as a whole. But it is a curious fact that in the "Thoughts," Burke does not classify Britain as a monarchy or as a limited monarchy. Indeed, he calls it by a variety of names—a "mixed government," a "free state," or "free commonwealth." He does use the word "monarchy" at times, but only when referring to the institution of the "crown," not to the constitution as a whole. He uses the phrase "monarchical government" once, but apparently only to qualify, not to classify, the constitution. He uses the word "kingdom" when referring to the country as a whole, but he leaves unstated the relation between the country and the constitution.[2] Why does Burke not classify Britain as a limited monarchy? To classify a country means to describe it as a whole. But countries seem to have a ruling element that presides over the good of the whole, rather than an obvious structure that can be viewed externally and described without reference to this ruling part. Hence to classify a country means to identify who rules in it. In someone who acts advisedly, failure to classify a country according to who rules implies a different conception of the constitution, perhaps a classification according to who controls. Burke's failure to classify the British regime requires us to test this expectation: Does he think that there is no ruling part in the constitution? That regimes are to be classified according to the controls on their government? That the constitution is the controls?

In Burke there is a connection among his failure to classify kinds of constitutions according to who rules, his conception of monarchy, and his reliance upon statesmanship. According to Aristotle, absolute monarchy is simply the best form of government, that "form" (if we can properly so describe it) which takes the fullest advantage of the virtue of a great man by giving unlimited discretion to his statesmanship. This arrangement is congruent with the probable range of virtue among men. For virtue is divided into ordinary virtue, attainable by the mass of men, and heroic virtue, far above the ordinary level, the end of great deeds rarely seen and within reach of only a few men. But if this is the likely range of virtue, the probability of heroic virtue is low; and absolute monarchy is revealed as fragile, though best. It is good only when at its best, because only the best men are capable of using unlimited power well.

So men may turn to limited monarchy, giving the rule to one man bound by laws. When the laws leave the most important powers to the discretion of one man, Aristotle consents to classify this constitution as a monarchy.[3] This kind of monarchy imitates the advantages of rule by one great man; for many things not already settled by the laws can be settled wisely enough if they are merely settled, and one man can do this most effectively, by substituting the single discretion of his will for the great man's wisdom. Yet the single direction of the will is ultimately impossible without wisdom, because a stubborn man will ultimately lose his direction after he loses his object; and he will ultimately lose his object if he is unwise. In both cases the advantage sought from monarchy is derived from the virtue of one man. It is the monarch's own virtue, not his deference to publicly established principles, that is reputed to be the advantage of monarchy. A monarch limited by laws must also obey the laws or restrictive institutions set over him. But he is retained as sole ruler (if he is supreme) to the end that his virtue, such as it is, may promote the common good.

We may call this supposed advantage of monarchy "the monarchical principle." Aristotle does not simply prefer either monarchy or the rule of laws, nor does he regard them as incompatible.[4] Since the laws define who is equal for the purpose of ruling, the advantage of monarchy can be known when the problem of the best man and the best laws is resolved. But Aristotle does not find arguments which resolve this problem without regard to particular circumstances; the problem remains for statesmen who have to act in circumstances. One must see whether Burke regards the question of the best man and the best laws as a problem and whether he considers the monarchical principle as a possible advantage of the constitution.

It must be conceded that the application of the monarchical principle is not absolutely essential to justify a reliance upon statesmanship. If statesmanship means doing what is best in the circumstances, however, then monarchy is certainly more congenial to the practice of statesmanship than democracy. Democracy cannot dispense with rulers, but it asserts that there is no natural difference between the rulers and the ruled and hence that men should rule over themselves. They themselves can exercise statesmanship. But to this one can object that doing what is best in the circumstances requires a certain division of labor, because reasonable men may disagree over what is best when the common good is dubious. It is reasonable that one man decide, and that he decide consistently over a period of time, rather than that reasonable men dispute without decision. Given a division of labor, or the necessity of office, actions become in a sense the private property of the officeholder; it is *his* administration.[5] It is not necessarily his because he is better fitted to act than those who are not officeholders, but because action requires that doubts be resolved or ignored. When doubts are genuine, they show that alternatives are equal, or nearly equal. Thus private property in administration arises, not from superior judgment, but from precisely the opposite—from a situation in which superior judgment is helpless. Then statesmanship is not incompatible with democracy, even as modified by officeholders; regarding the truly dubious action, democracy is more appropriate than monarchy, because it more closely reflects the helplessness of superior judgment by denying that some men are naturally superior in any capacity relevant to rule.

This argument for democracy would concede something to monarchy, but not to the monarchical principle. It would concede that a decision is necessary and that consistency of decision comes most surely from one man. If this concession were extensive, if the officeholders had wide powers, this kind of democracy would become the limited monarchy or limited aristocracy discussed earlier. According to Hobbes, there is no natural difference between ruler and ruled, but the disputability of the common good requires that all consent to an absolute sovereign, who is preferably an absolute monarch. By Hobbes's reasoning, the equality of men yields a drastic inequality in government, and monarchy follows from a *denial* of the monarchical principle. Having denied the need for superior judgment, democracy may have to concede much, or by Hobbes's argument concede everything, to the need for consistent decision.

But, on the other hand, situations in which superior judgment is helpless are rare; and, for the most part, statesmanship, which is the exercise of discretion in particular circumstances, thrives best when some men are thought to be more fit by nature than others to exercise that discretion, that is, when the monarchical principle is thought to be applicable, or possibly applicable. The argument that even for truly dubious actions statesmanship is needed, but not superior wisdom, indicates only the indispensability of discretion under even the best assumed condition for democracy, when all men are equally fit by nature to rule. It does not make the assumed condition probable.[6]

Now, Burke's conception of the king's power seems close to the Aristotelian idea of limited monarchy, which recognizes the problem of the best man and the best laws. Burke discusses the king in two places: in the first place the king as the crown, in the second place the king "in his personal capacity"; and he says that consideration of advantage to the latter aspect was the "grand principle which first recommended this system [the court system] at court."[7] But he implies that even if the court system brought advantage to the king in his personal capacity, this would not suffice to make it even tolerable to even his affectionate subjects. He brings up the supposed personal advantage of this system to show the King that even the original recommending principle, already overruled by other arguments, is false.[8] There is then a distinction between crown and king, and the crown is more important. When we turn to the crown, we find a further distinction that encourages a supposition of Burke's affinity to Aristotle: Burke distinguishes the laws which control the king from the "discretionary powers which are necessarily vested in the monarch" and adds that the latter are equal in importance to the laws. Burke is well known for his aversion to paper governments and to theoretical reasoning applied with blinkered complacency to political situations. Is this not an instance of his adoption (knowing or unknowing) of Aristotelian *phronesis*, the practical wisdom, the prudence of the statesman—combined with a prudent adoption (also endorsed by Aristotle) of a legal order to restrain the unlimited and unjust use of discretion?

One can sense the plausibility of this supposition by reading Burke's words; after saying that discretionary powers are equal in importance to law, he continues:

> The laws reach but a very little way. Constitute government how you please, infinitely the greater part of it must depend upon the exercise of the powers which are left at large to the prudence and uprightness of ministers of state. Even all the use and potency of the laws depends upon them. Without them, your commonwealth is no better than a scheme upon paper; and not a living, active, effective constitution.[9]

These ministers of state (in the British constitution) are the king's ministers, excluding the king himself in his personal capacity. The powers left to their prudence are important—executing the laws, nominating men to magistracy and office, conducting the affairs of peace and war, and ordering the revenue. But we pause to ask why the discretionary powers, which are said to be equal in importance to the laws in one sentence, are said to be the infinitely greater part in the constitution of the government, in the next sentence. The answer seems to be that the laws, though "fundamental," are "negative" and "defensive"; the discretionary powers are "next in order and equal in importance" because the more fundamental laws are inert by themselves. If the discretionary powers are infinitely the greater part of government, then the government, one might think, is less important than the laws—so that infinitely greater importance within the government can be balanced (by a nice interpretation) to a result of equality. Burke has said that Britain has a mixed government, composed of monarchy and of controls, one great end of which is "that the prince shall not be able to violate the laws." This is accomplished by the discretionary powers, however, since "the laws reach but a very little way." The "active part of the state," the prudence of ministers, makes the commonwealth "better than a scheme upon paper," makes it a "living, active, effective constitution." If this is so, whence the importance of the laws? So far, Burke seems to share Aristotle's appreciation of monarchy.

But if one has ordinary alertness and is warned by the fact that Burke does not classify the British constitution as a limited monarchy, one finds difficulties. The "discretionary powers," which seem to signal Burke's appreciation of the monarchical principle, gradually overcome this presumption of Burke's appreciation and finally require a different conclusion. First, the discretionary powers are "necessarily vested in the monarch," rather than placed there by choice. This distinction must be stated with caution: both Burke and Aristotle would agree that laws are necessarily defective, because they are unable to prescribe well for every situation of equity or emergency that falls under their literal meaning. Thus discretionary powers are in a way necessary. But Aristotle thought that discretion wisely exercised could improve upon the laws and that this wise exercise of discretion might in some circumstances reasonably be sought for in a monarchy, or limited monarchy—which would vest discretionary powers in one man by choice. Here Burke apparently takes the position that such an investment is simply of necessity; that the laws prescribe as well as possible, with some exceptions; that those exceptions are without doubt lamentable; and that therefore Britain must vest discretionary powers in the monarchy, not in the hope for more good but from the fear of having less. Discretion, as a remedy for the the imperfections of the laws, is not an opportunity for bettering the result of the laws, but only an attempt to achieve the same result as laws in areas where laws alone cannot succeed. Burke does not say this in so many words, but one can interpret the meaning of "necessarily vested" in this way: where Burke had the opportunity to state the virtue *par excellence* of monarchy, whether absolute or limited, he chose to ignore that virtue and to present the very same activity as a consequence of necessity.[10] This hint can be better appreciated if one sees more of the difficulties involved in aligning Burke with Aristotle.

Secondly, Burke states that the discretionary powers are to be "exercised upon public principles and national grounds, and not on the likings or prejudices, the intrigues or policies, of a court." He simply discards the possibility that the "likings or prejudices, the intrigues or policies" can be virtue in a king. In Aristotle, the advantage of monarchy is that it makes public the virtue of the king; here, a disadvantage of monarchy is that it makes public the private vices of the king, a disadvantage which may be cured by imposing public principles on the private dispositions of the king. Burke does not merely require that the court act for the public good rather than on its own prejudices; that would be unexceptionable. But he opposes the public to the court; what is for the public good cannot emerge from a court, but must be imposed upon it.

Public principles are to be imposed upon the court by ministers—a third difficulty in assigning to Burke the classical conception of monarchy. The discretionary powers, "vested in the monarch," are exercised by trustworthy ministers; the king does not himself possess these powers.[11] He is not permitted to act in violation of the laws because he is not even given the opportunity. This is limited monarchy in the modern sense of "constitutional monarchy," that is, no one-man rule at all—the limitation attacks the principle, not just the abuse, of monarchy. Burke's conception of monarchy in the "Thoughts" carries the limitation of the monarch far beyond practice contemporary to him and beyond other constitutional ideas of his time that were not frankly republican.

One can say more: Burke's conception is more antimonarchical than modern practice and ideas, for he carefully refers to ministers in the plural, avoiding the idea of a prime minister. The idea of a prime minister could not be unknown to him, for it had aroused controversy in the 1760's, especially when Pitt imperiously resigned in 1761. At that time Pitt's opponents condemned the idea of a prime minister as unconstitutional, an invasion of the king's task: the king is prime minister.[12] Modern scholars have praised the British constitution for the facility with which the king's prerogative has developed, without essential change, into the powers of the crown exercised by the cabinet under the prime minister. Burke takes neither side; he does not advocate a prime minister, but apparently on the grounds that the monarchical principle—one-man rule—is essentially in error, not just in need of limitation or democratization.

He says as much:

> But that form of government, which, neither in its direct institutions nor in their immediate tendency, has contrived to throw its affairs into the most trustworthy hands, but has left its whole executory system to be disposed of agreeably to the uncontrolled pleasure of any one man, however excellent or virtuous, is a plan of polity defective not only in that member, but consequentially erroneous in every part of it.[13]

It might seem that Burke argues only for limited monarchy, as opposed to "the uncontrolled pleasure of any one man." But this is not so, since "that form of government" is already limited monarchy and mistakenly entrusts only its "whole executory system" to one man. Since the monarch properly does not even have the whole executory system at his disposal, we suggest that Burke has even left the bounds of limited one-man rule. There is more in the passage to confirm this suggestion. What is to be feared from the "uncontrolled pleasure" of the superlatively excellent or virtuous man—since Burke invites us to form this hypothesis? Such a man, one might suppose, would either have a self-controlled pleasure in acting for the public good or an uncontrolled pleasure in controlling himself for the public good. But Burke does not allow differences in degrees of virtue to affect his conclusion; he takes each man on the level of the lowest and decides his attitude to one-man rule as if this one man were the lowest man. This does not necessarily mean that no man will use his discretion for the good. It may be that a good use of discretion leaves a bad example, as one man's daring may invite another's presumption.

This is a systematic decision. In Aristotle's conception, the "form of government" or constitution is the men who are supreme. It is they who make the laws; and the laws are well contrived because the men who made them were pleased to make them so. A monarchy was limited by laws because a king once wished to be so limited or was forced to accept limitations by others who wished to limit him. But in the passage above, Burke shows the primacy of the "form of government" or "plan of polity" over the rulers. "Form of government" is the subject of the sentence—as if one man, however excellent or virtuous, were incapable of overcoming with his virtue the bad design of the form which permits him to try to overcome it. Aristotle recognizes and allows for the possibility that Burke here denies. Just as it is necessary to remember that every form of government has been made at the uncontrolled pleasure of some man or men, so it is possible to conceive that one good man might be better than the best limited constitution.[14] But Burke seems to presume the superiority of a constitution to the monarchical principle, instead of regarding it as problematic. His statement above even recalls that of Jefferson: "May we not even say, that that form of government is the best, which provides the most effectually for a pure selection of these natural *aristoi* into the offices of government?"[15] Burke would deny that his "most trustworthy hands" are "natural *aristoi*," in Jefferson's use of that term. But both men, contrary to Aristotle, subject the best men to the "form of government"—Jefferson by supposing that the form can select the best men, Burke by supposing that the best man can never outweigh the ill effects of a form that encourages his uncontrolled pleasure and tolerates that of bad men.

To summarize: The discretionary powers of the king are "necessarily vested" in him; they are exercised on public principles by ministers, a result secured by a form of government that selects trustworthy ministers. These powers, according to Burke, are a part of the crown that is "equal in importance" to the other part, the laws. If discretionary powers give all their "use and potency" to the laws, however, how are the laws as important as the powers? The importance of the laws for Burke does not lie usually in the laws themselves, as they are negative and inert, but in their permeation of the realm of prudence with the idea of lawfulness. For prudence, as Burke thinks of it, is not outside the laws, but only an extension of the laws in which the laws' distrust of individual discretion is maintained and indeed improved upon, since areas where discretion should be distrusted are not distinguished from areas where it can be trusted, but tend to absorb them. The generality of the laws is maintained in the "public principles and national grounds" which are supposed to guide the statesman's exercise of discretion. These principles must be sufficiently free of exceptions to be accurate guides, though perhaps not sufficiently strict for legal enactment—they are rather like party principles in their quasi-legal character. There is also a sanction, other than the reproach of conscience, which secures the proper exercise of prudence; its exercise is removed from one man and given to a group of men who, we shall see, are externally accountable. The power of the crown, then, consists of the laws and lawful prudence. What the laws lack in importance, because of their inertness, they achieve through the example they impose upon the "active part of the state." Discretion, in Burke's view, turns out to have no higher aim than to enhance legality, and what he seems to give to the realm of prudence, as opposed to the realm of legality, he takes away by a conception of lawful prudence. It is one thing to say that discretion is needed to accomplish the end of the laws, which the laws themselves, because of their generality, cannot achieve. But Burke seems to care less for the end of the laws than for lawfulness, not only when dealing with a bad situation but systematically, even when facing the best and most mature constitution.

This discussion has dealt with the king in his public capacity, the crown. What of the "personal capacity" of the king? Is this a refuge for the ancient idea of monarchy? Even if the king must turn over his public capacity to ministers and forsake the active exercise of prudence, he might in his personal capacity exemplify virtues which are perhaps lower than the highest political virtue but which can be exhibited from a situation of inactivity. Shining honesty, solemn reverence, jovial avuncularity—these are virtues possible in such a station; prominently displayed, they might prove catching to the people generally, more as an example of obedience than as inspiration to greatness, yet still valuable. Some observers consider these or similar virtues to be the excellence of Britain's present monarchy.

But again, one finds in Burke no public advantage in the virtue of the king; that is, none but from the virtue of submissiveness to the people:

Independent of that greatness which a king possesses merely by being a representative of the national dignity, the things in which he may have an individual interest seem to be these;—wealth accumulated; wealth spent in magnificence, pleasure, or beneficence; personal respect and attention; and above all, private ease and repose of mind.[16]

The only greatness Burke mentions is that of being "representative of the national dignity"; that is, of representing the people's greatness—an idea opposed to setting an example of greatness, in some way, for the people to admire or imitate. The only greatness Burke seems to imply for the king is that of the magnificent or beneficent spender. But he quickly assimilates this implication to the foregoing assertion: "Nothing could be more unworthy of this nation, than with a mean and mechanical rule to mete out the splendour of the crown. Indeed I have found very few persons disposed to so ungenerous a procedure."[17] Thus the king can be a magnificent or beneficent spender because he represents the national dignity; the *nation* would be unworthy if it did not make a generous allowance to its king. Burke does not even let this point go as a matter of course—he has taken a poll to see whether the nation approves of his generosity in its name and found only a "very few" who do not!

But let us return to the "individual interest" of the king—wealth accumulated and spent, personal respect, "and above all, private ease and repose of mind." "These compose the inventory of prosperous circumstances, whether they regard a prince or a subject; their enjoyments differing only in the scale upon which they are formed." The king then is an ordinary man, a very unheroic man, whose pleasures differ in scale, not in kind, from those of his subjects; they differ in scale only because he represents the national dignity, that is, the dignity of his subjects. Burke says flatly that "the king is the representative of the people."[18] He thus has a derivative dignity, it would appear, to the extent that he stands for the dignity of his subjects. He would have less dignity than his subjects, who at least have the business of life to fill their thoughts; but, for the king, above all are "private ease and repose of mind." So far is Burke's monarch from the deeds of heroes that this idea is enough to recall the recent concern for the "burden of the Presidency" in the United States.

One may note two further indications that Burke requires no more of the king than of an ordinary man. The first is his attitude to the favorite of a king. We have seen that Burke depreciated the importance of Lord Bute, the favorite, as compared to the danger from the court system, a *system* of favoritism; we now see him deprecate the common opinion that the relation of king to a favorite is unnatural and bad:

If particular men had grown into an attachment, by the distinguished honour of the society of their sovereign; and, by being the partakers of his amusements, came sometimes to prefer the gratification of his personal inclinations to the support of his high character, the thing would be very natural, and it would be excusable enough.[19]

Burke uses this reflection to contrast an excusable favorite with the self-styled "king's friends," who are not true partakers of his amusements and thus do not contribute to his private ease and repose of mind. The "court," in Burke's usage, consists of the king in his personal capacity together with the favorites or "friends" he has chosen. It is thus distinguished from the crown, which consists of the king and his constitutional ministers, some of whom may belong to the court if they are personal favorites of the king. We pause only to record here that, for Burke, naked favoritism in the "court" is excusable, while the same thing in the "court system" is inexcusable and must be opposed.

Burke's undemanding conception of the king's office is also shown in his discussion of a debt of the civil list.[20] In the eighteenth century, the civil list was an allowance granted to the king by the House of Commons, in the case of George III without an annual vote or inquiry; it was like a settlement. The civil list included both the king's personal expenses (to which it is now confined) and some, but not all, of the "expenses of civil government." Accordingly, one writer has termed this division between governmental expenses paid from the civil list (for the most part not subject to parliamentary control) and those paid for by supplies voted by Parliament, a compromise which balanced the powers of the king and Parliament. If so, Burke did not consider himself a party to the compromise, for he shows a distrust of the king at least equal to that implied in modern practice. As a member of the Rockingham ministry of 1782, he introduced and secured the passage of an act whose purpose was to make the civil list as much as possible a subject of parliamentary estimates.[21]

The occasion of this discussion was an application to the Commons by the ministers in 1769 for payment of the debt of the civil list, that is, payment of expenses incurred on the civil list beyond its settled income. Fearing that such applications would encourage the use of the civil list to finance the court system, or (less seriously) that the debt had already been incurred to finance that system, Burke discussed the danger in this way:

There was a circumstance in that debate too remarkable to be overlooked. This debt of the civil list was all along argued upon the same footing as a debt of the state, contracted upon national authority. Its payment was urged as equally pressing upon the public faith and honour. . . .

It might be thought that Burke agrees with the compromise mentioned above and only thinks that the king has broken it—since he objects here only to payment of an excess in the civil list by the Commons as a matter of course, without inquiry, and not to the civil list itself, which covered many expenses for public purposes not included today. But the principle from which Burke argues is ultramodern, even if his application of it is less complete in not seeking curtailment of the civil list to the king's merely personal expenses.[22] For Burke completely distinguishes the honor of the crown from the honor of the public in this discussion. After stating the false argument of the ministers, quoted above, that debts of the civil list are simply public debts, he concluded by remarking on the character of the limitation to such future debts, which had been accepted by the crown:

> However, to put the matter beyond all doubt, in the speech from the throne, after thanking parliament for the relief so liberally granted, the ministers inform the two Houses, that they will *endeavour* to confine the expenses of the civil government—within what limits, think you? those which the law had prescribed? Not in the least—"such limits as the *honour of the crown* can possibly admit."
>
> Thus they established an *arbitrary* standard for that dignity which parliament had defined and limited to a *legal* standard. They gave themselves, under the lax and indeterminate idea of the *honour of the crown,* a full loose for all manner of dissipation, and all manner of corruption.[23]

Not only the honor of the king, but the honor of the crown cannot engage the public honor; such an engagement, we shall see, can be made only by the House of Commons, acting for the people. Burke clearly shows his preference for law over discretion, even when the discretion is exercised by ministers, and even when the subject of discretion, the civil list, is concerned with (though it is not confined to) the king's personal dignity. The honor of the crown is an arbitrary standard, not a legal standard. Nowadays suspicion of the "honor of the crown" has been relaxed; it is no longer considered to be an arbitrary standard, because cabinet ministers, connected by party to the people, vouch for the honor of the crown when they make engagements of the public honor. But Burke's stricter fidelity to the principle of distrust should not blind us to his fundamental agreement with modern belief and with Bolingbroke that the honor of the crown is an arbitrary standard. It remains to note that Burke does not bother to conceal or even to play down the fact that this phrase, "the honor of the crown," was spoken by the king, who thus appears as a puppet mouthing illegal doctrine. And this was some sixty years before the invention of the phrase "His Majesty's opposition."

Thus Burke's account of monarchy in the "Thoughts" ends on a strong and bold antimonarchical note. We can now venture to interpret a passage, at the beginning of the "Thoughts," where he apparently identified absolute monarchy with despotism:

This method, therefore, of governing by men of great natural interest or great acquired consideration, was viewed in a very invidious light by the true lovers of absolute monarchy. It is the nature of despotism to abhor power held by any means but its own momentary pleasure. . . .[24]

It is not merely that Burke supposes that absolute monarchy may quite easily degenerate into despotism and therefore prefers limited monarchy. If this were so, one could say that his calculation of the probable degeneration of absolute monarchy, reinforced by the practice of his times, which had been fixed by unhappy experience with Stuart despotism, rightly concluded in favor of limited monarchy. But by regarding the descent of absolute monarchy to despotism as a necessary, instead of a probable, occurrence, Burke steps past this conclusion. His identification of absolute monarchy with despotism separates him from the Aristotelian conception of monarchy and aligns him with the Lockian conception. One cannot be sure that Burke did not say with rhetorical vehemence what he would not always intend, but he could have spoken otherwise; he spoke the same on a later occasion; and elsewhere he spoke consistently with this conception.

Aristotle, as we saw, considers absolute monarchy not as a probable regime but as that regime which best shows the advantage to be gained from the rule of a man of pre-eminent virtue, that is, from statesmanship. Absolute monarchy shows best the advantage that is somewhat concealed in limited monarchy, where some of it has been traded for security and stability. Limited monarchy can do less evil than absolute monarchy because it can do less good—because it can *do* less. But the virtue of limited monarchy can be stated only in terms of absolute monarchy, for it is an attempt to achieve a lesser but similar advantage; otherwise the monarchical principle would be abandoned. The truth of this is clear in Burke's case: his rejection of absolute monarchy is so complete and drastic as to preclude acceptance of the monarchical principle. Burke concedes only a shadow of the absolute monarch's discretion to the British monarch's pleasure: the king has, in his personal capacity, the power to choose some ministers and to veto laws. The former power, as suggested in a treatment of cabinet government later in this chapter, is only a method of securing popular rule; and the latter power is only so important as it may be important to strengthen the laws (not important as a whole) with a new law.

We therefore conclude that the British constitution, in Burke's view, is not as a whole a monarchy, though it contains a limited monarchy; and that his refusal to call it a limited monarchy indicated this. One cannot deny that Burke regards the monarchy as an important institution; in a

later work he calls it "the essential basis" of the other parts of the constitution. But these other parts, he reminds us, are *republican* parts; and they
unite in the *crown*, not in the king.[25]

Bolingbroke, though also making use of the expression "mixed government," did call the British constitution a limited monarchy, thus recognizing, as one might expect, the importance (though not the sovereignty) of
the Patriot King. Yet, as with Burke, the king's private interest is not a
source of public advantage, for, privately, the king is likely to be very
much an ordinary man. On the contrary, the private character of the king
is dangerous: it may produce the "surprises . . . of the man on the king,"
to which great kings are especially susceptible. Bolingbroke's proposed
security against this danger is that the king should aim to be what he is
likely to be and that he serve his public interest by accommodating his
private character to the search for "popularity." To do this, the king must
not be proud from the knowledge of his virtue, but "free from every kind
of affectation."[26] Burke and Bolingbroke thus share a profound suspicion
of the monarchical principle, but Burke acts more boldly on that suspicion.

Burke does not say that one man is usually no better than another, and
that therefore men should exercise discretion in turn, subject to the laws.
On the contrary, he seems to say that a man is never good enough to exercise discretion, and that therefore no man should exercise discretion, but
men should submit their rulers to the laws, as far as the laws go; and to
lawful prudence, where the laws cannot reach. In his attack on monarchy,
Burke seems also to have depreciated statesmanship, although he need
not have done so.

Controls for the People

The first element of Britain's "mixed government" is monarchy;
the second consists of "controls on the part of the higher people and the
lower," especially Parliament. Since this inquiry seeks to find what Burke
considered the ruling part of the British constitution, so that we may
characterize that constitution as a whole, we can properly suppose ourselves near the objective; for Burke contrasts the dignity which Parliament
should have as "a national council" with the subservience it would have
as a "mere member of the court."[27] Parliament is closer to the nation than
is the court.

The corruption of Parliament is more to be feared than the corruption
of the crown in the misuse of prerogative; misuse of prerogative is only to

be expected, and since the Stuarts it has been subject to the scrutiny of a wary people. But corruption of Parliament infects the instrument of such scrutiny, indeed converts "the very antagonist into the instrument of power." Now Parliament has been corrupted and is in danger of mortal corruption from the misuse of the influence of the crown. The influence of the crown, here, means its influence in Parliament, which arises from its employment of M.P.'s and Lords in ministerial or subministerial capacity— those so employed, especially those in subministerial posts, being known as "placemen." Thus the abuse of this influence is an attempt on the independence of Parliament. This is of course not the first attempt on the independence of Parliament; there were many such in the heyday of prerogative; but it is a new attempt, more dangerous than the old attempts. The familiar effect of this new corruption is to turn Parliament, and especially the House of Commons, from a control on the monarchy to an abettor of its abuse of power:

> At the Revolution, the crown, deprived, for the ends of the Revolution itself, of many prerogatives, was found too weak to struggle against all the difficulties which pressed so new and unsettled a government. The court was obliged therefore to delegate a part of its powers to men of such interest as could support, and of such fidelity as would adhere to, its establishment. . . . This connexion, necessary at first, continued long after convenient; and properly conducted might indeed, in all situations, be an useful instrument of government.[28]

But it has not been properly conducted; instead of sharing its influence with men of interest (i.e., with the people) and fidelity, the court is on the point of *receiving* the power to exercise the crown's influence on its private favor alone. Burke delivers this masterpiece of circumspection:

> To get rid of all this intermediate and independent importance, and *to secure to the court the unlimited and uncontrolled use of its own vast influence, under the sole direction of its own private favour,* has for some years past been the great object of policy.[29]

It cannot now be surprising to see that Burke regards as corruption all use of influence under the direction of private favor, whether it be those powers granted to ministers after the Revolution or those powers retained by the court (the king and his "friends") at that time.

The true function of Parliament, then, is control of the monarchy in the name of the people. Burke's view of the independence of great men has been discussed in the previous chapter, and the conclusion was reached that their independence of the king was a consequence of their dependence on the people. The great men are for the most part in the House of Lords; what of the House of Commons? What is its independence? Is it the self-sufficiency of the country squires, secure in their domains, unabashed by their superiors in wealth and influence, who make up the large body of independents within the Commons, unattached either to the great men or to the king?

The independence of the House of Commons from the monarchy is also founded upon its dependence on the people. Burke describes two proper functions of Parliament, under the general title of controlling the monarchy, which "until of late" had been respected in the mature British constitution. The first is that "the laws should be the result of general consent" of the people. These are the laws that restrict the monarchy, which have already been discussed; we now find that the legislature is the combination of Parliament and the king's veto. But we should note that in this formulation of Parliament's proper function, Parliament itself is mentioned only indirectly, as that agent which procures "the result of general consent."[30] Moreover, the laws are the *result* of general consent. It is not that they are made so as to *secure* common consent, in which case it would be the duty of Parliament to make the best or wisest laws of which its members were capable, without overlooking the requirement that the people consent to them. Rather, the laws are made as the end of a process of securing consent, in which the feelings of the people supply both the beginning and the standard of success for law-makers, who act as mere agents of the people. Consent to the laws seems to take precedence over the wisdom of the laws, or almost to replace their wisdom; that is, the people themselves have sufficient wisdom in their feelings that these feelings can serve to indicate the need for legislation and to judge the success of it. If this is so, then the process of law-making would acquire greater importance than the content of the laws, since fidelity to popular feelings would be the chief element in good laws. This is a conclusion already suggested by Burke's treatment of the civil-list debt.

So far this is speculation on a slender phrase, but Burke rephrases the legislative function of Parliament in a way that seems to confirm this interpretation: "The people, by their representatives and grandees, were intrusted with a deliberative power in making laws; the king with the control of his negative."[31] *Their* representatives and grandees. And the people have "a deliberative power," that is to say, they have more than a consenting power to someone else's deliberation; the people deliberate "by their representatives and grandees" rather than consent to the deliberations of their representatives and grandees. The distinction is found in the words of Burke, and the words are not those which would tumble out casually from an unformed speculation.

"The laws reach but a very little way." The second and more important function of Parliament in controlling the monarchy is *"to refuse to support government, until power was in the hands of persons who were acceptable to the people, or while factions predominated in the court in which the nation had no confidence."* That is, to continue from the sentence quoted in the paragraph above: "The king was intrusted with the deliberative choice and the election to office [of ministers]; the people had the negative in a parliamentary refusal to support."[32] Again, Parliament acts as the agent of the people, and again its standard in so acting is what is acceptable to the people or what accords with the confidence of the people rather than what is best or noblest. Parliament seems to serve as the agent of the people, and in serving them, provides an expert skill that the people do not possess in order to produce a result acceptable to them.

Burke underlines this point on the next page, where he censures the choice of any minister who *"has no connexion with the interest of the people"* and who has *"no connexion with the sentiments and opinions of the people."* The latter case refers to the group of ministers who have got together "avowedly without any public principle," who have no connection with the sentiments and opinions of the people. Thus Burke appears to define the "public principle"—the only proper guide, as must be remembered, for the exercise of discretion—as a principle tenable in public, not a principle for the public good. If a principle is tenable in public, it is sufficiently for the public good. Similarly, the "interest of the people" appears to be their interest as they feel it, which is again sufficient; for Burke attacks ministers who have no *connection* to, rather than no *perception* of, the people's interest. In this second function, Parliament must use its veto on the king's choice of ministers so that the ministers will act as agents of the people, within the limits set by the interest, sentiments, and opinions of the people. This control provides a workable (not infallible) guide for the exercise of the king's choice "without any [of the] curious and anxious research for . . . abstract, universal, perfect harmony" characteristic of pretended supernatural virtue.[33]

This much is in Burke's first description of the court system; his presentation of its effects contains further remarks on the corruption of Parliament.[34] Here he comments upon the "spirit" of Parliament, especially the House of Commons, as opposed to its "legal form and power," already treated. Its spirit is sympathy with its "constituents"; it should "bear some stamp of the actual disposition of the people at large." If the actual disposition shared by the Commons were some "epidemical phrensy of the people," it would be an evil, but an evil that should not be corrected by disturbing the character of the Commons.

The virtue, spirit, and essence of a House of Commons consists in its being the express image of the feelings of the nation. It was not instituted to be a control *upon* the people, as of late it has been taught, by a doctrine of the most pernicious tendency. It was designed as a control *for* the people.[35]

Whereas Burke had previously urged that the Commons have a "connection" with the "interest" and "opinions" of the people, he now extends the fidelity required of the Commons to "infection" with the "disposition" and "feelings" of the people. This is an extreme statement on behalf of the people, and to it we may add another, which comes at the end of the "Thoughts." Burke says that "above all," the people

will endeavour to keep the House of Commons from assuming a character which does not belong to it. They will endeavour to keep that House, for its existence, for its powers, and its privileges, as independent of every other, and as dependent upon themselves, as possible. This servitude is to a House of Commons (like obedience to a Divine Law) "perfect freedom." For if they once quit this natural, rational and liberal obedience, they must find a support in an abject and unnatural dependence somewhere else.

Vox populi, lex Dei: this analogy occurs in the locus of rhetorical exaggeration, the end of the pamphlet, but it does no more than provide a culmination for the preceding expressions that have been noticed. Since the Commons cannot escape servitude of some kind, it should serve the people by sharing their feelings, a condition of "perfect freedom" (in inverted commas). This servitude does not extend to receiving the "authoritative instructions" of the people (or more likely, of a body of interested or enthusiastic advocates), which Burke decried in the "Speech to the Electors at Bristol" (1774).[36] But the Commons does properly accept the feelings of the people, the tone of popular opinions, as the authoritative basis for its deliberation. The people deliberate "by their representatives and grandees," who sympathize with popular feelings and rationalize them. The people cannot do their own speculation properly, and the House of Commons must supply this defect. But the Commons ought not to have its own feelings; otherwise it cannot supply the defect. To represent the people means to share their feelings and to refine their speculations; yet the distinction between popular feelings and speculations is operable only if popular feelings are sovereign. It is thus accurate to say that, according to Burke, the representatives must accept the *general* instructions of the people.

Control without Implication

Having examined the relation of the House of Commons to the people, one must mark the consequences for the constitution. Burke argues that the House must keep free from "the standing government"—a position which must be distinguished from the cabinet government of Bagehot's conception and of present times. In his declarations on the dissolution and election of 1784, Burke to some extent foresaw this distinction.

The Commons "was supposed originally," says Burke, "to be *no part of the standing government of this country.*"

This change from an immediate state of procuration and delegation [i.e., from the people] to a course of acting as from original power, is the way in which all the popular magistracies in the world have been perverted from their purposes.

For my part, I shall be compelled to conclude the principle of parliament to be totally corrupted, and therefore its ends entirely defeated, when I see two symptoms: first, a rule of indiscriminate support to all ministers; because this destroys the very end of parliament as a control and is a general, previous sanction to misgovernment; and secondly, the setting up any claims adverse to the right of free election; for this tends to subvert the legal authority by which the House of Commons sits.

As to the first symptom, Burke explains more fully his previously stated view that Parliament, when corrupted by the court system, becomes a positive instrument of tyranny, not just an impotent and innocent observer of it.

If they [the proponents of the court system] have any evil design to which there is no ordinary legal power commensurate, they bring it into parliament. In parliament the whole is executed from beginning to end. In parliament the power of obtaining their object is absolute; and the safety in the proceeding perfect; no rules to confine, no after-reckonings to terrify. Parliament cannot, with any great propriety, punish others for things in which they themselves have been accomplices. Thus the control of parliament upon the executory power is lost; because parliament is made to partake in every considerable act of government. *Impeachment, that great guardian of the purity of the constitution, is in danger of being lost, even to the idea of it.*

The consequence is that the people's confidence in the Commons is destroyed: "Whenever parliament is persuaded to assume the offices of executive government, it will lose all the confidence, love and veneration, which it has ever enjoyed whilst it was supposed the *corrective and control* of the acting powers of the state."[37]

Why should the court system be reduced to "indiscriminate support to all ministers"? The court system seeks this support because, as Burke has said, it affirms the adequacy of the reason, "that the king has thought proper to appoint them." This statement can be questioned. We have seen that neither Bolingbroke nor his political school maintains the adequacy of this reason; to do so would be merely to reoccupy, in Burke's phrase, "the shattered and old-fashioned fortress of prerogative."[38] Bolingbroke and his political school make a distinction between the great men and men of talent, a distinction that makes plausible "indiscriminate support to all ministers," once the king has been taught to apply it. Immediately afterwards, when Burke has the advocates of the court system advise the king to employ men "who are least infected with pride and self-will," he makes a possible reference to this distinction. As we cannot suppose him to be ignorant of so common a distinction,[39] it is easy to see why he would not advertise such a distinction if its plausibility works against him. Moreover, if his silence is taken for reluctance to mention it, his reasoning is also not hard to see: the distinction on which the political school relies would be misapplied by the king, and so men of talent would become tools of the king's pleasure, of his "arbitrary standard" of honor. The requirement that the king choose men of talent would mean, in practice, only the hope that he would do so. Burke rejects the use of the political school's distinction because he utterly disbelieves in the monarchical principle. The court system merely serves to raise up placemen and thus to reward their subservience.

In opposition to this distinction, Burke proposes another: namely, in a choice between ministers with and without a connection to the people, the king should choose the former. Burke's rule for the House of Commons would then not be "indiscriminate support for all ministers," but would be wariness against all ministers, as a control for the people. This is the sole authoritative instruction from the people to the Commons. The Commons is a check on the king's choice of ministers, by means of its separate connection to the people. But the ministers, that is, the crown, provide the "standing government" of the country; hence in Burke's view, the constitution does not have the same separation of powers as the United States Constitution. Parliament seems to have most of the law-making power, like the United States Congress; but for Burke, "the laws reach but a very little way." They are the passive and controlling, not the active, constitution—which consists of the exercise of powers left to the discretion of the ministers. Burke then differs with *The Federalist* in the importance he assigns to the laws (as distinguished from lawful prudence); the laws are not part of the standing government, as they are, according to *The Federalist*, in the United States Constitution. Accordingly, he sees the chief danger to the British government to come from a misuse of the discretionary power which is necessarily vested in the executory system, whereas *The Federalist* points to legislative usurpation as the "enterprising ambition" against which "the people ought to indulge all their jealousy and exhaust all their precautions." The House of Commons, though it makes the laws, does not share in the powers of a standing government, but stands outside it. On the other hand, the idea of separate and competing connections to the people, the idea which is the essence of the separation of powers in the United States Constitution, is fully present in Burke's "Thoughts."[40]

If Burke's view of the function of the House of Commons differs slightly from the function of the United States Congress, as seen in *The Federalist*, it differs greatly from present practice in Britain. Present practice is cabinet government with parties; it is a development from the cabinet government described by Walter Bagehot. Bagehot's view of cabinet government contained an element of Burke's view; he thought that the Commons itself did not rule, but chose its rulers between alternative cabinets. The choice which Burke left to the king, Bagehot gives to the Commons. For Bagehot, the Commons is still not part of the standing government, though it chooses the standing government.[41] This would produce, if one follows Burke's reasoning, a likely abatement in the wariness of the Commons toward the ministers, since the Commons would tend to look fondly on the object of its own selection. By keeping the power of choosing ministers in the king Burke achieves the stern confrontation of the legislature and the executive found in presidential government, as compared to Bagehot's cabinet government, which begins to implicate the people's control, the Commons, in the standing government. This result perhaps explains Burke's reason for allowing to the king the power of choosing ministers, despite his disbelief in the monarchical principle. His arrangement, apart from the introduction of sheer republicanism, with all its accompanying violence to the manners and calm of the nation, is that which best preserves popular control in its purity.

But present practice departs from Bagehot's view in a direction that is contrary to Burke's view, to say the least. Party discipline in the House of Commons has removed the choice of ministers from the Commons, which now gives almost indiscriminate support (and indiscriminate opposition) to all ministers. The people now have the choice of ministers by issuing authoritative instructions as they subscribe to party programs, which emerge as election mandates. But their making this choice virtually eliminates the Commons as a control *for* the people, in Burke's sense. The Commons has become thoroughly implicated in the standing government —though it has no prominent share in it—since members must vote with or against the governing party. In addition, the people themselves have become implicated in the standing government to the extent that the Commons became implicated, when, in Bagehot's view, it chose the ministers. Present practice stands condemned on Burke's principles.

Burke's position on the dissolution of Parliament in 1784 ought to be considered here, for it is apparently inconsistent with his view that the House of Commons ought to be, as a control for the people, the express image of the feelings of the people. The king ordered the dissolution after a period of some months, during which Pitt, his prime minister, was under heavy attack in the Commons, and during which he had suffered several major defeats from a majority in the Commons. Burke passionately opposed this dissolution as a punishment of the independence of the Commons. Yet the people in general supported Pitt at the time the Commons was opposing him, as evidenced by the gradual increase in Pitt's strength in the Commons and (less clearly) by his subsequent victory in the election following the dissolution. Burke must have known this, though he could not admit it publicly. Must one then convict Burke of a dishonest presentation of his views on the constitution, offered for a narrowly partisan purpose?

Some have said that this dissolution, the first under the Hanoverians to precede by intent the expiration of the legal term of Parliament, marked the beginning of cabinet government in Britain. It was the first time that a disagreement between the crown and the Commons was taken to the people for a decision. Others have replied that this is not so, because the King did not appeal to the people without a secure belief that the people would support him; his was not a true appeal to a disinterested observer for arbitration of a conflict, but only a demand from one partisan to another for aid.[42] Both views seem to be partly true: the second properly defines the nature of the appeal to the people; the first properly attributes this appeal to the beginnings of cabinet government, since dissolution remains even today a partisan device. Burke foresaw that this dissolution could become a precedent for something like cabinet government, that is, for a system in which ministers both rule as the crown and control in the name of the people.[43] The ministers pretended to a better knowledge of the feelings of the people than the Commons, he said; they made a claim to the virtue of the Commons as "express image" of the people's feelings. But this claim is dangerous, even if on occasion true. Though all branches of the government have a popular origin, only one can claim to be the express image of the people's feelings, and that one is the controlling branch.

Control of misrule by the people yields to an insidious implication of the people in misrule when the standing government bypasses the "natural guardians of the constitution," the Commons. For the standing government must then claim that intimate connection with the people which should function as a control upon itself. The people can no more prescribe the standing government and then control it, than the king can choose ministers and then control them, or than the ministers can act and then control themselves. "The people shall judge" means that the people can and must be non-partisan, not because they are above temptation but because they are below it. It was confidence in the non-partisanship of the people which was the guaranty of Bolingbroke's program for the Patriot King and the security of Burke's willingness to allow the feelings of the people to become the basis of government. The early promoters of party based their arguments for party on the non-partisanship of the people, which has not entirely failed them, despite the most earnest efforts of partisans today.

Control by Impeachment

How, in Burke's view, does the Commons achieve control of the ministers, apart from the previous security that the ministers must be connected to the people? Granted that "every good political institution must have a preventive operation as well as a remedial,"[44] what is the remedy, should the ministers fail in their trust? Impeachment is the chief remedial operation of the constitution, according to Burke. But he says that "impeachment . . . is in danger of being lost, even to the idea of it."

Of course this danger is now realized, and in present practice and opinion impeachment has been lost. According to more recent commentators on the British constitution, impeachment has been lost for good reasons: Erskine May says that it has been replaced by a more constant responsibility of ministers to the Commons (that is, through parties), which is fitted to a less drastic punishment in case of misdeeds; and A. V. Dicey says that it has been replaced by the increased volume of legislation and that an impeachable offense is now an illegal one, a breach of ordinary law.[45] The rise of party government and the increased volume of legislation are probably related, since they have the same effect of substituting for statesmanship. But that substitution is the problem of this study; hence one should try to recall the virtues of impeachment as an instrument of control. Burke believes impeachment to be the best means of control without implication; yet his idea of it and his conduct of the Hastings impeachment and trial exhibit the lawful prudence that seems to be his substitute for statesmanship.

What is the scope of impeachment? Sir William Blackstone, writing just before the publication of Burke's "Thoughts," says that "an impeachment before the lords by the commons of Great Britain, in parliament, is a prosecution of the already known and established law. . . ."[46] It is also a prosecution before the "High Court of Parliament." Blackstone thus anticipates (though he does not state) the view of Dicey, in declaring that impeachment must pertain to violation of laws. Burke, however, did not agree. He compared the House of Commons to a jury; as a control issuing immediately from the people, it "was in the higher part of the government what juries are in the lower."[47] Burke's opinion of the extent of the laws proper has been quoted. If impeachment went only so far as Burke thinks the laws reach, it could not be "that great guardian of the constitution." Impeachment must apply to the active constitution, that is, to offenses within the area of discretion that the laws permit. In likening the general function of the Commons to a jury, Burke states its particular function as the jury of presentment in impeachments. Thus, as the general function of the Commons, Burke may have in mind something similar to the practice in ancient assemblies of deliberating upon the praise or blame to be bestowed on the conduct of officials. Blackstone praises the British constitution above ancient assemblies, because the Commons, which represents the injured party (the people), only impeaches, and the Lords convict— while the people in ancient assemblies were both judges and accusers.[48] But Burke passes over the distinction between impeachment and conviction and does not mention the Lords; he may wish to imply, first, that impeachment is often conviction enough and, secondly, that the people ought to be both judges and accusers, since, as we saw in the preceding chapter, the Lords are also connected to the people.

But what is to be the standard for impeachable offenses, if not the law of the land? We can best answer this question by investigating Burke's part in the impeachment of Warren Hastings, one of the famous incidents in Burke's career, to which he himself attached great importance. Burke drew up the "Articles of Charge of High Crimes and Misdemeanors" against Hastings, which was presented to the Commons in 1786; and those charges concerned offenses for the most part outside the jurisdiction of the laws of England and of India. But Burke also had an opinion of the impolicy of Hastings which does not appear in the charges. We have, therefore, an opportunity to see what Burke regarded as impeachable offenses, of those not merely within the discretion permitted by the laws but also quite beyond the reach of the laws. The charges may be listed by subject:

(1) Hastings broke his word, the word of the East India Company and of England; this brought "high dishonour" to the company; it was "highly dishonourable to the character of the British nation"; it was contrary to "the principles of justice and honour," and to "all rules of justice." (2) In making charges without sufficient specifications against persons in India,

Hastings acted "contrary to the fundamental principles of justice." (3) In refusing a fair and impartial trial to the claims of the distressed Rajah of Benares, he opposed "the essential principles of natural justice" and committed a "high offense." (4) Again, it was contrary to the "rules of natural justice" not to give the Rajah time to answer the charges against himself. (5) Hastings, in seeking justification for a previously inflicted punishment, falsely imputed to the Rajah a criminal purpose contrary to "the principles of natural and legal reason." (6) It was "subversive of all principles of just government" for Hastings, a subordinate of the state, to act on his own private belief about the necessities of the state by levying an arbitrary tax. (7) It was "contrary to the sentiments and the law of nature" for Hastings to try to make the wife and son of the Rajah instruments of his oppressive designs against the Rajah; and it was an indecent spectacle in Asia, where one finds the utmost devotion to parental authority, for Hastings, a Christian governor representing a Christian nation, to compel a son to become an instrument of violence and extortion against his own mother. (8) Hastings, by instituting and confirming monopolies, infringed upon "the natural right of dealing with many competitors." (9) He disobeyed the instructions of the Court of Directors of the East India Company, which was "a high crime and misdemeanor." (10) Finally, he did what was "highly derogatory to the honour of this nation" when he accepted money for acting as he was bound to do.[49]

These are the charges that Burke distinguished with the most impressive epithets. Their character is legalistic. Most of them are concerned with violations of legal safeguards, as if Hastings were subject to a bill of rights or to the legal principles of the English common law, variously called essential or fundamental principles or rules of natural justice. It appears that Burke is not so far removed from Blackstone, after all. One instance departs from this pattern: the assertion that Hastings violated "the law of nature" in forcing a man's wife and son to act against him.[50] Nevertheless, Burke himself aligns this instance with a similar instance, which he does not so describe, but castigates as an impolitic and un-Christian spectacle. In general, Hastings has not violated specific commands of the law of nature; he has violated principles of natural justice which are legal.

Two objections may be made to this conclusion. It may be urged that we have exaggerated Burke's legalism, because the Hastings impeachment is not typical; or that we have understated Burke's legalism, which is best shown in the Hastings affair.[51] The latter view would take its sustenance, not so much from the writings already discussed, as from Burke's speeches at the trial of Hastings before the House of Lords, from 1788 to 1794. In these speeches, the impression is much stronger than in the Committee Report (to be discussed) and the "Articles of Charge" that in Burke's view, Hastings has simply violated the law of nature, and hence the law of God. Burke's conception of impeachable offenses would then be legalistic, not simply legal (since Hastings violated no promulgated law), but founded in a simple violation of a law, the law of nature. This view thus depends upon Burke's view of the character of the law of nature, into which we shall inquire at a later point.

Here we may note that the semilegal quality of prudence is very much in evidence in these speeches: ". . . all power is limited by law, and ought to be guided by discretion and not by arbitrary will—that all discretion must be referred to the conservation and benefit of those over whom power is exercised; and therefore must be guided by *rules of sound political morality*."[52] But Burke also reiterates that Hastings has violated, not the spirit of law, but "the law of nature which is the law of God," "the laws of morality," "that law which governs all law, the law of our Creator." "I impeach," he says, "in the name . . . of those eternal laws of justice which he has violated."[53] The references to God, both in oaths and in expressions of duty, are very frequent in these speeches in the Lords, more so than in the speeches on Hastings in the Commons and in the "Articles of Charge." Their peculiar regularity makes it difficult to assign them a simple meaning;[54] one must wait for later inquiry into Burke's religious beliefs.

Burke has left an indication in the trial speeches, however, that is similar to, yet clearer than, that which we shall see in the "Articles of Charge," that the law of nature is a consequence of certain natural rights:

We have shown you, that if these parties are to be compared together, it is not the rights of the people which are nothing, but rather the rights of the sovereign which are so. The rights of the people are everything, as they ought to be in the true and natural order of things. God forbid that these maxims should trench upon sovereignty, and its true, just, and lawful prerogative; on the contrary, they ought to support and establish them. The sovereign's rights are undoubtedly sacred rights, and ought to be so held in every country in the world; because exercised for the benefit of the people, and in subordination to that great end for which alone God has vested power in any man or any set of men. This is the law that we insist upon, and these are the principles upon which your lordships are to try the prisoner at your bar.

Also, the phrase "lives, liberties and properties" appears in the midst of a long passage containing Burke's fullest explanation of his conception of the law of nature.[55] This connection will be explored when the character of the law of nature is examined, together with the meaning of "human nature itself" or "the common nature in which I and all human beings are involved," also cited as a standard for impeachment.[56]

On the other hand, it might be objected that the "Articles of Charge" naturally show a legalistic bias suited to the occasion, because it is much easier to procure an impeachment if one can show that laws have been simply and directly violated. Thus their legalism would be evidence only for Burke's view of the proper method of impeachment, not for his view of impeachable offenses. This would be a dubious refinement, for the way of presenting the offense would soon come to define the offense. But this objection does not hold, because Burke does not accuse Hastings of acting illegally; he accuses him of acting wrongly, as defined in legalistic terms, yet beyond the laws. Hastings has not ruled illegally, but against the legal spirit of the laws; he has not comported himself in a lawful manner. He has violated, we should note, a natural right—"the natural right of dealing with many competitors." This leads us to the central impolicy of Hastings' regime in India.

The *impolicy* of which Burke complained is neither that which he called contrary to natural justice nor those charges called "high crimes and misdemeanors." It is best explained in the "Ninth Report from the Select Committee of the House," written by Burke, and it is scarcely stated in the "Articles of Charge." The impolicy is rapacity, as opposed to "beneficial commerce," that is, beneficial to both India and Britain.[57] As it stood, the profit from the India trade, according to Burke, was not honest gain. The East India Company, and especially Hastings, were milking the Indians for tribute, not promoting the prosperity of the Indians at all but advancing their own prosperity on an insecure and inhumane principle, the appropriation of private property by force. True policy required the restoration of "the main-spring of the commercial machine, *the principles of profit and loss,*"[58] hitherto repressed by state regulation and outright military intervention. Burke therefore approved of only so much empire as was necessary for this commercial purpose. Indeed Burke thought that it was "of absolute necessity" to abolish the forcible direction of the internal native trade by Europeans and to give it over to Indians—and that this reform could be achieved in the near future.[59]

Thus the impolicy of Hastings is scarcely found in the "Articles of Charge" against him; it has to be connected to them. The connection is clearest in Burke's single mention of a natural right whose effect is to place commerce above political restrictions. It is only a little less clear in Burke's accusation that Hastings acted on his private belief about the necessities of the state, the prudence of which was Hastings' own defense and the argument of his later defenders. The violations of natural legal safeguards, however, which make up the bulk of the charges, must be of lesser importance than the impolicy defined above; for they are either procedural, and do not prescribe an end, or they prescribe that level of morality necessary for commerce, such as keeping one's word. We are then entitled to suggest that the laws are for the sake of commerce. The principles of natural justice comprise the system of legality needed for commerce, and natural justice is inseparable from, even subordinate to, commerce or to "the natural right of dealing with many competitors," that is, of engaging in commerce. Burke's "Articles of Charge" do have a legal emphasis, as compared with his view of Hastings' impolicy; but this does not imply a merely rhetorical purpose, since commerce requires a steady legal basis.[60] Burke does imply that Hastings' impolicy—the substitution of conquest for commerce—cannot be corrected by legal or political prescription of an alternative goal. Commerce, "the commercial machine," must be allowed to re-establish itself on the basis which the law prescribes. In opening the trial of Hastings in the House of Lords, Burke noted that the "substantial excellence" of the British constitution was its "great circulation of responsibility." No man, except the king, "can escape the account which he owes to the laws of his country." Impeachment is not therefore based upon a "narrow jurisprudence"; on the contrary, it ensures that "those who by the abuse of power have violated the spirit of law, can never hope for protection from any of its forms." The spirit of law consists of "the enlarged and solid principles of state morality," which we have seen to have a legal and commercial character; hence the spirit of law does not transcend, but only complements, the law itself.[61] It goes without saying that the "commercial machine" requires a wider morality than the enforcement of fair reckoning. If the end of the state is commerce, the means are laws which release commerce from restrictions and permit the release of every man's commercial impulses. The laws being thus negative, the statesman's discretion is guided by the spirit of the laws. His prescriptions are less precise and less comprehensive than those of the statesman whose country's laws try to make men good.

The reader may object that we cannot assume that every impeachment will be like Hastings', that the end of the British nation in India—commerce—is not the sole end of the British constitution, of whose purity impeachment is the great guardian. But Burke spoke of *natural* principles of justice and of a *natural* right, without reference (in those crucial places) to the circumstances of Indian politics or to the fitness of Indians as factors in "the commercial machine." Hastings' fault was not misrule but ruling too much—or that form of misrule which is ruling too much. He was wrong to act upon his private beliefs about the state's necessities, and this impeachment is an assertion of public control over that action. This impeachment is an assertion avowedly modeled on Cicero's orations against Verres and was designed for the same general end that Burke attributes to Cicero:

> We have all, in our early education, read the Verrine Orations. . . . We may read them from a motive which the great author had doubtless in his view, when by publishing them he left to the world and to the latest posterity a monument, by which it might be seen what course a great public accuser, in a great public cause, ought to pursue; and, as connected with it, what course judges ought to pursue, in deciding upon such a cause.[62]

Such, then, is the standard for impeachable offenses; it is not precisely legal, but imprecisely legal. With the aid of this standard, there is no reason why the *idea* of impeachment would need to be restricted to the most heinous and infrequent offenses. In the first place, there is available a distinction made in the American Constitution between the sole penalty for conviction after impeachment—loss of office—and any further penalties, which must be inflicted by the ordinary courts after a prosecution for ordinary crimes. Impeachment could bring the punishment of ostracism, as in ancient practice, or as (in effect) in the case of Bolingbroke. If extraordinary in the legal sense, impeachment need not be uncommon, or drastic, though Burke allowed that it was "rare in its use." But, secondly, and more important, the idea of impeachment may be of more general use than as a guide for actual impeachments; it could serve as the guide for the typical activity of Commons as a control. It could define the usual *modus operandi* of Commons, such as would only infrequently result in actual impeachment.[63] Burke's description of the proper character of a candidate for the House of Commons sounds like the praise of a member of an investigating committee in the United States Congress: "A strenuous resistance to every appearance of lawless power; a spirit of independence carried to some degree of enthusiasm; an inquisitive character to discover, and a bold one to display, every corruption and every error of government. . . ."[64]

The idea of impeachment is control without implication. Impeachment is for crimes, whether defined by the ordinary laws or the principles of natural justice. Ministers are to be thought of almost as potential criminals, men who need the constraint of law, men from whom evil rather than good is to be expected. The Commons should keep its distance from them in order to judge them; it should not participate in ruling, as did citizens in Aristotle's definition. This forbearance, in Burke's conception, is not a restriction on the people, but an instrument of them. Were they to have the power to make particular recommendations or issue authoritative instructions, they could be seduced into a prior consent to misrule; and after their initial imprudence had been misrepresented as connivance, they could be prevented from making a searching examination and punishment of misrule. One may hazard a guess that party responsibility has now provoked just this result. It is no longer possible to secure an impeachment, because the attempt would be taken for a party maneuver; those of the people who share the partisan attachment of the miscreant official would immediately incline to regard themselves as his defenders, and their party principles as the defendant.

But Burke's conception of impeachment does not contrast fully with party responsibility. Like party responsibility, though to a lesser extent, it confines the range of statesmanship. For it does not require a judgment upon a ruler as a statesman responsible for the common good as a whole. It is satisfied with judging a ruler as a respecter of natural justice, which appears to be a means to a non-political end.[65] It applies the constraint of law not so much *upon* as *within* the statesman's discretion; he must follow rules that are legal in character rather than obey lawful commands and enjoy that discretion permitted by law. Burke's conception of impeachment occupies the same mediate ground of legality as that of party responsibility. Party responsibility means that party leaders should follow the rules laid down by the sovereign electorate. The rules do not state precise legal commands; they fix programs for the exercise of discretion. Party programs do not prescribe and permit, like the law; but they bring the use of legal definition into the realm of permissiveness, blending restraint into discretion.

Yet a difference remains. The modern conception of party responsibility engages the people and their representatives in the activity of ruling, though more by implicating them in the result than by granting them the power to affect the result. Still, by that conception, they do not stand aloof, in a stern posture of control. The people, by prescribing so much, lose the situation of innocence which, in Burke's view, would be the best protection for their rights; they cannot punish unrestrainedly. The power to punish rulers is more valuable than the power to issue authoritative instructions to them, because rulers may make the latter power into an instrument for enforcing a guilty compliance to misrule upon the people. It is true that impeachment as a whole is less important than securing trustworthy ministers, as we have seen; "every good political institution

. . . ought to have a natural tendency to exclude bad men from government, and not to trust for the safety of the state to subsequent punishment
alone . . . which has ever been tardy and uncertain."[66] But the conception
of party responsibility, which implies authoritative instructions in some
degree, combines and confuses the placement of trustworthy men and the
punishment of men who have been proved untrustworthy. Those who
adopt it punish, in a sense, because they try to correct what they had
left to be done on trust when they elected their rulers, and they punish ig-
norantly, without hearing the arguments or seeing the results; thereby they
lose the power to punish knowingly and with effect. Burke has less confidence than is found in the modern conception of party responsibility that
authoritative instructions, as distinguished from general instructions, can
sufficiently define the political situations that rulers meet. Authoritative
instructions have an overprecision useful only to rascals who flaunt their
particular successes in the midst of general ruin; such instructions, like
the laws, "reach but a very little way."[67]

Popular Favoritism

The first symptom of corruption in Parliament, "a rule of indiscriminate support to all ministers," has been discussed; the second is "the
setting up any claims adverse to the right of free election." Burke considers the second symptom in about eight pages—his treatment of the
latter part of the John Wilkes affair. Wilkes had been elected, and ob-
stinately re-elected, to Parliament in 1769 by the Middlesex constituency.
Eventually he was disqualified by the Commons, and the second-runner
seated in his place. At the time Burke wrote the "Thoughts," a host of
pamphlet-writers, including Blackstone and Dr. Johnson among the best,
and many others less well remembered, were praising and blaming this
action by the Commons. Sir William Meredith represented the Rockingham party with an able pamphlet. But Burke cruises over this battle,
neglecting the honor of engaging formidable men like Blackstone and
Dr. Johnson—who allowed themselves to be drawn into the event, though
they were not party men in Parliament—and passing up the opportunity
to succor his friends in distress; he only pauses to salute them with his
disbelief in their distress. Though not innocent of allusion to it, or without a conclusion upon it, his pamphlet "Thoughts" is utterly unconnected
with the circumstances of the Wilkes affair; that is, it would have no
effect upon that particular battle. Burke had no ordinary political purpose, no immediate partisan purpose, in writing his "Thoughts." He
brought out his pamphlet in the midst of the others, a modestly anonymous

pamphlet on the *present* discontents. Indeed, the essence of his rhetorical purpose, as we have described it, was to give his extraordinary political aim an ordinary setting. But the setting does not itself define Burke's intention.

Burke concludes that Wilkes's Middlesex election reveals the attempt of the House of Commons to assume a power to prevent a disagreeable person from sitting "without any other rule than their own pleasure." The fact that there is no appeal from the jurisdiction of the Commons does not mean that it has no rule in the exercise of its jurisdiction. What then is the proper rule for seating elected members? Burke has already mentioned the right of free election; the consequence is that he here supports the people's choice, Wilkes. Their actual choice must be seated; no legal subterfuge must in any circumstance substitute for it. The rule for the House of Commons is the pleasure of the people. Burke does not approve of Wilkes; he recalls that Wilkes is a libeler. But if it is excusable for the king qua ordinary man to have a favorite, it is the right of the people to have one. Burke displays his indignation that, while impiety and libel are rife, "the peace of the nation must be shaken to ruin one libeller and to tear from the populace a single favorite."[68] But those who deplore the attachment of George III to Lord Bute are closer to true belief than those who attack the attachment of the people to Wilkes. It is excusable for the king to have a favorite, but it is inexcusable that the king be taught to act on the principle of favoritism. It is also excusable for the people to have a favorite, even if he is licentious; but it is right that they be encouraged to have favorites. The right of popular favoritism needs to be understood against the wrong of court favoritism.

It is now possible to answer the first question about the Commons, In what does their independence consist? Burke says flatly: "The House of Commons can never be a control on other parts of government, unless they are controlled themselves by their constituents; and unless these constituents possess some right in the choice of that House, which it is not in the power of that House to take away."[69] The independence of the Commons comes from its dependence upon the people. In Burke's view, the *cursus honorum* of British public life should be made easier for the popular man, not more difficult. It is not right that the popular favorite should have to struggle against the advantages of "his court rival." "If . . . a pursuit of popularity exposes a man to greater dangers than a disposition to servility, the principle which is the life and soul of popular elections will perish out of the constitution."[70] That is to say, the pursuit of popularity should expose a man to no greater dangers than does that very timid passion, the disposition to servility. This was not the view of William Pitt, the people's favorite in the 1760's. He took pride in the dangers he had overcome in his career; and at his resignation in 1761, he sought the uncertainties of popularity, perhaps more than popularity itself, sustained by the knowledge of his great ability and not hampered by an ache for security. But Burke said that the favor of the people should be a surer and safer road to popular honors, such as election to Commons, than the favor of the court. Popularity has a poor reward from itself; it is necessary to add other rewards, those rewards presently monopolized by the King's friends.[71]

The reason is that the House would abuse its independence: ". . . all men possessed of an uncontrolled discretionary power leading to the aggrandizement and profit of their own body, have always abused it; and I see no particular sanctity in our times, that is at all likely, by a miraculous operation, to overrule the course of nature."[72] This assertion is astonishing, if we regard it not as a modern commonplace but in the light of Burke's reputation for holding traditional beliefs. All uncontrolled discretionary power will be abused; that is, the virtue which sustains the independence of men who know they are virtuous, and by which Pitt thought himself sustained (if the compliment is not too broad), is not likely or not dependable. Burke does not say that virtue, which means doing good voluntarily and therefore requires an "uncontrolled discretionary power," is impossible. He speaks only of all men in bodies, not of all men singly; and if virtue were impossible, the question would not arise. It is rather that sufficient virtue in a *body* of men cannot be dependably attained. There are not enough William Pitts; or, some would say, William Pitt himself cannot be trusted to remain untempted by court favor. Thus the House of Commons must be independent by its dependence upon the people, because it cannot be independent upon its own virtue. Popular favor is "surer" than its own virtue; consequently the good member is the popular member. Virtue is naturally weak, and it is necessary to fight servility to the crown with a kind of servility to the people.

Bolingbroke substituted the king's favor as the road to honor for the traditional virtues, because the king, if instructed how to be a Patriot King, would give favors on the basis of talents. Burke denies this. The education supplied to the Patriot King is spurious; it would loosen the restraint upon him without teaching him a new system. He would dispose of his favor unchecked, as a tyrant; and support for his favor would amount to servility to tyranny. Burke ends his treatment of the Wilkes affair by concluding that the true contest is between the electors and the crown, in which the Commons has become an instrument of the crown. This is the proposition which he intended to prove at the beginning. In the course of proof, however, Burke has substituted a system of popular favoritism for statesmanship. We have yet to see why he thought the people more worthy of the right to choose favorites than the king. It is safe to suppose that, while Burke endorsed the right of the people to choose Wilkes, he did so because he thought the usual choice would not be Wilkes. Popular favoritism is more reliable than court favoritism, but both are substitutes for statesmanship.

Burke's Popular Government

Our mixed government, said Burke, is "composed of monarchy, and of controls, on the part of the higher people and the lower." Having discussed monarchy and the controls upon monarchy, we come now to the referent of the two elements—the people. The people have already been discussed in their relation to king, the Lords, and the Commons, but we can begin with a summary.

The relation of the monarchy to the people is unclear, as it was left. The powers of the crown, that is, "the whole executory system," are to be vested in ministers who are "trustworthy" and who must act on "public principles and national grounds." The meaning of that quality and of those grounds has not yet been found, although they evidently have some reference to the people. The crown is separate from the king in his private capacity, and in this capacity (as in Bolingbroke's conception) he is not raised above the people. Indeed, the king has a connection to the people by feeling the same desires for wealth and ease as they. The Lords, as we saw in the preceding chapter, are defined by their wealth rather than by their honor and virtue; they are connected to the people because their wealth is the effect and pledge of the people's liberty. Indeed, they are frequently the people's subordinates, since most of those whom Burke regards as trustworthy ministers are Lords. One may consider their subordination to the people as a pledge of the people's liberty and as the proper relation to the people of ministers of the crown. The Commons is a control for the people; and it exercises its own judgment *in loco*, the people being absent, as well as for the people, who are deficient in judgment. Members of Parliament identify themselves with the feelings of the people in order to enforce the people's *general* instructions.

This being so, Burke's conception of a mixed constitution or government differs from the traditional conception. In Aristotle, a mixed constitution is a mixture of dissimilar elements, of which the popular element is one.

With Burke, each element of the constitution is connected and, one must add, subordinated to the people. The purity of the constitution, of which impeachment is the "great guardian," is its popularity. The mixture of the constitution (which includes both standing government and controls) results from the separation of its parts, despite their common origin and subordination. Burke's British constitution provides for popular government, indeed, "wholly popular" government, somewhat like the American Constitution described in *The Federalist*. The difference is that the British constitution, in Burke's view, is not composed wholly of parts connected to the people by direct or indirect election, as is the American Constitution (the judiciary partly excepted). The House of Commons, according to Burke, is the sole authorized representative of the people; the other parts have other connections to the people—the Lords by their wealth and standing,[73] the ministers by their reputation of respect for public principles, the king by his contentment with the virtue of an ordinary man. In a late work Burke distinguishes the natural from the artificial representatives of the people. The natural representatives of the people are the *public*, those with leisure for discussion, means of information, and subsistence above menial dependence, who number four hundred thousand in England and Scotland. The artificial representatives depend on the public more than on their legal constituents. But if Burke makes this distinction, then the people is composed of every adult, perhaps including women (who are not excluded from the public).[74] This popular constitution collects and composes those different channels to the people that have been made gradually and kept by habit and custom.

"Popular government" seems to be the best name for Burke's view of the British constitution. He does not himself call it that, and it is not popular government of the traditional kind. We have seen that the people do not rule, but control the rulers. This was indicated at the beginning of the "Thoughts" in Burke's reference to the capacity of the citizen as permanent and distinguished from the temporary capacity of a magistrate. Aristotle defines (or describes in various ways) the citizen as one who participates in rule, if only by electing magistrates.[75] Burke distinguishes the citizen from the ruler; and in the context of the distinction, he declares that the virtue of the citizen is forbearance from rule. Although the people do not rule, the British constitution is nonetheless popular government, in Burke's view, because the traditional question of who rules has lost its central importance.

The laws, for Burke, are more important than who rules; and the laws therefore define the nature of a government. The laws are made by the legislature, which includes the Commons, Lords, and the king; they are partly made outside the standing government. Now Burke identifies the "standing government" with the "whole executory system";[76] that is, the rulers execute the laws. But the reason for the rulers' discretion is that the laws by themselves cannot rule; the laws rule through lawfulness, or lawful prudence, or "principles of natural justice," or "rules of sound political morality." The discretion of rulers is a means for the rule of laws, not a complement to the rule of laws; the aim of their discretion is not an end beyond the laws, but lawfulness and the morality attendant to it. Rulers do not rule; the laws rule, although they rule chiefly by rules, not directly. We are also told: "The laws of this country are for the most part constituted, and wisely so, for the general ends of government, rather than for the preservation of our particular liberties."[77] But what are the "general ends of government"?

They cannot yet be defined. But we have seen that the end of government in India was legality, so as to secure certain natural rights. In the "Thoughts," there are fifteen references to the ends of the government or the constitution as a whole, in addition to the implication of the title of the pamphlet, which promises a search for the cause of the present discontents and thus seems to imply that the discontents are the most obvious evil. Burke argues, of course, that the constitution is in great peril; one would suppose that the most obvious evil would be in this circumstance the most important evil. One is then tempted to conclude that the most important evil is a corruption of the most important good, the end of the constitution, which in turn appears to be popular contentment. This is not a necessary conclusion, but it is confirmed by the very title of the "Thoughts" and by references to the ends of the constitution in the "Thoughts." These ends are recommended: composing the minds of the subjects, bringing good-humor to the people, putting an end to disorder and confusion and to weakness in the regular authority of the state or in the powers of executory government, and promoting the glory, power, and commerce of England.[78] Burke seems to say that the end of the constitution is contentment, meaning order and security—not pride in virtue, for the good life is absent from the explicit ends of the constitution. The rules of prudence seem to be largely prescribed by the system of "political economy," in the study of which Burke took such pride.[79]

Moreover, the burden of Burke's accusation against the court cabal is that it enfeebles government, not that it is unjust. Here we may summarize Burke's analysis of the danger to the constitution. The influence of the crown, operating on the interest of active men in the state, seduces the House of Commons, making it a positive instrument of tyranny, that is, the rule of the private pleasure of the king. This seduction could not succeed without the influence of Bolingbroke's theory, for his theory not only encourages the ambition of active men, but removes the check to their ambition in the public opinion that the strongholds of government should be held by trustworthy men, connected to the people. But it has not succeeded. The people, alarmed by the loss of their institution of control and puzzled by the restless revolving of government based on court favoritism, have lost confidence in the beneficence of government. Thus feeble government is further enfeebled.

It may be objected that this evidence is not sufficient to show what the "general ends of government" are. The constitution may be endangered by a threat to a subordinate end, one which is necessary to the ultimate end, virtue, but not identical with it. It is true that there seems to be an end beyond security in the "Thoughts," but that end is freedom. Burke says that there is "a peculiar venom and malignity in this political distemper." Formerly "the projectors of arbitrary government" attacked the liberties of their country, but in so doing they exalted the grandeur of the state and secured at least this lesser advantage. But the present court scheme "tends to produce neither the security of a free government, nor the energy of a monarchy that is absolute."[80] The court scheme has neither the subordinate virtue of a free state nor the consoling virtue of an absolute monarchy—from which it is evident that both security and energy are subordinate to freedom, in Burke's opinion. Thus the end of the constitution is to secure freedom. Yet the use of freedom, on the evidence so far, is commerce: the crime of Hastings was the violation of commercial legality and morality; and the rules for the statesman's prudence are found in the spirit of the laws or the method of political economy. Burke seems to believe in the modern view of the free state, which claims that a state does not aim to produce good men but first establishes, then watches, the self-regulation of private interests.[81]

If this is Burke's view, then clearly in a double sense, the question of who rules is not decisive for the British constitution. The laws rule the "executory system" chiefly through lawful prudence; they are more important than the statesmanship of their executors. Secondly, Burke has attenuated the meaning of "rule" so that the laws only guarantee the basis for freedom, an attenuated morality, but do not chiefly concern themselves with the virtuous use of freedom. Both parts of the question have declined in importance—"who" and "rules."

It is consistent with this supposition that Burke in effect abandons the traditional threefold classification of regimes in the "Thoughts." He uses the words "monarchy," "aristocracy," and "tyranny," but not to classify regimes. The operative distinction of regimes in the "Thoughts" is the modern one—lawful government and arbitrary government.[82] Lawful government secures freedom, and arbitrary government destroys it; so lawful government is also called free government. We have already considered the connection between statesmanship and the traditional classification of regimes; there is a corresponding connection between this modern classification and the depreciation of statesmanship. In the modern classification, there is only one good regime, or legitimate regime, whose essence is the rule of law, as opposed to the corruption of the good regime, which is the rule of discretion or, as it is argued, of arbitrary discretion. The lawful regime, in the conceptions of Locke, Montesquieu, and their followers, remains lawful not by assuming for itself a discretion which it denies to others, but in part by its internal arrangement, by a separation of powers. In Burke's formulation, this separation of powers takes the form of a division between the standing government and the controls, a division that cuts across the Commons, the Lords, and the king. No one part is responsible for the whole, for the common good; that is, in the strict sense, no part rules. Nor is the government as a whole responsible for the common good. The common good emerges as the result of the interaction, perhaps the competition, of the parts of the government and society. There is only this one "law of nature" defined in the "Thoughts": "Whoever is necessary to what we have made our object, is sure, in some way, or in some time or other, to become our master." This law is applied to the meaner adherents of the court cabal, but more generally it states the essential precaution of the British constitution, according to Burke. Designed for popular freedom, the constitution avoids the selection of any single agent to do the task of government (though only the House of Commons properly undertakes to represent the people) and thus avoids this enslavement to an indispensable agent. The constitution therefore stands on a "nice equipoise"; its elements, each popular in its way, compete and co-operate as agents, direct or indirect, of the people.[83]

But what of Burke and Bolingbroke? It is apparent that Burke has made very considerable concessions to Bolingbroke. Burke argues that a monarchy, absolute or limited, does not have virtue dependably sufficient to support a constitution whose end is freedom. An institutional arrangement is necessary to substitute for virtue, an arrangement connected to the people, with its energy drawn from and its limits posted to their feelings and interests, as opposed to a regime that seeks the wisdom and virtue surely confined to a few. Bolingbroke's conception of the British constitution has a closer resemblance on the surface to the traditional or Aristotelian constitution. Bolingbroke agrees, as we have seen, that an institutional arrangement should be substituted for virtue; and, like Burke, he distinguishes, as of the first importance, the regimes that do so (free constitutions) from those that do not (arbitrary regimes). Bolingbroke insists upon a distinction which Burke not so clearly, but still apparently, makes, between constitution and government. The constitution is based upon "fixed principles of reason," upon a strict contract recognizing the "rights of the subject," while the government is the "whole administration of public affairs," including the arrangement of offices, which is judged by its efficacy in supporting the constitution. Hence both follow the distinction of Locke between the "commonwealth" (the organization of society) and the "form of government" (the agent entrusted with the protection of the commonwealth).[84] For Burke, the constitution is the "standing government" and the "controls"; and the people are drawn, by their connection to the "controls," to a closer and more active inspection of the "standing government" than is implied in Locke and Bolingbroke.

Both Bolingbroke and Burke prefer "mixed government" as the form of government best designed to protect the constitution, but Bolingbroke differs from Burke in his conception of mixed government. For Bolingbroke, mixed government is not an "equipoise" of agents of the people, but a "balance of powers," not all popular but all serving, in their contrived independence and dependence, to protect the "rights of the subject." Bolingbroke says that mixed government is a mixture of the "simple forms," that is, of monarchy, aristocracy, and democracy.[85] Each part is therefore permitted a certain independence—derived, to be sure, from its situation, not from the virtue of its discretion—rather than required to maintain a connection to the people. Accordingly, while Burke says that the House of Commons ought to be the express image of the feelings of the nation, Bolingbroke says that the Commons may serve to keep the people quiet; while Burke says that greatness in a peer is the effect and pledge of the people's own importance, that peers are "the higher people," Bolingbroke says that peers depend upon neither the king nor the people but mediate between them;[86] while Burke says that the king's discretionary powers are vested in ministers, Bolingbroke allows the king sufficient independence to choose and to dominate his ministers—and so refers to the British mixed government as "limited monarchy."

Yet Burke does not fully accept the premise of the doctrinaire conception of separation of powers, the premise that the circumstances of a regime may be largely disregarded if its parts are duly arranged. He is surely *the* defender of prudence and statesmanship in modern times, and, in the "Thoughts," against the system and program of Bolingbroke. Burke's statesmen were gentlemen, the "natural leaders" of the people; if one studies his statesmanship, his views on the natural leaders and their relation to the people must be examined. Burke uses the phrase "the people" with great frequency; the implication is that the people can be moderate as a whole. They can be moderate if they are led by their natural leaders rather than by John Wilkes. But their natural leaders are traditional; they connect to previous times and claim former distinctions. Burke radically reinterprets Britain's limited monarchy, as tradition praised it; but he does not go so far as to give it a new name, popular government. His view of the constitution is very similar to that of the constitution called by *The Federalist* "wholly popular"; but, unlike Madison, he never flaunts its novelty.[87] This discussion of Burke's first remedy for the present discontents—popular control—has led us to his second remedy. It is our next task to see how Burke combines popular government with the rule (in its attenuated sense) of gentlemen.

CHAPTER SEVEN

The British Constitution: The Rule of Gentlemen

We have come to the tentative conclusion that in Burke's understanding, the British constitution is popular government. The difficulty with this conclusion is that popular government does not always produce good government; it is in general a problem, not the solution to all problems. Particularly, the Bolingbroke party is a problem for Britain's popular government. How does Burke meet this problem? Does his solution, the rule of gentlemen in parties, depend on statesmanship and the virtue of statesmen; or does it seek independence from statesmanship for the sake of security?

In this chapter Burke's "Thoughts" will be compared with his "Reflections on the Revolution in France," because they present different treatments of the problem of popular government. The treatments differ because both works are by intention rhetorical; for Burke recognizes the need to speak differently on different occasions. Whether they are also inconsistent on the problem of popular government will be a question for investigation, not the subject of an assumption.

In the "Thoughts," the people, through the Middlesex constituency, show themselves to be deficient by selecting John Wilkes as their remedy for the present discontents. Wilkes has made Lord Bute his enemy and has proposed, more by the implication of his outrageous provocations than by any direct insinuation, that the king discard him. But Wilkes, in so proposing, and the people, in approving of this proposal, are "fifty years, at least, behind-hand in their politics." They seek to remove the Favorite, as if the present danger of tyranny were the same as that under the Stuarts—as if it were enough to remove a favorite, without touching the system of favoritism.

In the "Reflections," the error of the people is different. There they have been misled not by history but by philosophy; the error is more profound. Yet curiously the error is in both situations involved with the doctrine of the natural rights of man. The people in 1789 were themselves aligned with the attack on the old regime, in the name of the natural rights of man; in the 1760's they were involved in a mistaken attempt to support the old regime against a political school owing its origin to Bolingbroke's modified doctrine of the natural rights of man. In 1789 the people were in a manner for Rousseau, not for John Wilkes and against Bolingbroke's influence. Of course, in the "Reflections," it is the French people who make this mistake; but Burke fears that the British people will follow their example, that is, that the British people are capable of doing so.

This new possibility, that the people will adopt the error they formerly opposed for the wrong reasons, does not change the problem of popular government but poses it in a different way. For Burke, it requires a defense of the old regime, of its "establishments,"[1] a defense which could be assumed in the "Thoughts," and was concealed by the economy of its rhetoric. But the "establishments" are not wholly concealed in the "Thoughts," for Burke's remedy for the present discontents amounts to the rule of gentlemen—"so to be patriots, as not to forget we are gentlemen." Thus, for the interpretation of the "Thoughts," our question is: How is the rule of gentlemen consistent with popular government? But the rule of gentlemen is one of the "establishments" defended in the "Reflections." Thus an inquiry into the consistency of the "Thoughts" can be aided by an inquiry into its consistency with the "Reflections," and because of the one-sided rhetoric of the "Thoughts," one needs such help.

The Introduction of Party

Let us review Burke's treatment of remedies for the present discontents. The remedies he discusses are five in number: first, he demands a complete restoration of the right of free election to the people; second and third, he rejects a place bill and more frequent elections; fourth, he recommends, at this conjuncture, the "interposition of the body of the people itself"; and fifth, he defends and encourages the practice of party. In the preceding chapter, the first and fourth remedies were considered under the heading of popular control; we can now discuss the fifth remedy, party.

Burke precedes his famous definition of party with an encomium upon the "great connexion of Whigs in the reign of Queen Anne":

> These wise men, for such I must call Lord Sunderland, Lord Godolphin, Lord Somers and Lord Marlborough, were too well principled in these maxims upon which the whole fabric of public strength is built, to be blown off their ground by the breath of every childish talker. They were not afraid that they should be called an ambitious Junto; or that their resolution to stand or fall together should, by placemen, be interpreted into a scuffle for places.
>
> Party is a body of men united, for promoting by their joint endeavours the national interest, upon some particular principle in which they are all agreed.[2]

But this passage is only the last term in a procession which serves to introduce the definition—a magnificent procession whose color and variety of allusion attract our love of parade and whose order of march impresses our love of logic. To lead us to the thought through the excellence of the rhetoric, we should pause to describe the members of this rhetorical train.

Heading the parade are Solon and other legislators, who go "so far as to make neutrality in party a crime against the state." They are overstraining the principle, barking for advance, as is typical of first discoverers. Next follow "the best patriots in the greatest commonwealths," who are more serene, having "always commended and promoted such connexions," led by Cicero the philosopher. They regard each other, and *idem sentiunt de republica.* Then come the practical and powerful Romans, whose spokesman is Cicero the orator, who carries the same principle a fortiori and looks upon it "with a sacred reverence." The Romans are a whole people and take some time to pass our eye, as they tramp out their devotion to private honor and public trust. Then suddenly Molière the comedian appears, shouting through his Fool, *"plus sages que les sages,"* and bowing in "all the wise and good [English] men who have lived before us." Last among these are the great Whigs, who are not only wise and good, but great in success, having governed according to this principle "in one of the most fortunate periods of our history." Addison is there with his trumpet, not really to play the Whigs' tune, but to play a tune that he knows they and the people like. "The Whigs of those days" tread lightly, their sympathy reaching out to the sufferings of their friends, their imagination untempted by a desire to sacrifice their tenderest connections to the bloody idol of Milton's Moloch.[3] And so we come to "these wise men," who embody the definition of party, being so "well-principled in these maxims." The definition itself, freed from its quadruple incarnation, stands with a classic simplicity that brings quiet to the noble and venerable ceremony of its introduction.

But the definition cannot silence our surprise, after we have admired its introduction. The parade was made up of a mingled train of practitioners and praisers; but the practitioners, especially the Whigs, do not speak; and the speakers do not praise *party*. Addison, who is the test case, because "he could not applaud . . . for a thing which in general estimation was not highly reputable," praises desert, long-tried faith and friendship— but not party. The four wise men, who so staunchly embodied party maxims that they safely disdained "the breath of every childish talker," kept clear of the recommendation of party which Burke makes for them. In short, we learn from this parade what was mentioned in chapter i, that there is a traditional view of party which does not mention party.

Then if Burke would follow the Whig wise men, he should not speak their praise, but repeat their deeds. He cannot point to writings for precedent, he can only point to actions. Clearly, then, the actions are insufficient or inappropriate. In speaking praise of the Whigs, Burke is refusing to follow their example. Their example must be inapplicable: just as the tyranny they fought now wears a new guise, so the remedy they applied will not work now. As we have said before, there is a very great difference between using party and praising it; this difference marks the distance of Burke's reform. Why, then, did Burke believe it wrong or useless to follow the example of the Whig connection of the reign of Queen Anne? One must dispose of this question before trying to understand Burke's definition of party, because his reform is less in the *content* of his definition of party than in the *giving* of it.

The Whigs as Conspirators

Burke has high praise for the Whig statesmen of 1688 and of Queen Anne's reign. In the "Thoughts" he calls them "these wise men"; in the "Reflections" he calls them "great lawyers and great statesmen" and "great men"; in "An Appeal from the New to the Old Whigs," a sequel to the "Reflections," he calls them "those great men," "men of deep understanding, open sincerity, and clear honour."[4] This praise surpasses the very mild approbation of "particular peers," perhaps those living in the 1760's, to which we have alluded in chapter v in a discussion that can be sufficiently recalled with this quotation:

If any particular peers, by their uniform, upright, constitutional conduct, by their public and their private virtues, have acquired an influence in the country;

the people on whose favour that influence depends, and from whom it arose, will never be duped into an opinion, that such greatness in a peer is the despotism of an aristocracy, when they know and feel it to be the effect and pledge of their own importance.[5]

This approbation is not an isolated assertion, gratuitously repeated, but the unfeeling demand of an argument, coldly required. As we have seen, it is not even inconsistent with this approbation, as it seems surely without reluctance, that Burke next says: "I am no friend to aristocracy. . . ." Yet how does one reconcile such coolness for aristocracy in the usual sense, where it means men of property, with warm praise of the "Old Whigs"?

Perhaps the Whig leaders of the 1760's are not so competent as the Old Whigs, and cannot follow their example; perhaps this is why Burke was unable to follow their example. But Burke joined Lord Rockingham's party in 1765 and frequently issued compliments to him; there is one in the "Appeal," given after Rockingham's death, which almost equals the same esteem he expressed above for the "Old Whigs."[6] In the "Thoughts" and in his "A Short Account of a Late Short Administration," however, his praise for Rockingham's administration is moderate, as if to confess by implication its inability to oppose the court system. It was the King who expelled Rockingham, but he did so because Rockingham was unable to prevent him from thinking meanly of his ability. In Burke's *Correspondence* can be found several of Burke's letters of this period to Rockingham, gently reproving him for missed opportunities and urging more determined action against the court system. In 1777 Burke wrote to an acquaintance that his "chief employment for many years has been that woeful one, of a *flapper*"—which is a poor reference for his employers.[7] In any case, it is not implausible to suggest that Burke believed Rockingham to be less remarkable than the four wise men of Queen Anne's reign.

Two passages in the "Thoughts" support this suggestion and give three reasons for the recalcitrance of the Whigs of the 1760's. In accounting for the early success of the court system, Burke points, first, to the pleasure of the Whig statesmen (no doubt of the Duke of Newcastle in particular) that Pitt was the first victim of the court cabal, and says, secondly:

To the great Whig families it was extremely disagreeable, and seemed almost unnatural, to oppose the administration of a prince of the House of Brunswick. Day after day they hesitated, and doubted, and lingered, expecting that other counsels would take place; and were slow to be persuaded, that all which had been done by the cabal was the effect not of humour, but of system.

A third reason can be found in a passage which is part of Burke's proof that "he that supports every administration subverts all government." Such support is a license to the caprices of a court:

All good men at length fly with horror from such a service. Men of rank and ability, with the spirit which ought to animate such men in a free state, while they decline the jurisdiction of dark cabal on their actions and fortunes, will, for both, cheerfully put themselves upon their country.[8]

It is not only that "men of rank and ability" do not wish to be put upon by "dark cabal"; they do not wish to be placed where they must protect themselves against "dark cabal."

The unremarkable Whig statesmen of Burke's time indulge their jealousy for a man of great but transient popularity because, as we have previously supposed, their own sense of self-sufficiency is defective. They are "rooted in the country"; their popularity is more permanent than Pitt's. But they are not above the need for support from the people in the consciousness of their popularity, since they are not, according to Burke, self-sufficient by the consciousness of their virtue. They are not rooted in anything more steady than popularity, which is essentially fitful, even when it is recurring because it is derived from wealth; hence they cannot know that their popularity is permanent, and they are jealous.

Yet while jealous, they are not properly fearful. They are too impressed by the success of the Whig statesmen of Queen Anne's reign to imitate them; that is, being impressed with the fact of success, they do not perceive the causes of it. They attribute to the Whig system alone the success that was partly caused by its good fortune; consequently, in the present danger, they attribute to "humour" or to bad fortune the evil which is a consequence of a defect in the Whig system. For it seems to be a defect in the Whig system which permits the success of Bolingbroke's opposing system. If the present Whigs did not exaggerate the virtue of the Old Whigs, they would not exaggerate the durability of their settlement. Besides, the present Whigs have a distaste for intrigue; they want to be where "they will be supported against any intrigue." They need public support from Parliament in their rule, again because they have insufficient internal resources in their virtue. Their fortunes— the wealth which connects them to the people—make them sober with that undiscriminating sobriety which neglects the occasional necessity of daring. Their prudence results not from their wisdom but from their privilege.[9]

To summarize: The present Whig families are unfit for conspiracy, but following the example of the Old Whigs requires conspiracy. As we have noted, in the past even those who practiced the *use* of party avoided the *praise* of party, because party was considered to be at best divisive, hence an instrument dangerous to praise even when it was necessary to employ. This traditional opinion deferred to and encouraged the distaste for conspiracy found in "men of rank and ability." But conspiracy was nonetheless necessary; indeed, the sturdy loyalty of the Old Whig connection grew from its common experience of the greater need for loyalty in conspiracy.[10] Even the popular reputation of the Old Whigs implied their conspiracy. In the public mind, they were saviors, if not founders, of the constitution, secret friends opposed to its public enemy; their public reputation was the greater because, as later appeared, they had performed their task outside the view of the public.

Moreover, the need for conspiracy is clearly implied, although only implied, in Burke's treatment of the Old Whigs in the "Reflections" and the "Appeal." These are artful works; in general, they are designed to tell the British people what their views on their constitution are at present and have been, in order to distinguish those views from the new proposals derived from the theory and practice of the French revolutionists.[11] It is therefore necessary to conceal the fact that the French revolutionists drew their theories from an English source. The name of John Locke is not mentioned in the "Reflections" or the "Appeal," although there is a possible reference to him in a later work, where Burke shows his awareness of the problem of French revolutionism within the English tradition.[12] It is also necessary to distinguish the Old Whig justification for revolution from the French, or New Whig, justification; the Old Whigs acted upon a perception of the absolute necessity of resistance, whereas the New Whigs promise to rebel by virtue of their arbitrary pleasure, as Burke explains. But if revolution properly waits for the last provocation from tyranny consistent with success against tyranny, it must be achieved by conspiracy. Burke does not explain this implication, since an explanation would qualify the distinction he wishes to recommend; but an explanation is not necessary.

All this can be said in support of the first reason for Burke's reform upon the example of the Old Whigs, that the Whig families of the 1760's were unremarkable men, incompetent to follow the example of the Old Whigs. But this much is not enough. If he had wished to imitate the Old Whigs, Burke himself could have taken a more forward role. He could have sought to form a coalition of statesmen against George III, like the coalition of wise men he praises, instead of the party discipline he recommends in the "Thoughts."[13] For Marlborough and Godolphin, unlike

Sunderland and Somers, were by no means doctrinal Whigs; if they had been, the Old Whig connection could not have ruled under the Tory Queen Anne. Pitt was available to lead, in place of Lord Rockingham, whom Burke vainly urged to effectual party action; others talented in details or gifted in compliance could complement the power of his elevated vision. There would be great difficulties in such a course: the jealousy toward Pitt, the bitterness between the Whig factions, the lack of reversionary resource after the death of the Duke of Cumberland in 1766. But these difficulties were no greater than those in the menace of the French Revolution, against which Burke spent his fading energy alone, though in public. He could have tried the role of the "Trimmer," Lord Halifax, a role and a man whom he does not mention in his account of the Glorious Revolution;[14] or, if too inconsiderable himself, he could have urged this role on another. If this had been too presumptuous, he could at least have refrained from acting so as to harden party enmities among the Whigs or only from priding himself upon having so acted.[15] In short, Burke could have urged party action privately instead of publicly.

If this possibility of private action reveals a genuine problem in the explanation of Burke's reform, one must seek a complete explanation. But even if Burke could not have acted differently, his praise of the Old Whigs can hardly be taken seriously. For it is evident to historians, and easily within Burke's comprehension, that the Old Whigs made a mistake in the impeachment trial of Dr. Sacheverell. That trial "was carried on for the express purpose of stating the true grounds and principles of the Revolution. . . ."[16] Yet the distinguishing principle between the New and Old Whigs was that revolution is just only in a situation of absolute necessity, and absolute necessity is undiscoverable by Whig or by any other principles.[17] The Sacheverell trial produced a doctrinal defense of a solution that could not be decided by a doctrine. Indeed, it was embarrassing in this respect for both Whigs and Tories at the time: the Whigs tried to fix a doctrine for exceptions to the general duty of obedience without unsettling the composure of the monarch whom they had seated by means of an exception, while the Tories tried to state a doctrine which opposed any exception, except that exception in favor of the reigning Tory Queen.

The trial is a set piece to illustrate the fatuousness of theoretical rigidity in politics, of the bad habit of mooting cases on the ruin of the constitution[18]—the evil object of so much Burkian declamation, and the very evil of which he accuses the French revolutionists. And yet his parody of his French opponents of the "Reflections" and the "Appeal" serves as the solemn authority for the authentic Whig and the authentic British principles in those same works! If the Old Whigs were as statesmanlike as Burke reported them to be, they would not have conducted the Sacheverell trial. The Whigs of the 1760's, even if less remarkable men, may be able to avoid their mistake. Burke did not discuss their mistake, which would have given the New Whigs a chance to misrepresent Whiggism; and his account of the Sacheverell trial conceals the embarrassment of the Old Whigs by a drapery of quotation and praise. In interpreting Burke's account, one must choose between gross naïveté and a certain artfulness, to describe his purpose.

The difficulty in the Whig justification for revolution is this: it is best to act only in the case of absolute necessity and to say nothing in public, for the public will make a category of an exception and forget the circumstances of the necessity. Yet it is very difficult, and perhaps impossible in a free country, not to speak. Burke saw this difficulty, for he comments in the "Thoughts" upon the "wonderful convenience" of "retrospective wisdom and historical patriotism," in serving "admirably to reconcile the old quarrel between speculation and practice." It is possible to speak about the past successfully, without defeating the aim of one's practice by speculation, because no passions deceive us about the past and because "the whole train of circumstances . . . is set in an orderly series before us." The past is settled in books for the many who judge "without the exertion of any considerable diligence or sagacity."[19] History is the proper resource for a statesman forced to speak about an absolute necessity after he has been forced to act upon it. The statesman should produce a historical example, we suppose, to justify his action as the result of an absolute necessity and to avoid the formulation of a damaging rule. But, as we have seen, the Whig statesmen of the 1760's are themselves under the deluding influence of history. Bemused by the success of the Whig revolution, they are in no position to make a successful use of its example—Burke must make it for them. He must bemuse them with history by praising the Old Whigs, while he actually departs from their example.

One can reach the same conclusion from another remark in the "Thoughts": "They who can read the political sky will see a hurricane in a cloud no bigger than a hand at the very edge of the horizon, and will run into the first harbour." Such is the foresight of "prudent men."[20] But Bolingbroke's influence is a plausible danger; current statesmen do not see the hurricane in the cloud and may not see it until too late. It is not safe, therefore, when there are no recognizable signs of tyranny, to wait for a situation of absolute necessity before resisting tyranny. The danger of tyranny is not only hidden; it is recurring, because it results from the application of a theory. In this, it resembles the danger from the Whig theorizing at the Sacheverell trial; the danger from Bolingbroke's influence is like the danger which arises from the mistake of the Old Whigs. Then the Whig statesmen of the 1760's must not follow the example of the Old Whigs, even if, urged in some way by Burke, they were able to do so. Burke wishes to lead them to something new, which is party.

Party Replaces Conspiracy

The subtle relation of party to necessity can be found in this passage at the end of the "Thoughts":

> There is . . . a time for all things. It is not every conjuncture which calls with equal force upon the activity of honest men; but critical exigencies now and then arise; and I am mistaken, if this be not one of them. Men will see the necessity of honest combination; but they may see it when it is too late. . . . They may at length find themselves under the necessity of conspiring, instead of consulting. The law, for which they stand, may become a weapon in the hands of its bitterest enemies; and they will be cast, at length, into that miserable alternative, between slavery and civil confusion, which no good man can look upon without horror. . . . Early activity may prevent late and fruitless violence. As yet we work in the light.[21]

We are now in a critical exigency, says Burke; but it still permits "early activity." Our argument suggests that Burke seriously propounds this implausibility—that there is an absolute necessity to act in the anticipation of a situation of absolute necessity. Only early activity will be successful; the moment of absolute necessity must be pushed forward, as compared to the example of the Old Whigs.

This passage decisively shows that Burke rejected the example of the Old Whigs. At the same time, it shows that party is a resort of absolute necessity or critical exigency; Burke did not claim that the practice of party was a good thing in the best circumstances, but that it was needed in bad or critical circumstances. This is the last moment when tyranny can be successfully opposed, since only "early activity may prevent *late and fruitless* violence" (emphasis added). Modern students of party sense a truth, in Burke's opinion, when they justify party as a necessary institution, rather than as a good institution, which should be chosen for its own sake.

It is necessary, Burke believes, to have a regular means of anticipating cases of absolute necessity. Honest men "may find themselves under the necessity of conspiring, instead of consulting." Honest men do not conspire well; they have a distaste for dark cabal and an open trust of their rulers. At their best, they are "persons of tender and scrupulous virtue."[22] They act well only "in the light." But conspirators acting for the good have a more delicate task; they must think in private, plan public deeds in private, act out their private plans in public, and speak in public.[23] Conspiracy involves a subtle shading from private thought to public speech that is beyond the discrimination of bluff, honest men; each step must succeed in its own compass, while looking forward to the conditions of success in the following steps. Conspiracy thus requires acting well in light and in dark and in twilight; unless aided by luck, a conspirator must be able to shift the purchase of his faculties calmly and rapidly, in a manner impossible to sensitive, honest men, who often cannot refrain from showing their virtue in a display of anguish.

Only a very remarkable man, in complete command of his faculties—as distinguished from honest men with virtues less skilfully ruled—can be a successful conspirator in a good cause. But states are regularly supplied only with honest men, not with remarkable men. If a regular supply of lesser virtue is considered more important than the best virtue, infrequently seen, then states should do away with the necessity of conspiracy by good men, in times of critical exigency, since conspiracy requires remarkable men. But eliminating the necessity of conspiracy requires itself the offices of a remarkable man, like Burke—perhaps even of an especially remarkable man—since in Burke's view, it may be greater than great to obviate the need for greatness. The founder of party has to see the absolute necessity of early activity, when honest men are complacent and when even remarkable men, taught by the example and doctrine of the Old Whigs (as reported by Burke), are patiently awaiting the last tolerable provocation of tyranny.

Party regularizes the wise man's precaution, so that honest men do not have to scan the horizon for hurricane clouds. They may consult, instead of conspiring. They have an organization in being, whose business is the prevention of occasions that necessitate conspiracy: "Every good political institution must have a preventive operation as well as a remedial." Party is a preventive operation whose remedial counterpart is impeachment. But what must be done to regularize the prevention of the necessity to impeach or to resist (the king himself cannot be impeached)? Consulting instead of conspiring is the regularization of conspiracy, because "instead of" means "in anticipation of." Burke's idea is to render harmless, by rendering honest, the practice of conspiracy. The example of remarkable men plotting in a good cause will not, by doctrinal extension, give license for scoundrels, since the "plotting" will now be publicly sanctioned consultation. And since it will be so, honest men will lose their embarrassment about plotting against an established regime, while their distaste for dark cabal is left inviolate. Burke's party is a re-enactment of revolution or resistance to tyranny, but a hidden re-enactment, cautious and traditional in its presentation, rebellious only by its anticipation of the need to rebel. Burke's concealment has been successful, for he is not known as a revolutionary, though he is known for having made party respectable.

Thoughts and Observations

Party enables honest men to act in the light, anticipating the task of remarkable men, who act in all degrees of light and dark. Party brings clarity to the gray shadows, natural and artificial, of conspiracy, making (so far as is possible) honest men clever, and clever men honest. Since conspiracy is always a possible necessity, especially when the monarchical principle is as little valid as Burke believes, party brings clarity to politics generally. Burke's presentation of the clarity that party contributes to politics has two stages, the first in the "Observations," the second in the "Thoughts." We now turn to a comparison of the remedies proposed in those pamphlets, as promised earlier in the treatment of the "political school."

Burke says in the "Observations" that the "canker-worm in the rose" is "a spirit of disconnexion, of distrust, and of treachery amongst public men."[24] His remedy is that ministries be established "upon the basis of some set of men, who are trusted by the public; and who can trust one another." How are such men to be recognized? Burke considers and rejects the test of trustworthiness described by the "political school" and by Bolingbroke, "under the name of *men of ability and virtue*"; this conveys no definite idea at all, and "all parties pretend to these qualities." There is a clearer test, one which "with certainty discriminates the opinions of men": ". . . if the disease be this distrust and disconnexion, it is easy to know who are sound and who are tainted." Men show their unshaken adherence to principle by means of their attachment to a party, for such men obviously put their private trust and faith above their interest in office, or guide their ambition by their private trust. Then the "great strong-holds of government" will be "in well-united hands," because the king will be unable to choose according to his pleasure.[25] He will be forced to choose a party composed of men who demonstrate their trustworthiness to the public by their trust in each other. In the "Observations" Burke recommends party discipline, that is, party action.

As in the "Thoughts," Burke's desire for clarity through party action attempts to repair a defect in public men; these persons "of the first families, and the weightiest properties" are honest men.

> This body will often be reproached by their adversaries, for want of ability in their political transactions; they will be ridiculed for missing many favourable conjunctures, and not profiting of several brilliant opportunities of fortune; but they must be contented to endure that reproach; for they cannot acquire the reputation of *that kind* of ability without losing all the other reputation they possess.[26]

Thus a reputation for constancy to the public good is incompatible with a reputation for cleverness—which we would not contest; but in addition, Burke does not wish to rely upon the ability of the truly clever man (who is also the good man) to acquire an honest reputation by concealing his art with more art.

But one must pay closer attention to Burke's rejection of the distinction proposed by Bolingbroke's school for bringing greater clarity to politics, "men of ability and virtue"; for this is Burke's most visible difference with Bolingbroke's politics. For Bolingbroke and his school, "men of ability and virtue" were understood in opposition to men of false honor and piety. The adoption of this distinction in the constitution would clarify politics, because "ability and virtue" simplified the traditional end or ends of the constitution. "Ability and virtue" mean the ability to contribute to national strength and wealth, which is a simple goal compared to the difficult and ambiguous idea of the common good, as discussed by Aristotle and as patronized by the aristocracy (that is, the great families). Burke does not dispute the idea of seeking a simpler substitute for virtue, but he does dispute Bolingbroke's particular substitute for virtue, because he believes that traditional honesty, which includes a certain respect for honor and piety, is more durable and reliable than Bolingbroke supposes and should not be re-educated to exclude this respect.

In order to show his objection to rule by "men of ability and virtue," Burke provides a satire on their decline from friendship to inhumanity, in a passage at the end of the "Observations." A powerful interest, "often concealed from those whom it affects" debauches the man of ability and virtue from his legitimate connection, which would be based on mutual trust. He gets new friends with his new office. "A certain tone of the solid and practical is immediately acquired. . . . The very idea of consistency is exploded. Then the whole ministerial cant is quickly got by heart." This person, by "frequently relinquishing one set of men and adopting another," grows into a "total indifference to human feeling, as . . . before to moral obligation." According to Burke, the phrase "men of ability and virtue" is, first, self-deception, then ministerial cant; it is a cover for the "interest of active men in the state"; it is a justification for simple ambition. It is so because, in hawking this phrase, the "political school" tries to make a man's public reputation depend on his cleverness, instead of his constancy.

But the curious consequence of Bolingbroke's idea is to give constancy to cleverness, and therefore to pervert cleverness. "The very idea of consistency is exploded," but not the consistent *practice* of the man who learns from a flattering phrase to prefer himself to his friends and to the public. He may begin by deserting a doltish aristocratic patron to accept a post where his talent can be exercised; yet he learns from this experience not his true worth, but the principle of desertion. His corruption shows the power of constancy, even against the renouncement of it, for the man of ability and virtue becomes as undiscriminating in his "cleverness" as the aristocratic patron who is puffed up by traditional pretensions. "Men of ability and virtue" strut as foolishly and awkwardly with their new pretensions as do "men of rank and ability" with their traditional pretensions. It does not seem possible to do away with pretensions or with the dull vanity of honesty. For this reason, honesty is in a sense more durable than Bolingbroke supposed.

Honesty is also more reliable, since those distracting aspects of honesty that Bolingbroke wishes to eliminate can be used for public purposes. The private faith of men in each other, which grows only with prolonged acquaintance and which therefore requires a stability of association found only in aristocratic status (that is, aristocracy in the usual sense), can be used to test their public trustworthiness. It is better that the great men prove their sympathy with the people than that they merely profess it. But since the interests of the people and of the great men, properly pursued, do not diverge, the great men can show their sympathy with the people by proving to be trusted friends not of the people, with whom intimacy is impossible, but of each other.

The necessary condition for this transformation of private trust into public trustworthiness is a free society where the wealth of the great men is the effect and pledge of the people's liberty. Such a free society is a commercial society—a society in which, according to the method of political economy, everybody shares in the wealth as the wealth increases by virtue of the release of private interests. In a free, commercial society, wealth gives the great men a common interest with the people, though both sides must be taught to recognize that interest. Since all share in the fruits of commerce (though not equally), the division of the rich and poor, which so occupied the older tradition of political philosophy, has been blurred if not eradicated; and the fear of partisanship, which was rooted in a fear of the poor as well as in a fear of religious fanaticism, has been in proportion reduced. At the same time, the great men and the people are connected—not so much by the public spirit of the great men, who act for the common good, as by a hoped-for harmony of *private* interests. The respectability of party is the respectability of partial and partly private loyalties, and partial loyalties are much enhanced when private wealth-getting is encouraged. A commercial society is not by itself the sufficient condition of party government, but it helps make party government possible by making parties tolerable, in two ways: it turns men's attention from collisions of religious faith, in which only the elect are saved, to divergences of economic interest, from which all can gain; and it eases the conflict of the poor with the rich.

Since it is the task of party to anticipate conspiracy, and thus in a sense to engage in conspiracy, honesty does not quite replace cleverness, but remains in need of cleverness. Honest men may shrug off their scruples against conspiracy, if they work in the light, but they cannot supply themselves with all the cleverness they need. Clever men, in Burke's conception, will not hover around the king but around their more trustworthy aristocratic patrons; there they will be able to do less mischief. Yet, to make clever men honest, a price must be paid: "As to leaders in parties, nothing is more common than to see them blindly led. The world is governed by go-betweens. These go-betweens influence the persons with whom they carry on the intercourse, by stating their own sense to each of them as the sense of the other; and thus they reciprocally master both sides."[27]

We have seen to what extent the "political school" constituted a party and how Burke interpreted the danger of its influence. In sum, their teaching and their example permit dishonest men to act in public, "in the light." Burke's desire is to make it easier for honest men to counteract the influence of this school; the "political school" has made necessary the reform that makes party respectable. Then the suggestion that Burke's party is a hidden enactment of revolution by anticipation must be revised to say that it is a hidden *counter-revolution* against Bolingbroke's party. Bolingbroke's party is in being; Burke's praise of party is a reply to it: "When bad men combine, the good must associate. . . ."[28]

However, as a counter to the Bolingbroke party, Burke found it insufficient to recommend party action, as he had done in the "Observations." In that work he discussed and rejected the distinguishing principle of the "political school," the advancement of "men of ability and virtue." In the "Thoughts," he notices another plausible maxim of Bolingbroke's political school, "Not men but measures"—a maxim of which the phrase "men of ability and virtue" is a consequence. This maxim asserts that political consistency can be discovered in measures or principles, but not in men. Hence the statesman (especially the rising statesman) should find his support in "men of ability and virtue," who are to be judged by the standard of "measures" (those that state the common good more simply in terms of national strength and wealth), not in the independent great families, who consist of "men" bound together by private trust, as well as by "measures." "Not men but measures" is an anti-party slogan, if parties are made of independent aristocrats—even if their independence is derived from the people. Yet it also comes close to describing rule by party program, as opposed to rule by statesmen.

Burke denies that this maxim serves as a guide to consistency in anything but subservient ambition. The attachment of men in parties, he maintains, is the best test of attachment to principle rather than interest. Thus, again for Burke, party has the purpose of bringing clarity to politics: "When people desert their connexions, the desertion is a manifest *fact*, upon which a direct simple issue lies, triable by plain men. Whether a *measure* of government be right or wrong, is *no matter of fact*, but a mere affair of opinion, on which men may, as they do, dispute and wrangle without end."[29] For the sake of "plain men," consistency in political conduct is preferred to the delicacy of statesmanship, because consistency can be made clear if men will judge it by party loyalty.

Thus "not men but measures" is the pretense of a court party or cabal, and the same is true of the slogan "men of ability and virtue," discussed in the "Observations." The earlier pamphlet directly attacks another opposition party, now out of office like the Rockingham party. Here Burke shows that the phrase "men of ability and virtue" encourages desertion by the satire upon a place-hunter who first deserts and then is deserted—a satire which is intended to bring the lesson home to the opposition. But desertion means desertion of one's friends for power; thus there is a somewhat greater stability of association in the neighborhood of power, in the court. This is the court party, or cabal, located where all "men of ability and virtue" aim to be. The use of this phrase by the court party is an advertisement for members from the other, more aristocratic parties, which are based on private trust; such a phrase spreads the spirit of distrust, which is the cause of feeble government and consequently of popular discontents. Recruitment for the court party masquerades, and quite successfully, as hostility to all parties. In order to stop this recruitment, therefore, it is necessary to recommend not only party action, as is done in the "Observations," but party itself, by name.[30] By this extension, Burke's attack on the court party becomes a general recommendation of party.

The "Thoughts" is more general than the "Observations" because it concentrates upon the court cabal, that is, upon the successful rather than upon the unsuccessful deserters of party. It does not answer a particular pamphlet, but a school of pamphleteers, who are inadequately identified; and it answers with an august vagueness appropriate to constitutional pronouncements. As an inducement to action, the "Thoughts" relies on a "legend" to evoke indignation, but removes the obvious targets of indignation—Lord Bute and the King. The "Observations" contains a careful analysis of English finance and reaches a satisfied conclusion on that account; it ends with a biting indictment of the Grenville party that more evidently serves the purpose of the Rockingham party than does the "Thoughts." The "Observations" is a first step, tentative rather than necessary, in the direction of Burke's innovation; coming so soon before the "Thoughts," it indicates an awareness of innovation and caution in causing it.

We may summarize the meaning of public praise of party. Party has been distinguished from cabal or faction by its disciplined independence, not by the goodness of its end. Party thus brings clarity to politics; by this added clarity, politics is made easier; it is within the capacity, not of the common man able to understand party principles, but of honest men, who Burke argues are the aristocrats (in the usual sense of the word). Party permits honest men to act publicly while they are resisting tyranny. Thus statesmen need be no more than simple, honest men—perhaps aided by go-betweens. They do not have to question the value of honesty by the occasional use of dishonest means, or of dark cabal, to thwart dishonest men and to restore the primacy of honesty in the constitution. Burke's reason for introducing party then agrees with the view of some modern students of party—that party conflict replaces violence. The advantage of party, as presented in the "Thoughts," is that it does not demand great ability; honest men can fight tyranny openly without causing a civil war. The disadvantage may be that party conflict, even when it successfully replaces the use of violence, does not avoid all the evils of violence. As it allows the discrimination of public men to decay in a party conflict made continual by the prudent anticipation of all sides, does it not also, by frequent calls to action, encourage cynicism in rulers and inattention in the people?[31]

Such is Burke's reform of the practice of the Old Whigs. It confirms the view that party government is opposed to statesmanship, but one should observe that Burke does not suppress the alternative. There remains in the "Thoughts" and in the "Reflections" a tension between party government and statesmanship, between "these great men" (the Old Whigs) and the great families, the present Whigs whose sole rule would be "austere and insolent domination," but who supply the constitution with a fund of honest and trustworthy ministers.

A Party System

There are many kinds of party: Which kind does Burke defend? Let us return to his definition: "Party is a body of men united, for promoting by their joint endeavours, the national interest, upon some particular principle in which they are all agreed." Party is a part of the nation acting for the whole—the traditional definition of party. But there is an obvious difference between the traditional definition and this one. Burke, though himself a party member and here an advocate of party action, does not define party from the standpoint of a participant but from that of an observer. He clearly distinguishes "*the* national interest" from "*some* particular principle," whereas the party member, from his standpoint, would consider the two identical. Burke's definition, while defending party, is skeptical of its claims. The part acting for the whole *is* the whole, in a way, like the government of a country; but if the part acts only "upon some particular principle," does it not remain a simple part, only contributing to the whole? The difficulty is that Burke defines "party" in the singular, but also in the universal. The first inquiry, then, must be: Which does he mean? Is party the means of applying true principles, as for Bolingbroke, in which case only one party is legitimate; or is the legitimacy of a plurality of parties desirable, as in a modern party system?

Certain remarks of Burke strongly suggest the latter:

If he [a statesman] does not concur in these general principles upon which the party is founded, and which necessarily draws on a concurrence to their application, he ought from the beginning to have chosen some other, more conformable to his opinions.[32]

Preferring this connexion, I do not mean to detract in the slightest degree from others. There are some of those, whom I admire at something of a greater distance, with whom I have had the happiness also perfectly to agree, in almost all the particulars, in which I have differed with some successive administrations. . . .[33]

It seems that several parties, which can be identified by their adherence to various principles (sometimes coinciding in application) though not to any special principles, are legitimate, if not equally desirable.

Any other conclusion would be improbable, if we remember the division into parties of British politics in Burke's day. Speaking in such general terms, Burke cannot have supposed that his praise of party would cause the Bedfords and Grenvilles to merge with the Rockinghams; on the contrary, its effect, if any, would be to encourage the maintenance of division. On October 29, 1769, Burke wrote to Lord Rockingham, contrasting their party with "the Bedfords, the Grenvilles, and other knots, who are combined for no public purpose, but only as a means of furthering with joint strength the private and individual advantage."[34] The Rockinghams are singular in fulfilling the role of a true party; other parties should follow their example, but do not have to join them.[35] Burke does not rule out "healing coalitions"; but he does not require them, and he sees great danger in spurious coalitions: "No system . . . can be formed, which will not leave room fully sufficient for healing coalitions: but no coalition, which, under the specious name of independency, carries in its bosom the unreconciled principles of the original discord of parties, ever was, or will be, an healing coalition."[36] Coalitions should be permitted, in order to heal the wounds of the original party discord; but Burke implies that wounds do not necessarily result from such discord, and hence that coalitions need not attempt to *prevent* party discord.

On the contrary, the Whigs and the Tories, at least in the past, "by their collision and mutual resistance have preserved the variety of this constitution in its unity."[37] Burke notes that these parties, by their union, saved the country in 1688. This statement must be compared to Burke's praise of the Old Whigs, discussed earlier; for it continues the criticism of the Old Whigs implied in the refusal to follow their example. Was it the Old Whig party, acting for the common good, that saved the constitution in 1688 and protected it thereafter? Or was it a union of parties, perhaps led by the Old Whigs, who formed a healing coalition? Burke seems to say the latter. What is desirable is not the protection of the common good by a part which acts for the whole, but the assurance of variety, which was achieved by a duality of parties in the past, and at present perhaps by more than two parties. In a crisis, the parties will unite, as after a truce; no single party will step forward to act for the whole. Thus, in the present crisis, with "a division of public men among themselves," Burke proposes that public men stand together against the court cabal, each in his own party, not all in the Rockingham party.[38] Burke has a preference for a particular party over the other parties, but he prefers the existence of a variety of parties to a single party, even that of the Old Whigs, one may suppose. We may note that the Old Whigs did not have such a tolerant view of the Tories, one of whom—Dr. Sacheverell—they took pains to prosecute.

We conclude that Burke meant to defend a party system, because of its variety, that is, for the sake of liberty, rather than a single party which would apply true principles to politics. "What is right should not only be made known, but made prevalent. . . ."[39] What is right is liberty, which must be defended against the court cabal, but not at the cost of variety, not by "some particular principle" of a single party. Hence, as noted earlier, the common good is not under the care of a single agent but results from the action of several agents, none of which is fully dependable in its own right. Burke's conception of party thus not only implies but includes in its definition the paradox of urging party action in general. He presents as the main virtue of party a result which is visible only to an observer of a party system, not to a party member; his definition does not explain, indeed it depreciates, the motive of the party member. As distinguished from Bolingbroke, Burke is the first partisan of the two-party (or multi-party) system. Of course, not every group is a true party; some are factions. The difference between a party and a faction is that a party has principles, other than common ambition, which serve to make it independent of the court. These principles, we shall see, support the "establishments" of the constitution.

Necessitudo sortis

If there should be several parties, how should they differ, and who should belong to them? According to Burke, there are two ways in which men become party members: by family and by shared experience in government. Both are in some sense natural, for party is natural—or, rather, parties are natural. Both sources of party are plural, compared to the single source of true first principles of Bolingbroke's party. Consider the first source: "Commonwealths are made of families, free commonwealths of parties also; and we may as well affirm, that our natural regards and ties of blood tend inevitably to make men bad citizens, as that the bonds of our party weaken those by which we are held to our country."[40] Here is of course an analogy between family and party, not a statement of identity or of relation; party bonds are like natural family ties. It is a peculiar analogy, since it likens two parts of the commonwealth that seem dissimilar: the family is a part that usually claims to be no more than a part, while a party is a part that claims to act for the whole.

But could party have its basis in the family tie, such that free commonwealths display the natural articulation (in families) of all commonwealths? Party is concerned with rule, which is always the subject of some claimed superiority. Parties whose basis is in the family would have their basis in the best families or in the aristocracy, for example, "the great Whig families." When Burke discusses the aristocracy in the "Thoughts," he identifies its leading characteristic as the possession of property, not as good birth.[41] Aristocrats are not so much the well-born as they are "men of property"—which is to imply that wealth attracts rank. Families have histories; their wealth is settled wealth; hence the best families are the settled or landed wealthy who have rank. In the first instance, then, parties are family parties, when family is understood as an institution founded in property, because property as power should be permitted "its natural operation," and property as the consequence of liberty should stand as "the effect and pledge" of the people's liberty.[42] Natural family ties, in this sense, prevent the party conflict (as in the Wars of the Roses) which results from the claims of family honor; for family honor inspires men to claim to be more than a part of the state and tends to make men bad citizens. Family property, however, is secured by a general recognition of property rights, a recognition that is not only compatible with patriotism, but *causes* it, since the insecurity of property is a prime motive for the original contract.[43] On the other hand, we have seen that Burke mutes the claim of party to act for the whole; so, with this interpretation, his analogy of family and party holds.

Burke's view of the family as a source of party is so undynastic that one must examine the other source he gives—common experience in government. "The great Whig families" are families of substance that have descended from the men who shared the responsibility for governing or watching the government for three decades following the Revolution; these "Revolution families" were not necessarily the most ancient families. In a previous discussion, it was suggested that rule is a kind of private property because it requires many individual judgments whose line of consistency marks an individual path. Sharing in rule is thus almost always a memorable experience. The experience of governing (or of opposing) becomes the private property of a group, and the memory of it becomes the *raison d'être* of the group. Proud of its achievements and aspirations while in office, the group stays together to repeat or to vindicate its achievements and to fulfil its aspirations. Thus a party develops the "history" which constitutes its character and usually comes to dominate the souls of its members; this healthy development works to unify the party like a "healing coalition."

This source of party is like the Roman *necessitudo sortis,* which Burke explains at the end of the "Thoughts." The Romans, he says, carried the the principle of *idem sentire de republica* a long way.

Even the holding of offices together, the disposition of which arose from chance, not selection, gave rise to a relation which continued for life. It was called *necessitudo sortis;* and it was looked upon with a sacred reverence. Breaches of any of these kinds of civil relation were considered as acts of the most distinguished turpitude.

The relation of *necessitudo sortis* was not merely of passing significance for Burke, because he used as his motto on the first page of the "Thoughts" a passage from Cicero's impeachment of Verres, in which Cicero accuses Verres of faithlessness to his fellow consul by *necessitudo sortis:* "Hoc vero occultum, internum, domesticum malum, non modo non existit, verum etiam opprimit, antequam perspicere atque explorare potueris."[44] The present discontents are caused by feeble government, which is caused by distrust among public men, distrust whose operation Burke characterizes in this quotation. *Necessitudo sortis* seems to be the relationship whose proper functioning Burke wishes to restore.

But Burke does not conceive of party exactly as the Roman *necessitudo sortis*. In the British constitution, obligation arises from shared rule; rule is not given by fate, however, but awarded by selection. Burke wants rule by selected trustworthy ministers, men of property and therefore men of a certain ambition. Men of property naturally reach for political power, but their ambition is trustworthy, because they are not desperate. Is the principle of selection, then, merely to reward the ambition of an undesperate group? Does this ambition have to be associated with the common good? Burke does seem to require such an association:

> Men thinking freely, will, in particular instances, think differently. But still as the greater part of the measures which arise in the course of public business are related to, or dependent on, some great *leading general principles in government,* a man must be peculiarly unfortunate in the choice of his political company if he does not agree with them at least nine times in ten.[45]

We observe, first, that he does not specify a single general principle of government, not even the common good, but rather welcomes a plurality of principles, which would doubtless conflict with one another in practice. The *"leading general principles in government,"* here so haughtily italicized, were "a mere affair of opinion" on the previous page. It seems still that Burke insists upon "principledness," rather than upon any particular principle. Secondly, Burke distinguishes thinking freely about particular measures from choosing political company. Choosing one's political company is not inconsistent with thinking freely, because measures which arise in the course of public business are "related to, or dependent on," general principles. "Disagreement will naturally be rare" because another party "more comfortable to his opinions" is available to the dissenting party member. What causes this neat division of public measures according to several leading principles which gives every man not "peculiarly unfortunate" the opportunity of 90 per cent agreement with his friends?

It is impossible that the cause is the law of nature in the traditional sense, for the operation of natural law upon men's consciences would produce a simple unanimity of opinion, if it produced any harmony. It would produce neither the harmony which results from the interplay of conflicting opinions nor the partial harmony of like-thinking men. At the same time, Burke's description of political opinion as if it were found in compartments is not consistent with our experience, or with his statement elsewhere,[46] of the difficulty and unclarity of practical judgments. It is not true that men, in the face of the circumstances of politics, come to conclusions so readily reconciled. The solution to this problem seems to be that the cohesiveness, as well as the plurality, of parties is caused by the development of party "history" through common and different experiences in governing. The different party histories are the means by which public measures are related to leading general principles; when a man enters the House of Commons, his choice is easy because he is confronted with several parties, each with a consistent history developed from a certain common experience.

Yet if a man chooses a party, he must first have chosen clarity; that is, he must have decided not to try to exercise his practical wisdom in isolation. He has chosen to act in concert rather than merely to "think freely." Then he does not merely adhere to a party because of some principle but acts in pursuit of some private ambition; for if he adhered to party on principle alone, in the absence of simple, true principles like Bolingbroke's first principles, parties would not have the high cohesiveness which Burke attributes to them *in potentia*. And if such a man were not free to act on ambition, it would have to be admitted that party discipline would impose upon his freedom. According to Burke, there is a law of nature on which parties base their development and with which they have occasional correspondence. When applied, however, this law of nature yields no clear choice of political company, no obvious leading principle of government; it must somehow be reconciled to the history of parties, which is apparently based on their experience and acquired without obvious reference to such a law.

Private and Public Trust

Parties are formed for both the higher and lower reasons for which men agree—and we suggest that, in Burke's view, association for the higher reasons is made possible by the lower:

When I see in any of these detached gentlemen of our times the angelic purity, power and beneficence, I shall admit them to be angels. In the mean time we are born only to be men. We shall do enough if we form ourselves to good ones. It is therefore our business carefully to cultivate in our minds, to rear to the most perfect vigour and maturity, every sort of generous and honest feeling that belongs to our nature. To bring the dispositions that are lovely in private life into the service and conduct of the commonwealth; so to be patriots, as not to forget we are gentlemen.[47]

Generous and honest feeling and lovely dispositions seem to be less than virtue; in the context, they are opposed to angelic virtue. They may be identified as the causes of private trust, which Burke says make up the foundation of public trust—or of adherence to leading general principles in government. But private trust among gentlemen (by whom Burke means men of property) cannot be separated from their natural inclination to secure the political power which corresponds to their wealth. "The dispositions that are lovely in private life" might therefore seem to be poisonous in public life, at least in tendency, because they cause oligarchical cabals. But Burke seems to believe, on the contrary, that private trust, precisely because it establishes a certain collective selfishness in public life, makes possible adherence to principle in public life. A detached man may be virtuous, but he is weak;[48] only men acting in concert have strength. Men acting in concert who have common experience in governing will achieve consistency on public measures merely by virtue of their *amour propre*. Their ambition, or concern for private property of one kind, counteracts their avarice, or concern for private property of the usual kind. Consequently, their private trust, which is mingled with avarice when they have no chance to act in government, is mellowed by ambition, when they do have the chance to act. At the same time, their avarice counteracts their ambition, because their property is settled and would be endangered by political instability.[49]

Their motive is not pure, for they are not simply acting for the common good; they are defending their past deeds, including their misdeeds. But public consistency, in men of some private standing, makes such men independent in public, which is sufficient for Burke's mixed government.[50] Burke provides for the obvious danger of mere consistency—that it may bring a consistent evil—by defending (though indirectly) a plurality of parties, that is, by defending a kind of inconsistency. Defense of the plurality of parties is a recognition that mere principledness, without reference to the common good, is insufficient. It is also a recognition of the composition of motives that gentlemen have in joining a party, as well as a security against the possible ill effects of that composition. And finally, it is a limitation upon his preference for the Rockinghams. Burke does not say directly that party permits the use of private vices or of dispositions which can become vices to turn private trust into public trust, but we believe that no other interpretation finds his meaning. He does say the following:

> It is never . . . wise to quarrel with the interested views of men, whilst they are combined with the public interest and promote it; it is our business to tie the knot if possible, closer. Resources that are derived from extraordinary virtues, as such virtues are rare, so they must be unproductive. It is a good thing for a monied man to pledge his property on the welfare of his country; he shows that he places his treasure where his heart is; and, revolving in this circle, we know that "wherever a man's treasure is, there his heart will be also."[51]

In some current opinion, Burke is considered to be naïvely hopeful by having held that parties can be based upon principle rather than interest. This view underestimates Burke's realism in composing principles of interests, and in substituting *any* public principle (that is, principle known to the public) for *the* common good, as the basis of party. Burke saw that "not men but measures" was the excuse of unprincipled men, as well as a high-minded slogan. He proposed that men of principle be held to the standard of private trust, in order to keep unprincipled politicians from claiming the right to desert their friends. But the standard of private trust is imperfect: among men of property, it allows collective avarice; and among oligarchical politicians, it allows collective ambition. In order to prevent the dangerous effects of Bolingbrokian humbug, Burke was forced to accept the dull vices of gentlemanly privilege. His parties of principles are tinged with interest so that they may be more than a mere cover for interest.[52]

For Burke, the "program" of a party is found in its history, what it has done, not in its plans for the future. Consistency is a rationalization of past judgments of public measures, and a party sustains its history when it insists upon being "not inconsistent with our former behaviour in the last opposition," as Lord Rockingham once put it.[53] Burke never wrote a program for the Rockingham party in the sense of a modern party program—that is, a demonstration of the advantages to be gained from the enactment of particular public measures derived from an application of the party's principles. But he did write "A Short Account of a Late Short Administration," which listed the achievements of the Rockingham administration of 1765–66. The conception of the party history as a program accords with eighteenth-century practice in Britain; as another example, one may recall the stubborn attachment of the Grenville party to the wisdom of the Stamp Act. Yet this conception does not simply describe eighteenth-century practice: a majority of the House of Commons were still independents; and there was a growing number of "men of ability," with a taste for administration and a sliding attachment to the party in office. Burke castigated the former for their tendency to support every administration, and the latter for their subservience to the king's private pleasure.

When the party program is a history of party judgments and decisions, it is bound to include hostility to certain persons, as that of the Rockinghams for Pitt, which memorialized certain disagreeable incidents of the past. The modern party, seeking to apply its party principles, attacks its opponents for their principles with a hostility whose source is less personal, whatever hatreds it looses. One of the changes made in the "Thoughts," after Burke had circulated it to his party, was the moderation of its aspersions upon Pitt.[54] The following is an evident allusion to Pitt, perhaps a moderated aspersion:

> In a connexion, the most inconsiderable man, by adding to the weight of the whole, has his value, and his use; out of it, the greatest talents are wholly unserviceable to the public. No man, who is not inflamed by vain-glory into enthusiasm, can flatter himself that his single, unsupported, desultory, unsystematic endeavours, are of power to defeat the subtle designs and united cabals of ambitious citizens. When bad men combine, the good must associate; else they will fall, one by one, an unpitied sacrifice in a contemptible struggle.[55]

Yet this recommendation of group action is not only an allusion to Pitt; it also upholds the basis of the modern party program by lessening the reliance upon statesmanship. A party's history begins with the statesmanship of its members; but Burke encourages what might have been deplored, that judgments made in certain circumstances become, by virtue of the vanity of party members, the standard of political wisdom in later circumstances. This concession to the vanity of a party is intended to prevent the weakness of individual vanity and to procure the strength of group action; group acts are always stronger, or always more dependably strong, than the deeds of an individual man. This does not dissolve the traditional distinction between party and faction, but it does reverse the presumption of that distinction: connections in politics, Burke says, are "essentially necessary for the full performance of our public duty, accidentally liable to degenerate into faction."[56]

Parties are necessary, rather than simply good; they are contingent for their good upon the evil circumstance of "ambitious citizens." But their tendency to degenerate is only accidental. This is a very important change from the traditional view of party,[57] which we must pause to record. The

traditional view was that party functioned as an occasionally good instrument, whose use even by trustworthy men was subject to some, though
not to all, of the evils of faction; for good men who conspired set an
example of which bad men might take advantage. In this view, healthy
politics excludes the recognition of the regular necessity for party, because party has the inevitable tendency to degenerate into faction. In
this view, the deeds of great men, which show the virtue of statesmanship, and the deeds of individual men, which show the need for statesmanship, conform to the nature of politics, whose complexity Burke has
chosen to simplify with the introduction of party. One cannot deny that
this reference to Pitt, if such it be, is a fine statement of the need for and
the methods of political responsibility. A wise statesman must wish to
give weight to his wisdom and must be willing to sacrifice his pet ideas
for his fundamental design and to shake off the irritations caused by his
necessary associates. He must act in concert with others, perhaps in a
party. But acting together, we have argued, does not require the respectability of party. A statesman can act without the assurance of success or
ease or immunity and take the consequences of failure as a result of a
poor or unlucky connection. In a free society, he might suffer no more
than the taste of opprobrium. But when party is respectable, connection
is regularized and almost unavoidable; a statesman loses the advantage
of his judgment in choosing how and with whom to connect and learns
to march and shout. In the "Thoughts," Burke has argued from the use
of connection to the imposition of it.

Yet Burke regarded party as natural; how he did so is as yet unclear.
We have a partial answer to this inquiry: Parties are properly composed
of men of property who have, in the past, acted together in public. Party
thus depends upon the "natural operation of property" and upon the
natural fondness of men of property for their own past deeds. These
causes produce a natural grouping of parties, such that a man entering
the House of Commons can find a group with which he can agree nine
times in ten. But the relation of party to the law of nature that guides
a statesman's prudence remains obscure; it will be considered in the next
chapter.

Party as an Establishment

The next topic is the relation of people and party, and the two remedies for the present discontents involving the people. The first remedy
is the complete restoration of the right of free election to the people—
which seems dubious because it endorses the election of an acknowledged

rascal like Wilkes. But party, when recognized as part of the public constitution, makes this right harmless, since party tolerates and moderates ambition. When the people's favorite enters the Commons, he finds that he can rise to office only by submitting to party discipline, if the Commons insists upon party consistency as the ticket to office. If he prefers applause to power and "thinking freely" to agreeing nine times in ten, however, his "spirited disposition" will help Parliament to control the standing government.

Burke's second remedy involving the people is "the interposition of the body of the people itself" whenever its representatives seem, by some flagrant act, to claim for themselves an arbitrary power, as in the denial of the right of free election in Wilkes's case. "Standards for judging more systematically upon their conduct ought to be settled in the meetings of counties and corporations. Frequent and correct lists of the voters in all important questions ought to be procured." Burke allows this to be a "most unpleasant remedy,"[58] and it certainly approaches the idea that the people should issue authoritative instructions to their representatives; but it only approaches this idea since there must be provocation from the Commons, and the provocation must be flagrant. Moreover, the people would aim only at the restoration of the proper duty of the Commons, that is, control in the name of the people, by temporarily enforcing the connection that ought to be naturally felt.

The purpose of interposition is not only to enforce the proper connection between the people and their representatives but also the proper connection among the representatives. Interposition should enforce party consistency by seeking "standards for judging more systematically upon their conduct." The Commons can properly control the standing government only by holding it to party consistency; if Commons fails in this, the members must be led to their duty by the people.[59] Party is a control, in the name of the people, on the standing government. Yet the party in office *is* the standing government. Burke's conception of the function of party shifts, by an unmarked extension, from the apprehension of tyranny to investment "with all the powers of government," or from an early alarm against power to a regular contender for power. This is the result of prudent anticipation of tyranny by its possible opponents, who come to spend their time of peace in lesser conflict, in the hope that they may escape their time of war.

Now interposition in the Commons is a most unpleasant remedy because, as we surmised in the earlier discussion of popular government, the people should not have active power in the state. Burke says this in the "Appeal":

> ... no legislator, at any period of the world, has willingly placed the seat of active power in the hands of the multitude; because there it admits of no control, no regulation, no steady direction whatsoever. The people are the natural control on authority; but to exercise and to control together is contradictory and impossible.[60]

Then is there not a danger that party as a contender for power over the people conflicts with party as a control in the name of the people? In the modern conception, party is a control for the people because it serves as a governing instrument for them by application of the party program. This conception is clearly "contradictory and impossible," in Burke's meaning. But how does Burke's own conception escape this difficulty?

Party must have a dual function. Party is a control for the people, as the practice of party consistency is enforced by the Commons; and a control on the people, as it also functions as the standing government. Control for the people through party requires only the application of the *idea* of party consistency, not any particular party program; only principledness, not any principle; only general instructions, not authoritative instructions. Thus the people can use the idea of party as control or, what is better, the Commons can make such use of the idea of party without that involvement in the standing government which disqualifies anyone from controlling the standing government. But this is not the chief advantage of the dual function of party.

The people are not *the* people merely by original contract, according to Burke. His argument can be quickly sketched, because it is the theme of the "Reflections" and the "Appeal." The people make a contract to escape their "naked, shivering nature," but the contract is only the first step of that escape. The government then established must make a record of continuing success in two respects. It must satisfy the wants that made men seek government, and it must subdue the passions whose conflict makes the satisfaction of wants without government impossible. A record of success in satisfying wants is necessary because men will not submit themselves to authority when they are told that they have a right to protection of their rights. Such promises will only inflate their demands, cause conflict, and prevent their escape from, or force their return to, the barbarism of prepolitical life. Men must not be told that they possess the natural rights of men, though they do have them in the state of nature. Instead, they must be shown that they have a government which, on the record, has protected them by occasional intervention in areas of private liberty to allay grievances. Such intervention is reform, as distinguished from innovation, which is substantial novelty. A successful record makes a government legitimate by prescription, and prescription must be substituted for enlightenment of men as to their natural rights, which is dangerous and insufficient.[61]

This prescription is secured by establishments. Not the original contract, but establishments give form to the people. These establishments are institutions whose present function owes little to the manner of their founding or to the intention of their founders; they have grown by occasional and gradual accretion of purpose, in response to emergencies. Their growth has not been guided by founders with a view of the whole, but by adjusters with a view to the parts most urgently defective. The form of the people is a "nice equipoise," built over centuries and maintained by habit; it is a complex of heterogeneous parts that is never visible as a whole, except to such a man as Burke.[62] The final end of the people, happiness and security, is produced only by balance and counterbalance, so that the people see only the immediate and not the more remote agents of their happiness. The people are not a mystical whole; but because they are not formed by a comprehensive, purposive act, they are not a self-conscious whole. A man is a Briton by virtue of his place in Britain, not because of the end of Britain.

In the "Reflections," Burke discusses the church, the monarchy, and the aristocracy as establishments. These are parts of the people, be it noted, not parts of the constitution which are separated from the people and act upon the people. These establishments give structure to the people, but do not impose upon them or rule them from outside. Yet, as separate parts of the people, they restrain the other parts of the people; consequently, as a whole, the people are restrained.[63] This is a delicate distinction, for which we must have recourse to Burke's words:

> Government is a contrivance of human wisdom to provide for human *wants*. Men have a right that these wants should be provided for by this wisdom. Among these wants is to be reckoned the want, out of civil society, of a sufficient restraint upon their passions. Society requires not only that the passions of individuals should be subjected, but that even in the mass and body, as well as in the individuals, the inclinations of men should frequently be thwarted, their will controlled, and their passions brought into subjection. This can only be done *by a power out of themselves;* and not, in the exercise of its function, subject to that will and to those passions which it is its office to bridle and subdue. In this sense the restraints on men, as well as their liberties, are to be reckoned among their rights.[64]

Government is then a part of society, not outside it; society, or the people, is begun by the original contract. At that time, "each man has a right, if he pleases, to remain an individual." "That he may secure some liberty, he makes a surrender in trust of the whole of it."[65] It is therefore a requirement of society that men be ruled "by a power out of themselves," out of their original consent and out of their present control. The natural rights of man require that in the beginning every man first consent to join the society or the people, but they do not require that every man consent to the acts of the standing government, as in active popular government. Quite to the contrary, they require that the people absolutely abandon the right to participate in government. The people must not become involved in government; they have a right to be restrained by government.

Yet the original contract is still of fundamental importance, for it satisfies the people that the restraints upon them are founded in their rights. The equality of restraints and rights, of standing government and controls, is characteristic only of civil society, because a man is rightfully restrained only when restraints are mutual among all members of society. In the original contract men consent to the equality of restraints and rights. And though each succeeding generation does not repeat this consent, yet it is a legitimate inference that each would do so, as long as this equality continues.[66] The people accept the duties of society by feeling the benefits of society, not because they make a formal act of consent. But they should feel the benefits of society, instead of consenting to society, only because their feelings are more accurate than their imaginations in reckoning benefits. The contractual relation between benefits and duties, or between rights and restraints, remains. For the sake of security, Burke did not think that the original contract should be consented to in each generation. A re-enactment of consent should occur only in a case of absolute necessity. The Revolution of 1688 was just, according to Burke, because the Old Whigs sought to repair a breach of the original contract in a situation of absolute necessity, not because they sought merely to redress an imbalance of development in the constitution.[67] The original contract is not sufficient to make government legitimate, as the formal statement of consent does not fully create a society. But this formal consent is the model for the presumption of prescription that a people well governed owes duties to its government. In this way the original contract sets the terms on which society, having made its benefits felt, becomes legitimate; although it is only the first step toward society, it tells which future steps must be taken to go in the right direction.[68] Therefore, restraints, though equal to rights in civil society, are originally and continually based on rights.

Human wisdom is to provide for human wants. The wants are those of ordinary men. Hence, human wisdom, as it is used in government, serves the wants of ordinary men. "There is no qualification for government but virtue and wisdom, actual or presumptive."[69] But these qualities serve only to find the means to satisfy ordinary human wants; virtue and wisdom are limited to the ends of the people, a limitation expressed in the original contract, though defined only after experience. The means to human wants include restraints upon those wants, but do not, as it seems, imply a transcendence of ordinary wants.

The people are kept from rash enthusiasm not by their knowledge of their right to self-preservation, but by their habitual experience of the protection of their rights. Protection of their rights requires that the passions that inflame the imagination be subdued, in order to permit the operation of natural feeling. Natural feeling is love of our own, of our "little platoon," of the establishments of society. It is not boundless, as is the imagination;[70] it is a mild kind of vanity, compatible with settled dispositions and hence with security and stability. It clings to private property of all kinds; it is tenacious rather than grasping and makes possible the civilizing growth of prescription. Since "the desire of acquisition is always a passion of long views," we may tentatively describe natural feeling as passion subdued, or disciplined.[71] It is the task of statesmanship to subdue popular passions and to satisfy the natural feeling that develops through the establishments of civil society.

It is not necessary to teach men to thirst after power. But it is very expedient that by moral instruction they should be taught, and by their civil constitutions they should be compelled, to put many restrictions upon the immoderate exercise of it, and the inordinate desire. The best method of obtaining these two great points forms the important, but at the same time the difficult, problem to the true statesman.[72]

This task is compatible with, indeed it is required by, the condition of popular government, described earlier, that statesmen must rule in accordance with the general instructions of the people by sympathy with their feelings. The reconciliation of the rule of gentlemen and of popular government is made by the establishments—the private platoons of the people in which they are taught patriotism. The establishments are tended by gentlemen whose public spirit is protected, if not inspired, by their private interests and whose public position is the result of their private independence. The establishments restrain the people and support the gentlemen by allowing public duties to emerge from settled private rights, rather than by forcing duty upon interest.

Party is important in this reconciliation, since it is both a control on the government and the standing government itself. In Parliament it helps to subdue popular passions by putting a damper on ambitious demagogues elected to the House of Commons, like Wilkes. In the standing government, the idea of party consistency prevents an alliance between a demagogue and court favor, such as Burke feared might be a practical consequence of Bolingbroke's principles. Party prevents the success of a Patriot King, or a patriot minister (both were advocated by different members of the "political school"), or even a combination of both, by giving solidity to popular favor. It permits groups of honest men of property to occupy the public stage, shuffling through successive scenes, ruling tolerably because of their connection to the people, and justly because of their independence from the people. Party particularizes the general instructions of the people without involving the people in active government.

It was Burke's intention, then, in the "Thoughts," to make party an establishment in society. He did not explain the need for establishments in the "Thoughts," however, as he did in the "Reflections" and the "Appeal"; the "Thoughts" is an ostensively popular pamphlet, openly favorable to the people, displaying their discontents as the symptom of public evil; the "Reflections" and the "Appeal" support authority. But a different emphasis does not necessarily mean inconsistency, nor have we actually found an inconsistency. Burke believed, as we shall see, that consistency in politics *requires* an unbalanced emphasis on different occasions. Moreover, it was a problem in the "Thoughts," the relation of controls and standing government, that forced us to seek the solution offered in the "Reflections" and the "Appeal."

Party as Majority Rule

Burke's view of the relation of the people to party is opposed to, and we believe designed to oppose, the view that Thomas Jefferson later advanced in America. Jefferson believed that the people could give authoritative instructions to their rulers through the Republican party program; these instructions would become authoritative when a majority of the people, reasoning on the basis of their natural rights, voted for the Republican ticket. Party, for Jefferson, was an expression of majority rule without establishments; its purpose was to revive the institutions of the Constitution with the spirit of the original contract. Party was revolutionary, to Jefferson; it attacked the "monarchical" Federalist administration in the name of the principles of 1776.[73]

In his writings on the French Revolution, Burke attacked this kind of party. The rights of man exist by nature, Burke agrees. But they give no title to rule by majority, whether at the time of the original contract or later, to inspire society with the original principles of the contract, or in the ordinary course of rule. For the principle of majority rule gives license to conspirators to begin a majority on any point, and to flatterers of the people to gather a majority. Majority rule is arbitrary rule, to Burke, because it encourages popular rule without the establishments and hence without restraints.[74] At the original contract, or at any subsequent fundamental change of contract, only the submission of each individual person makes government legitimate; a majority decision would be simple usurpation.[75] When it was necessary to inspire England with the principles of the original contract, in the Revolution of 1688, it was sufficient that a small group of men, led by the Old Whigs, act to protect the rights of all. Ordinary rule, according to Burke, is standing government not by the people through majority decision but by several institutions with a connection to the people, or by several parts of the people.

The party of majority rule has the disadvantage of active rule by the people—by involving the people in rule it incapacitates them for the control of rule. The people cannot control "their infamous flatterers." It follows that Burke is opposed to what is now called "responsible criticism." "Responsible criticism" is the speech of an "alternative government," the party in opposition. It is or can be responsible because those who speak may have a later chance to act; thus, their ambition, guided by their knowledge of the problems of rule and by their sympathy with rulers in difficulty, should restrain their tendency to criticize what cannot be improved and to flatter the people for the wisdom of impossible desires. The alternative government, as a regular institution, is an attribute of party government in the modern sense, for only a party united in its program and on its record can responsibly imagine its future exercise of power.

But clearly Burke prefers independent criticism to "responsible criticism." Because it combines control and government, "responsible criticism" is self-contradictory. "Responsible criticism" will be tainted, not restrained, by ambition, since its basis will be the aims of the ambitious, not the aims of the people. Popular government requires that the general aims of the people be sovereign and that those aims be the basis of criticism of the government, unmixed with sympathy for rulers. Sympathy is owed from rulers to people, not from people to rulers, because the necessities of rule derive ultimately from the rights of the people. There should be no profound inquiry into the necessities of rule, such as an alternative government professes, and no knowing acquiescence in the opinions of rulers, to hamper later criticism. True criticism is dependent upon the desires of the people and judges independently of the necessities of rule. Consequently, independent criticism can come only from a source independent of ambition. It is true that the people have a right to their restraints, but the fundamental implication of this assertion is that government is restrained to protecting the people's rights.

Party and Statesmanship

But when we have said this much to distinguish Burke's view from modern practice on the dual function of party as control and government, we must ask whether Burke's solution is successful. It would seem that Burke's own party, as it became consolidated through its common experience in government and opposition and grew disciplined under the influence of Burke's defense of party, drew away from the function of control in the name of the people. Burke broke with the Foxite Whigs on the question of the French Revolution, because he said that these New Whigs had lost their appreciation of British principles, which the "Reflections" and the "Appeal" had been written to recall. Burke would have avoided the "alternative government" which derives its discipline from a party program, but he did encourage the alternative government which was based on a party history. How strong, then, is the difference between a party program and party history? The Foxite Whigs did not have a program in the modern style, but by assimilating their view of the French Revolution to their experience in opposing the British war against the American Revolution, they came to an acceptance of the French Revolution. The view was variously expressed but rigidly held; it disgusted Burke and kept Whigs out of power, suspected of near-treason, until 1832. When the rights of man are the subject of current slogans, ready for appropriation, a party history may become as rigidly hostile to the establishments of society as a party program; it may actually become a revolutionary party program.

Besides, even though a party history is more compatible with statesmanship in its composition than is a party program, is it any more compatible in its operation? It is our opinion that Burke intended to make party an establishment of British society. Yet party is not mentioned as among the establishments in the "Reflections," where they are defined and listed. If it is an establishment, party must be a peculiar one. It does not seem to be a fully natural growth within the constitution. It is a highly refined contrivance that alters the teaching of the most obvious example of defense against tyranny—the Old Whig use of party—so as to render tyranny impotent and honest men effectual by anticipation of the need for conspiracy. For this complicated function, party needed a complicated defense from a far-seeing statesman—the more complicated because party must be made to seem a simple, honest recourse. Then, after 1790, his party proves to be too confining to the same statesman, so he leaves it and almost attempts to destroy it. Party needs a far-seeing statesman to set its limits, as well as to establish its respectability. In a sense Burke's public defense of party and his public demonstration of the limits of party correspond to the Old Whigs' use of party to eliminate the need for party. Yet Burke's acts—both the beginning and the limiting—required a much more subtle statesmanship than the use of party required from the Old Whigs (though the introduction of party was intended to reduce the need for statesmanship on the part of others). For it is easier to stop using party when its use has not been made respectable.[76]

Burke was not of the great families; he was a newcomer, a man of ability. His conception of party does allow for such as himself; party is by no means strictly familial and does permit the slow and well-tested rise of men of ability. But his conception does not allow for his sovereign decisions to begin and to limit party respectability. These decisions were taken by himself, as a man of ability in the highest practical sense, not in nine-tenths agreement with his party in Parliament. It is true that the honest men of his connection mostly agreed with his first decision, and that many of them agreed with his second; but they did not know, as he did, what they were agreeing to. The problem of reconciling the "Thoughts" with the "Reflections" and the "Appeal" is found in this tension between party and statesmanship, more than in the tension between popular liberty and authority. In the "Appeal" Burke expressly refrains from defining the limits of party; but in the "Thoughts," limits are not mentioned as such, though of course party is not intended in its modern form. Burke expresses only this desire to experiment, guarded by a politic modesty: "My aim is to bring this matter into more public discussion. Let the sagacity of others work upon it." Thus we have come an important distance, by an important descent, from the subtlety of the beginning of the "Thoughts," a subtlety required by the delicacy of the task of introducing a remedy, to a blunt invitation to the honest men of party to work upon this matter.

Burke's conception of party cannot account for his defense of party and the limits to party; these are acts of which a party man is incapable. Having completed our discussion of party and our analysis of Burke's "Thoughts," we are left with a tension between party and statesmanship in Burke's thought, which we must go beyond party to resolve. Since Burke's acts with respect to party are what cast doubt on party, his opinion of himself or of those men like himself should be used as the guide in this inquiry.

CHAPTER EIGHT

Presumptive Virtue

We begin our inquiry into the problem discerned in the "Thoughts" with this impressive statement from the "Reflections": "There is no qualification for government but virtue and wisdom, actual or presumptive." The reader who knows the basic political principle of the classical political philosophers, the rule of the wise, will readily perceive its resemblance to Burke's words, but wonder at the difference. There are men of actual virtue and wisdom and men of presumptive virtue and wisdom. What is the meaning of presumptive virtue? Why is actual virtue insufficient, so that it needs a presumptive companion? And if it is possible at all to presume upon virtue, why is presumptive virtue insufficient, so that it allows the claims of actual virtue? If we find the rule of gentlemen to be the rule of presumptive virtue, how is this reconciled with the claims of actual virtue? "Virtue" and "gentlemen" are not much in the speech of present-day political scientists, but Burke's understanding of these terms leads him to something like the modern conception of "leadership."

Actual Virtue

Wherever actual virtue and wisdom are found, Burke says,

they have, in whatever state, condition, profession, or trade, the passport of Heaven to human place and honour. Woe to the country which would madly and impiously reject the service of the talents and virtues, civil, military, or religious, that are given to grace and to serve it; and would condemn to obscurity everything formed to diffuse lustre and glory around a state!

For the encouragement of actual virtue, Burke accepts the principle of equality of opportunity, but with a qualification:

201

I do not hesitate to say, that the road to eminence and power, from obscure condition, ought not to be made too easy, or a thing too much of course. If rare merit be the rarest of all rare things, it ought to pass through some sort of probation. The temple of honour ought to be seated on an eminence. If it be opened through virtue, let it be remembered too, that virtue is never tried but by some difficulty and some struggle.[1]

This is a very short discussion of actual virtue; it stands as an apparent introduction to a long discussion of presumptive virtue. Actual virtue must not be madly and impiously rejected, but it must not be welcomed. It is neither mad nor impious to keep virtue on probation, and thus to cause difficulties for it. Now why should rare merit be thus employed? If Burke thought himself to be a man of rare merit, perhaps there is an answer to this question in his own life. Certainly an observer finds it puzzling that such a man as Burke would submit with deference to this extensive probation.

Burke has been blamed for his deference to his aristocratic associates in politics.[2] Men far less remarkable than he were willing to accord him some of the prominence due to his merit, yet they were met with the freezing condescension of a man apparently in need, who turns down help. He never claimed the place that he could have taken, or even that which he would have been given. But this deference was chosen, and chosen for a reason that implies a certain independence; it was not a mere confession of inferiority. One can study it in two episodes at the beginning and end of his career.

Burke had a violent quarrel with his first patron, William Gerard Hamilton, whose pension he resigned and service he left, in the opinion that he was *"perfectly* in the right."[3] Burke explains his opinion in a statement in which he refers to a letter he had written to Hamilton to state his position:

There is a turn of expression in this Letter which being more submissive and professing than is common with E. B. to any man, and as it may surprise his acquaintance will need some explanation and will serve to throw more light on the genuine intention of the writing in Question—Mr. H was in the habit of frequently expressing to E. B. his regard to him; The pleasure he received from his Company and The Sense with infinite exaggeration, of the Services he did him. E. B. was always fearful Lest H. should imagine he took advantage of his strong frequent expressions to impose difficult Terms on him. His delicacy in this respect has betrayed him into a mode of expression very unusual with him and of the consequences of which he was not at all aware.[4]

Burke denies that submissive language is habitual with him, but justifies its use in circumstances which, after 1765, were to become usual for him. There is danger to men of ability, Burke says, in the praise of men of rank, for men of rank do not mean the respect their speech implies. They praise ability in order to use it. A man of ability, if he is a man of true ability, of actual virtue, will avoid such flattering servitude. Burke submitted to Hamilton's rank so as to avoid a worse submission to his praise. Burke's courtliness was the consequence of a desire for independence.

"A Letter to a Noble Lord," written in 1796, is Burke's famous self-assertion; and we should examine its most famous passage:

> I was not, like his Grace of Bedford, swaddled, and rocked and dandled into a legislator; *"Nitor in adversum"* is the motto for a man like me. I possessed not one of the qualities, nor cultivated one of the arts, that recommend men to the favour and protection of the great. I was not made for a minion or a tool. As little did I follow the trade of winning the hearts, by imposing on the understandings, of the people. At every step of my progress in life, (for in every step was I traversed and opposed), and at every turnpike I met, I was obliged to show my passport, and again and again to prove my sole title to the honour of being useful to my country, by a proof that I was not wholly unacquainted with its laws, and the whole system of its interests both abroad and at home. Otherwise no rank, no toleration even, for me. I had no arts but manly arts. On them I have stood, and, please God, in spite of the Duke of Bedford and the Earl of Lauderdale, to the last gasp will I stand.[5]

Burke was a proud man. The measure of his pride is the reference, six years after he wrote the "Reflections," to his passport. His is a manly passport, the other was the "passport of Heaven"; but they are the same passport, because Burke met and passed the same searching examination as the man of actual virtue. One may conclude that Burke regarded himself as a man of actual virtue and, consequently, that his life, as he saw it, is further evidence for his conception of actual virtue.

Yet Burke, in this work and in his statement about Hamilton, did not seek to show his pride. He wrote "A Letter to a Noble Lord" because the Duke of Bedford had criticized the pension granted him when he retired from Parliament. The Duke claimed that Burke's ability, as shown in his opposition to the French Revolution, did not deserve reward; Burke was forced to assert himself by the Duke's refusal to accept the presumption that the crown rewards merit. The Duke could have been like the gentle, heraldic historians, who "dip their pens in nothing but the milk of human kindness," with whom "every man created a peer is first a hero ready made."[6] But instead he chose, in imitation of the philosophers of the rights of man, to deny the presumption, which, in Burke's case, was so obviously well founded. Burke sought to make the danger of attacking presumptive virtue most forcefully apparent to the Duke by comparing his own actual virtue, not to the Duke's (a comparison that he scorned), but to that of the first Duke of Bedford, whose fortune and character had caused the presumption in favor of the present Duke. Burke says that the virtue of the first Duke of Bedford, "a prompt and greedy instrument of a *levelling* tyrant,"[7] was only presumptive and therefore was improperly presumed. Burke himself had done real public service, not least as an economist and reformer, and had done this in a connection of "men of high place in the community," that is, men of presumptive virtue, who, unlike the present Duke, pursued a liberty inseparable from order, virtue, morals, and religion.[8]

But Burke asserts that actual virtue must work in the service of presumptive virtue, because one can be sure of actual virtue only if it is tested in service, not if it is permitted the full scope of its pretensions from the beginning. Indeed, the greatest pride of actual virtue is in its submission to this test. A man of actual virtue has pride in great deeds, and great deeds are difficult; but the most difficult deed, that in which Burke himself takes most pride, is not that which a great man would choose as great, but that which is imposed on him by lesser men. The test of his rare merit is administered by men of presumptive virtue, according to their standards and through the establishments, since serving men who claim the highest honors as privileges is the most dependable test of men whose end is actual virtue (in public service) and not ostentation alone.[9] It is therefore impossible to do without presumptive virtue, even when actual virtue exists, since without presumptive virtue there would be nobody to administer the test to actual virtue.

A man receives a presumption of virtue when he exchanges the "passport of Heaven" for noble rank; a searching examination of this "passport" is the condition of unquestioning acceptance of his rank. But this test must take place in the man's lifetime, before his rank is conferred; otherwise the idea of presumptive virtue will be undermined. The first Duke of Bedford, "prompt and greedy," did not have to run the course of actual virtue, and his rank was not deserved; but the present Duke should have his rank, because his example shelters the idea of presumptive virtue and brings good out of original evil. Burke apparently believes that presumptive virtue is necessary and that actual virtue depends upon presumptive virtue. His pride is real, but muted and tentative.

Actual virtue properly consists of public service, Burke has said; but it becomes presumptive virtue through families. We have seen that Burke replaced individual statesmanship by family parties of statesmen; his reason for this is involved in the present inquiry, since he defers to noble families and his hope was for a family of his own. That is, Burke's pride is family pride; but it is for a family yet to come, or in his case, not to come, since his son had died.

"Had it pleased God to continue to me the hopes of succession, I should have been, according to my mediocrity and the mediocrity of the age I live in, a sort of founder of a family. . . ."[10] He thinks himself as good as the first Duke of Bedford and, hence, by the presumption that the crown will reward his merit, as good as the present Duke. This presumption cannot be anticipated, because actual virtue must be tested; so Burke remains deferent. The man of actual virtue must forego personal pride, except as the founder of a family. Only a family member, hence only a member of the best families, a nobleman, can rightly and fully feel the pride of a good man. A man of obscure condition can be considered only tentatively good until his acts have found acceptance from honest men and from the king, who acts as the representative of honest men. If a condition of pride is membership in a family, then a condition of goodness is public acceptance. The good man, the man of actual virtue, takes pride in his goodness only when he has made it politically acceptable; so his greatest deed is to fashion his goodness for acceptance. He cannot make a constitution as a legislator in the fullest sense: if he could do so, he would surely have to suit his legislation to the temper of the people; but also he could change the temper of the people by changing the establishments. In the classical view, the legislator in the fullest sense does form the people and make the establishments. According to Burke, however, the establishments, which are the parts of the people, are not to be changed. In a free constitution, the people and the honest men who lead them are sovereign over actual virtue; they force the men of actual virtue to make their way, not over families as a legislator in the classical sense, but through families. Actual virtue is held to public service because actual virtue is contained by the establishments. One fundamental purpose of the establishments is to make difficulties for the best men.

Men of actual virtue have two roles in relation to the family, founder and defender. It might seem that the family founder's task is greater, since it is he who must pass the tests set by the men of presumptive virtue. The tests are difficult for the man of actual virtue not because they put demands on his capacities, but because they require restraints to his pretensions. But the family defender may have a yet more difficult task as successor to the founder. He may have to defend the presumption that he enjoys by interpreting, for present times, the actual virtue of the family founder. Such an interpretation must not be a simple recounting of heroic deeds in the past, but that recounting qualified by a perception of the conditions for their acceptance in their day and of the force of their example in the present. Burke's celebration of the Old Whigs had this problematic character; it was part praise, part adaptation.

In "A Letter to a Noble Lord," Burke celebrated himself in the same way, causing his own pretensions, though original and based on actual virtue, to stalk behind the honest men who regard liberty and order as inseparable. In the passage succeeding his expressed desire to be the founder of a family, Burke says that he would have left a son not inferior to the present Duke, or to any other in his line. As his successor, his son would not "resort to any stagnant wasting reservoir of merit in me." One deed his son would have done is to defend Burke; hence Burke says: "I owe to the dearest relation (which ever must subsist in memory) that act of piety, which he would have performed to me; I owe it to him to show that he was not descended, as the Duke of Bedford would have it, from an unworthy parent." Thus Burke defends himself; he is both family founder and defender. The best family defender is a man of actual virtue, then, not a man who tries to live on a "fund of inexhaustible merit." One might suppose that this is precisely what presumptive virtue means—that a man is presumed to have actual virtue. But it is more virtuous to have merits which are original and personal than to have merits which for some reason require a presumption. Hence there seems to be, in Burke's view, a distinction in *virtue* between actual and presumptive virtue; actual virtue is greater virtue than presumptive virtue.

But men of presumptive virtue think that they *are* good, not just that are presumed good; they are not eager to learn that they may be more privileged than deserving. They are easily seduced by the slogan "men of ability," for they are taught that it does not exclude them. It is therefore a more subtle and more difficult task to be a family defender than a founder, because it is easier to pass tests set by men of presumptive virtue than to defend the idea of presumptive virtue. Not every presumption can be defended: the "actual virtue" of the first Duke of Bedford should be shorn of its presumption, since to be the instrument of a leveling tyrant is a poor example for present times, when the menace is a leveling tyranny.

We must mark the importance of family for Burke by a comment upon his grief at his son's death in 1794. The depth of his grief can be seen in a letter to Lord Fitzwilliam, in reply to condolences:

I am told by some wise and good friends—that I ought to endeavour the prolongation of my being here, to suffer firmly whatever providence may have yet to impose for my ultimate good. Otherwise I had and have a serious Doubt, whether it is of good example to the world that I should conquer the just feelings that God and nature have implanted in men, and which indulged, would soon place me in the grave of my dearest Son and impanelled friend.

He contemplated suicide, or something akin to it, for public example, until persuaded, though imperfectly, by others' arguments that he should submit to providence.

Burke's desolation at this event can be explained, we believe, only by his decision to perpetuate himself through his family by ennoblement (which was apparently under consideration before his son's death), rather than more directly, through his personal fame.[11] Fame is the reputation of actual virtue among honest men; and of fame, Burke throughout his life sought only so much as would serve to establish a family. With abilities no meaner than those of William Pitt, George Grenville, Charles Jenkinson, and Lord Mansfield, and from a condition hardly more obscure, he never reached for the eminence to which they aspired. It is not merely that Burke's "passport" was frequently examined; he always held it out to be viewed. Regarding party, Burke spent the years from 1766 to 1782 in opposition, constantly urging the relaxed men of property whom he served to act in accordance with his conception of party, when he could have improved his career, established his fame, and tested his virtue with power—all with perfect prepartisan propriety—by accepting a post in the government. Therefore, those who accuse him of a deference contrary to nature are partly right, since Burke restrained the actual virtue given to his nature; but they should realize that he chose deference and should examine his reasons.[12] He preferred the mediation of fame through property to the direct influence of personal fame upon the people. The people should not receive an idea of actual virtue by the direct example of a hero, Burke felt, but by the steady presence of presumptive virtue in the great families. Burke's intense desire for family fame shows his belief that men of actual virtue should perpetuate their heroism in this fashion.

In the discussion of actual virtue it is evident that Burke gives anything but unqualified support to honest men who have only presumptive virtue. He recognizes a virtue that is greater than theirs, and he seems, in "A Letter to a Noble Lord" and elsewhere, to locate that virtue in himself, for one. But Burke's pride, or actual virtue in general, is somehow defective, since it must perpetuate itself through presumptive virtue. Its leading defect seems to be ambition against property; the men of active virtue in the "Reflections" seem to be the men of ability, or "the political school," criticized in the "Thoughts." But falsely ambitious ability cannot be true ability; true ability or true active virtue would have the self-restraint of Burke in serving presumptive virtue. The defect of actual virtue must apply to the presumptuousness of men without property, as we have seen in Burke's most basic criticism of Bolingbroke. Ability is a "vigorous and active *principle*";[13] that is, the encouragement of ability, or of actual virtue, becomes a principle used by schemers to achieve a position which they have neither the property to be presumed fit for nor the virtue to reach patiently. It is not actual virtue itself that is dangerous, but the misapplied principle of actual virtue. Yet this misapplication cannot be avoided; and actual virtue must suffer in curtailment and probation for the potential ill consequences of its corruption. But when Burke's claims for presumptive virtue are studied, it can be seen that actual virtue is not only easily misapplied as a principle but essentially incapable of rule.

Presumptive Virtue

What does "presumptive virtue" mean? It could mean actual virtue that *probably* exists. But another possibility already stated is that presumptive virtue means a lesser virtue than actual virtue, but more certain and dependable. After settling this problem, we can inquire into the relation of natural law to presumptive virtue, for Burke's "presumptive virtue" is a novelty which seems at first sight contrary to reliance on natural law.

We may return now to the passage in the "Reflections" from which the discussion of actual virtue began, to find the following introduction to presumptive virtue:

> Nothing is a due and adequate representation of a state, that does not represent its ability, as well as its property. But as ability is a vigorous and active principle, and as property is sluggish, inert and timid, it never can be safe from the invasions of ability, unless it be, out of all proportion, predominant in the constitution.

Burke immediately identifies presumptive virtue with property and states that property must be represented in the constitution "out of all proportion" to its natural energy, to be safe from the invasions of ability. His argument is that property fixes a man's place, that a man's place determines his duty, and that a man's place assures the performance of his duty.

In regard to the first point, there is a problem in the relation of ability and property. When men of ability achieve property, as they will in a free constitution under the system of political economy, they will also achieve political power; this is "the natural operation of property" already noticed.[14] Property, however, depends on its recognition by others; it is a right, not a product. When men of ability get property, they receive something they did not and cannot make, the permanence of property. To protect its permanence, property must be hereditary and settled, and it must be represented in the constitution "out of all proportion." It is therefore not contradictory for Burke to say that property will be powerful in its natural operation and that property must be made powerful beyond its natural energy. Burke combines the right of acquisition and the right of inheritance: men "have a right to the fruits of their industry; and to the means of making their industry fruitful. They have a right to the acquisitions of their parents. . . ." It follows that a man's place is not fixed by hereditary privilege; the criterion for rank is the slippery principle of property.[15] But society should ensure that rank is not an *immediate* consequence of wealth, because hasty men from obscure condition who become wealthy rapidly do not understand the conditions of their rise. They forget that the protection of their property requires not only the original contract but also the establishments which developed through prescription. Thus ability gets its due from society slowly for its own protection—which means that rank, or place, is a consequence of hereditary wealth.

Secondly, "the place of every man determines his duty. If you ask *Quem te Deus esse jussit?* You will be answered when you resolve this other question, *Humana qua parte locatus in re?*"[16] Persius would not have recommended reading of the Bible for the answer to the former question; but he did include another question, *"Quis modus argento?"* which is quoted by Burke in a footnote, but not asked on his own account. For Burke, *argentum* determines place; God has not commanded a limit to the desire for it, or determined how much is appropriate to one's place. The only limits to acquiring property are implied by the regulations for keeping it.

The third point can be seen in a long passage from the "Appeal," whose importance for the present discussion of presumptive virtue and for the previous discussion of the rule of gentlemen requires quotation in full:

A true natural aristocracy is not a separate interest in the state, or separable from it. It is an essential integrant part of any large body rightly constituted. It is formed out of a class of legitimate presumptions, which, taken as generalities, must be admitted for actual truths. To be bred in a place of estimation; to see nothing low and sordid from one's infancy; to be taught to respect one's self; to be habituated to the censorial inspection of the public eye; to look early to public opinion; to stand upon such elevated ground as to be enabled to take a large view of the wide-spread and infinitely diversified combinations of men and affairs in a large society; to have leisure to read, to reflect, to converse; to be enabled to draw the court and attention of the wise and learned wherever they are to be found—to be habituated in armies to command and to obey; to be taught to despise danger in the pursuit of honour and duty; to be formed to the greatest degree of vigilance, foresight, and circumspection, in a state of things in which no fault is committed with impunity, and the slightest mistakes draw on the most ruinous consequences—to be led to a guarded and regulated conduct, from a sense that you are considered as an instructor of your fellow-citizens in their highest concerns, and that you act as a reconciler between God and man—to be employed as an administrator of law and justice, and to be thereby amongst the first benefactors to mankind—to be a professor of high science, or of liberal and ingenuous art—to be amongst rich traders, who from their success are presumed to have sharp and vigorous understandings, and to possess the virtues of diligence, order, constancy, and regularity, and to have cultivated an habitual regard to commutative justice—these are the circumstances of men, that form what I should call a *natural* aristocracy, without which there is no nation.[17]

This is, to repeat, "a class of legitimate presumptions, which, taken as generalities, must be admitted for actual truths." They lead to the surprising conclusion that the opportunity for virtue sufficiently guarantees the practice of it. But actual virtue is higher than presumptive virtue. Therefore in Burke's intention, presumptive virtue is lesser, but more certain, than actual virtue. It is not probable actual virtue but lesser virtue which is presumed from one's place.

Burke proclaims the body which requires these presumptions to be nothing less than "a true natural aristocracy." When the classical political philosophers applied the principle of the rule of the wise to ordinary circumstances, they concluded that the rule of gentlemen who had been favored by such advantages as Burke recounts would be usually the best, because probably the wisest. They would have agreed with Burke that gentlemen have less virtue than men of actual virtue but are more in supply. But for the classical philosophers, the aristocracy or the natural aristocracy retained its literal meaning, the rule of the best, or the wise. They never lost sight of the highest virtue when they sought more easily secured virtue; hence they never supposed that virtue was secured when lesser virtue was certain. In classical political philosophy, the gentlemen had to show their "passports," since the presumption was that only actual virtue gave title to rule. Burke retains a distinction rather like that between heroic and ordinary virtue, found in Aristotle's *Ethics*. But he hands a presumption to ordinary virtue; so, as he tries to fix the distinction, at the same time he reduces the distance between ordinary virtue and vice, between aristocracy and oligarchy.

In considering the British constitution, we saw that, for Burke, the rule of gentlemen solves the problem of popular government without transcending the desires of ordinary people. It can now be added that the rule of gentlemen is the rule of presumptive virtue. Presumptive virtue means "to be bred in a place of estimation"; it is a simple attribute of place. A place of estimation is a part of the people; it is defined by what the people esteem; to be in such a place gives rise to legitimate presumptions which must be admitted for actual truths. An elevated place is "a sort of cure for selfishness and a narrow mind."[18]

"Statesmen are placed on an eminence, that they may have a larger horizon than we can possibly command. They have the whole before them, which we can contemplate only in the parts, and often without the necessary relations. Ministers are not only our natural rulers, but our natural guides."[19] Indeed, they are guides, or leaders, rather than rulers; they lead, direct, and moderate the people.[20] On the basis of presumptive virtue, Burke substitutes the relation of leaders and led, so common in the language of modern students of party, for the Aristotelian relation of rulers and ruled. Burke's statesmen are leaders; however eminent, they are part of the people. They mingle with the other parts of the people the better to represent them, not to rule them. They have the whole before them, but they cannot rule it, because society as a whole is "infinitely diversified." They have a public duty and an education in public concerns, but they are nevertheless essentially a *private* aristocracy. Their virtue is presumed for them from their *private* place; their property is not a consequence of their public duty, but their duty a consequence of their property. Where they are is the cause of what they do, not the reverse. The security for the award of presumed virtue to them is their connection to the people, of whose liberty they are beneficiaries. Although only men of this group can be presumed trustworthy ministers, they must be watched by the "controls for the people" in order to constrain their rule to leadership.

The necessary condition of presumptive virtue in the leaders of the people is good humor in the people: ordinary statesmen can be presumed to be good enough if the people can be presumed to be quiet enough. Leadership is not too difficult if the people are tractable; and the people will be tractable in a free society if they are not forced to be better than they desire, if they are not ruled. In the "Thoughts," Burke presents the statesman's presumption, by which the people are presumed sound enough to permit effective action by statesmen. In his later writings, he presents the idea of presumptive virtue, by which men of property are presumed to be effective statesmen. These two presumptions are so far from contradictory that they are necessary to each other: the leaders must be capable of leading and the led capable of being led. But in effect, the leaders are led by popular desires and so the led are leaders; there is no rule in the relation.

Presumptive Virtue and Natural Law

What, then, is the lesser virtue which we have shown to be presumptive virtue? It is clear that Burke accepts some kind of natural law, and one must see whether presumptive virtue is defined by natural law. The problem is: Why is presumptive virtue necessary if natural law exists? Why is it necessary to presume a lesser, but more certain, virtue in high places if virtue is supported by the law of nature? In the natural law according to Aquinas, virtue is supported chiefly by the natural inclinations in the human conscience to live sociably and to know God; in Hobbes and Locke, justice is supported by the natural desire for self-preservation. In either case, nature is thought to have a *law*, because nature has some means of enforcement to support the virtues. Then does not presumptive virtue, by which Burke discounts the support in nature for actual virtue, seem to be a substitute for either kind of law of nature?

The phrase "law of nature" does not frequently occur in Burke's works; in fact, it occurs much less often than do words of praise for prudence and cautions for circumstances. But this means only that Burke's interpreter must find a conciliation of natural law and prudence which includes an understanding of presumptive virtue. Burke has made sufficient solemn pronouncements upon the law of nature to require an interpreter to take them seriously; he is not simply a precursor of latter-day utilitarianism, which is offered without a conception of natural law. It becomes a question, then, whether his conception of natural law is modern, as in Hobbes and Locke, or traditional, as in Aquinas. The reader will have already noted much evidence for the former description. Burke concludes, from an examination of the state of nature, that man has natural rights, including the natural right to the acquisition of property, which has been modified through prescription. He says that the first fundamental right of uncovenanted man is to judge for himself and to assert his own cause, and that the right of self-defense is the first law of nature—assertions which approximate the Hobbesian view that self-preservation in the state of nature requires each man to be his own judge of the means of preservation.[21] Knowing this much, we shall try to prove that Burke's conception of natural law is modern by showing that it is composed of natural feeling and prudence. We shall consider how Burke's religious views suit

his conception of natural law and compare those views with Bolingbroke's deism in order to explain the relation of parties and religion.

If natural law exists, there must be a reason why presumptive virtue is
necessary. Actual virtue must be incapable in some way; however superior
to presumptive virtue, it must have little or no support in nature. Burke
shows his belief in the incapacity of actual virtue by his use of the term
"duty." He never contrasts duty and virtue, and when he speaks of duty,
he seems to leave no place for unforced virtue.

"Duties are not voluntary. Duty and will are even contradictory terms.
. . . Look through the whole of life and the whole system of duties. Much
the strongest moral obligations are such as were never the results of our
option."[22] It is true that he sometimes says "virtue" when he means the
virtue available to ordinary men, as in the phrase "presumptive virtue";
but at such points he means duty.[23] An example of a particular virtue
understood as a duty is the following: "Our physical well-being, our moral
worth, our social happiness, our political tranquillity, all depend on that
control of all our appetites and passions, which the ancients designed
by the cardinal virtue of *Temperance*." But "that control," in the context,
turns out to be what Aristotle called "continence."[24]

According to Burke, moreover, duty in general is continence: ". . . men
love to hear of their power, but have an extreme disrelish to be told of
their duty. This is of course; because every duty is a limitation of some
power."[25] Men in general sense their powers, and far from desiring to
do good with them, must be forced to relinquish the exercise of them,
in some degree. Duty has to do with this limitation, not with the education of the passions to desire the right things. It is a lower order of virtue
(as continence is below temperance), because the man who resists temptation has to feel the temptation. This defect he shares with the man
who does *not* resist temptation.[26] The man of actual virtue, one may assume, has an unforced desire to use his powers rightly; but the man of
actual virtue is not man in general. Considered politically, men must be
considered generally. Only an enforced virtue, or duty, can be generally
presumed; so presumptive virtue must be duty.

Burke's distinction between actual and presumptive virtue seems Aristotelian—a rejection of the rule of philosopher-kings in favor of the rule
of gentlemen. Actual virtue is too rare in nature to be relied upon for
government; men must arrange for a lesser virtue when they gather in
political communities. But Burke denies that the role of legislator (in
the full sense) is possible for the man of actual virtue. According to
Burke, the establishments of society cannot be formed by the wisdom of

a legislator; rather, they must be respected and cultivated by the prudence of statesmen. For Aristotle also, actual virtue is not politically viable, and it must submit to the decent but inexact rule of gentlemen. But occasionally it is possible that an extraordinary man can form a society by giving it a rationally planned constitution. For Aristotle, the possibility of a legislator is crucial for the possibilities of man: it is the link between the best life of man—the life of reason—and the usual, necessary life of man—the life of politics. For Burke, this link does not exist.

According to theories of natural law, the connection between the life of reason and the life of politics is direct: reason (or practical reason) gives to the statesman his guiding principles. According to these theories, whether traditional or modern, nature legislates for man by providing natural penalties for the failure to follow the way of life which nature recommends. For their transgressions, men will suffer the agonies of conscience, in the theory of Aquinas; or the agonies of the fear of violent death, in Hobbes's theory. The legislator does not form the constitution of a society in these theories; he only adapts the natural law to local circumstances, adds to the natural penalties for wrongdoing, and fills in the gaps between the laws of nature. Natural law does not need to be legislated in the classical sense; natural law means that the law for man is available in the nature of man. But if the law for man is available, it must be fairly obvious: there could be no law suitable for communities of men which was not on the level of the capacities of most men. Thus theories of natural law, traditional or modern, tend to abolish, or at least to reduce, the political importance of the Aristotelian distinction between moral (or political) virtue and intellectual (or philosophic) virtue.[27] They suppose that the laws by which men should live are visible to gentlemen, because there are sufficiently obvious natural penalties for failure to obey them. These natural penalties make the legislator in the full sense unnecessary and thus substitute for the legislator of classical political philosophy.

Now what is singular in Burke's political philosophy is the combination of the distinction between actual and presumptive virtue with natural law. Burke's actual and presumptive virtue correspond to Aristotle's intellectual and moral virtue. They are not the same, because, as we shall see, actual virtue for Burke could never be intellectual virtue in Aristotle's sense; but they correspond. This distinction implies great freedom for the statesman, who must make up for the rarity and inapplicability of actual virtue with many, various adaptations to imperfect men and conditions. Yet Burke, as we said, refuses to allow the statesman to form the establishments of society; that is, he refuses to allow him to be a legislator. To compensate for this limitation of the statesman's freedom, Burke introduces the natural penalties of the natural law. Not only does nature negatively suggest the need for presumptive virtue by means of the rarity of actual virtue; nature positively supports presumptive virtue in the natural law. But first, what could be the natural penalties which provide the sanctions for Burke's natural law? "Presumptive virtue," as an attribute of settled property, seems to be supported by the necessity of property: if men of property have no respect, then property has no respect, and society relapses into anarchy. But property is something private, and the law is something public. What makes the virtue presumed of property authoritative for the public law of society? And, secondly, how could these natural penalties become visible to gentlemen-statesmen? If such men cannot successfully plan the constitution of society, how can they read the law of nature? To provide for these difficulties, Burke must deny the natural penalties of Aquinas' natural law and modify those of Hobbes's natural law.

We have seen that the establishments are the restraints of men, "by a power out of themselves," that form them into a people. Such restraints "are to be reckoned among their rights."[28] The establishments become effective restraints when the people know their duty to them. Unless subdued by the notion of duty, the people will listen to extravagant flatterers, undismayed by the wholesome menaces of their leaders. But how do they learn duty? Duty is an inner restraint; but as a restraint, it is still in a sense "a power out of themselves." It could be an inner restraint placed in the soul by an outside power, such as conscience in the traditional conception of natural law. But in an extended discussion of duty in the "Appeal," Burke fails to mention conscience, nor does he discuss it elsewhere in his writings, though he occasionally uses the word. In the "Thoughts" he says that a politician plausibly argues that he follows his conscience only when he has "great visible emoluments":

> It is . . . very convenient to politicians, not to put the judgment of their conduct on overt acts, cognizable in any ordinary court, but upon such matter as can be triable only in that secret tribunal, where they are sure of being heard with favour, or where at worst the sentence will be only private whipping.[29]

This remark has the aroma of Hobbesian cynicism and seems to contain the substance of Hobbes's view of conscience. At least it rules out the possibility that conscience operates according to traditional natural law.[30] In that conception, conscience is allied to a natural human inclination toward good, and thus provides a sanction for the natural law. But in

Burke's view, the use of conscience in politics is the right only of those who have acquired property in the natural way.

To Burke, duty is not the command of conscience; it is an inner restraint. Unlike the traditional conception of conscience, it is a restraint given to the self by the self:

> Neither the few nor the many have a right to act merely by their will, in any matter connected with duty, trust, engagement, or obligation. The constitution of a country being once settled upon some compact, tacit or expressed, there is no power existing of force to alter it, without the breach of the covenant, or the consent of all the parties. Such is the nature of a contract. And the votes of a majority of the people, whatever their infamous flatterers may teach in order to corrupt their minds, cannot alter the moral any more than they can alter the physical essence of things.[31]

That is to say, the moral essence of things is contractual. In this passage Burke argues against Dr. Price's conception of the natural rights of man; but he does so on the ground that Dr. Price misconstrues the nature of a contract, not on the ground that duty is not contractual. The original contract is more solemn and serious than Dr. Price believes; it cannot safely be repeated for every generation, either in fact through a revolution, or in imagination by frequently mooting cases on the supposed ruin of the constitution. Now if the moral essence of things is contractual, the *source* of duty, rather than its *content,* must be the most important question. For a contract is a way of taking on an obligation, whatever that obligation may be. Since "consent is the origin of the whole," the origin of duty must be in the original contract. But for Burke the origin of duty in the original contract is not the source of duty today. From his criticism of Dr. Price, one concludes that duty must have a source for its current operation other than the frequent recall, by actual revolution or by imagination, to man in the state of nature.

That source is natural feeling, as it develops in manners. The distinction between natural feeling and the passions has been noted previously; natural feeling is love of one's own, as defined by the establishments, and is therefore limited in extent, whereas passion is under the influence of imagination, and therefore infinitely excitable. Natural feeling is defined by the establishments; it is developed by the manners of civilized life, the pleasing illusions, the decent drapery, the "chastity of honour." Manners engage the public affections of love, veneration, admiration, or attachment; they are the means whereby individual men look beyond their own speculations and interests: "There ought to be a system of manners in every country, which a well-formed mind would be disposed to relish. To make us love our country, our country ought to be lovely."

Manners cause the natural feeling of honor, as Burke explains in the "age of chivalry" passage in the "Reflections":

> It was this opinion which mitigated kings into companions, and raised private men to be fellows with kings. Without force or opposition, it subdued the fierceness of pride and power; it obliged sovereigns to submit to the soft collar of social esteem, compelled stern authority to submit to elegance, and gave a dominating vanquisher of laws to be subdued by manners.[32]

The reader will recall the earlier discussion, in which we found that Burke surprisingly agreed with much of Dr. Brown's criticism of the traditional conception of honor. That early impression may now be reinforced. Burke does not regard honor as the external reward of virtue, or as pride, the internal consciousness of virtue; he regards it as a manner or an opinion, whose effect is to *subdue* pride. Honor is not the inequality of treatment or estimation due to a superior man, but the *mitigation* of the fierce pride which is falsely advanced by a "dominating vanquisher of laws," by a tyrant.

Honor, in Burke's conception, facilitates the association of noble men, whereas in Aristotle's view, honor is the cause of isolation, as it is the consciousness of true superiority; and honorable men can be understood to associate only on the basis of another principle, friendship, or proportionate friendship. Burke's conception of honor is less demanding than Aristotle's, since it asks only for a proper modesty from kings and for a certain inflation of the pretensions of private men. It is also less problematic, since it suits the needs of men in civil society, while it ignores, in accordance with Burke's disbelief in the monarchical principle, the claims of the truly superior man.

Honor suits the needs of civil society by replacing the motive of fear as a source of obligation. Having surrendered their natural liberty in the original contract, men desire continuing protection from government without experiencing fear. Fear causes "the precautions of tyranny" on the part of both kings and subjects; both sides act from suspicion with "preventive murder and preventive confiscation."[33] This is the reason why the original contract is insufficient, in Burke's view; he thought, contrary to Hobbes, that men could not rely solely or securely upon fear, to escape "the state of unconnected nature." A reliance upon fear leads to civil war and reduces men to the state of nature; the "precautions of tyranny" must be avoided, at the cost of some of the advantages of monarchy. By his defense of party, Burke meant to transform those precautions into open and harmless transactions which would produce public trust and be based, as we now see, upon natural feeling or honor.

Natural feeling, then, cannot be found entire and effective in the submission to the original contract; it develops, through manners, into those powerful instincts which make "duty as dear and grateful to us, as it is awful and coercive."[34] But that aspect of duty which is "awful and coercive" remains; indeed one should say that coercion on the occasion of the original contract makes possible the milder aspects of duty. The subduing of greatness—or more precisely, of presumed greatness—is the condition for the awakening of the milder affections of ordinary, modest men. One of Burke's references to this subduing has been noted; another is in his description of the effect of the fate of Louis XVI upon the people. "We learn great lessons," he says; "our weak, unthinking pride is humbled" when we see, in such an example, "the tremendous uncertainty of human greatness."[35] Burke seems even to identify the subduing or humbling (rather than the thwarting) of greatness as tragedy. Tragedy, whether real or imitated, is a kind of re-enactment of the original contract, when pride or vanity was first conquered, when man gave up the right "to assert his own cause"[36] so that natural feeling could develop. The result of the realization that human greatness is uncertain is a natural feeling of awe; it makes men content with the little that they have and eager to conserve that much. Love of finite things begins with the demonstration that love of greatness brings disaster. Tragedy, in Burkes' theory, teaches the lesson that is taught by the natural right of self-preservation, in Hobbes's theory—the lesson that human vanity must be conquered to make society possible. Tragedy does not quite substitute for the original contract, but its effect on the people substitutes for the re-enactment or frequent reconsideration of the contract. For Burke, natural feeling originates with the coercion of the contract and retains in one respect the awe of this coercion through real or imitated tragedy, which is like Hobbes's stress on the fear of violent death, but is not the same.

In its milder aspect, natural feeling is also, in a sense, the result of a contract. In a passage quoted previously, where Burke contrasts imagination and feeling, he says: "Remove a grievance, and, when men act from feeling, you go a great way towards quieting a commotion."[37] That is, the people's grievances must be met; their natural feeling is satiable when it is regularly satisfied. Natural feeling, and the sense of duty it forms, require the regular satisfaction of popular desires. Otherwise the people will seek out demagogues, as they have done in the past, long before the Enlightenment.[38] The government must not try to remove ineradicable grievances, like poverty, for the people will come to expect, and afterward will condemn, what is vainly attempted or promised. Indeed, government must avoid the "officious universal interference" of the French *ancien régime*, which, though not the cause of its fall, gave means for its destruction by gathering the odium of all reasons for failure. Yet the need for caution in attempting to satisfy popular grievances emphasizes the need for satisfying those grievances which can be defined and limited; love and veneration from the people must be requited with public peace, public safety, public order, and public prosperity.[39]

Natural feeling is proportionate to place. Place is fixed, so far as it can be, by property. In order to see that natural feeling, and hence duty, are also contractual, it will now be shown that place is a consequence of contract. Civil society, Burke says, might be at first a voluntary act, but the duty of obedience attaches to anyone born into a place in society thereafter.

> This is warranted by the general practice, arising out of the general sense of mankind. Men without their choice derive benefits from that association; without their choice they are subjected to duties in consequence of these benefits; and without their choice they enter into a virtual obligation as binding as any that is actual.[40]

Again Burke does not deny that duty is contractual, but only specifies, differently from Dr. Price, how contracts may be entered into. The exchange of one's duties for one's benefits remains; and without the benefits, men could legitimately withdraw their obedience, under the leadership of their "natural aristocracy." Burke goes so far as to call the duty of obedience for those who receive benefits a "virtual obligation." Men are put in their places by God:

> Taking it for granted that I do not write to the disciples of the Parisian philosophy, I may assume, that the awful Author of our being is the Author of our place in the order of existence; and that having disposed and marshalled us by a divine tactic, not according to our will, but according to his, he has, in and by that disposition, virtually subjected us to act the part which belongs to the place assigned to us. We have obligations to mankind at large, which are not in consequence of any special voluntary pact. They arise from the relation of man to man, and the relation of man to God, which relations are not matters of choice.

However, men are not bound by duty to stay in their places because they must obey God's mysterious will; on the contrary, "But out of physical causes, unknown to us, perhaps unknowable, arise moral duties, which, as we are able perfectly to comprehend, we are bound indispensably to perform."[41] This expression might be biblical or might refer to the traditional notion of conscience, but Burke shows that he has a more modern meaning. Every man is able to comprehend his duties; hence, comprehension may be reduced to consent:

> Children are not consenting to their relation, but their relation, without their actual consent, binds them to its duties; or rather it implies their consent, because the presumed consent of every rational creature is in unison with the predisposed order of things. Men come in that manner into a community with the social state of their parents, endowed with all the benefits, loaded with all the duties, of their situation.[42]

Again, benefits are balanced with duties. Because the predisposed order is such as to win consent from every man, whether or not he actually does reflect and consent, he is bound to the duties of his place. But his place, defined by property, is changeable: ". . . the laws of commerce . . . are the laws of nature, and consequently the laws of God."[43] Hence God predisposes an order which is fixedly commercial and so as changeable as commerce, and able to secure men's consent. If this were not so, then Burke's arguments for duty would dissolve. Of course, Burke is at pains to emphasize that men are not free to accept what duties they will, at pleasure. But in Hobbes's theory also, men are not free to engage in the social contract for any purpose; they should bind themselves only when they are dominated by the fear of violent death, a domination that Hobbes supposes to be the result of freeing their passions from mistaken opinions. One must conclude that, for Burke, place is contractual and ultimately dependent upon the performance of God. Burke's theory has an external resemblance to the Thomist moral order; but the idea of divine order has been assimilated to the idea of contract, rather than the reverse.[44]

Burke opposes the natural duties of man to the natural rights of man. The duties of man are natural, because their source is natural feeling. Natural feeling yields a "natural sense of right and wrong,"[45] or conscience, in Burke's usage. But what is naturally sensed to be right is not duty primarily, but those duties which secure certain benefits. The natural duties of man, because they are contractual, ultimately depend upon the natural rights of man: if duty depends upon benefits to oneself, men must have a prior and natural right to those benefits. Burke's language says nothing less: men's restraints are to be reckoned among their rights. If we take his word at face value, it means that he intended, while opposing duty to rights, to make duty depend upon rights. Duty is a restraint given to the self, by the self, and for the sake of the self. Its effect is to transform short-run self-interest into long-run self-interest, as in the modern conception of natural law. Men must understand "the nature of a contract"—that it is not continually renegotiable on the basis of short-run interest—and they must include, in their calculation of advantages, all the benefits of society which Dr. Price and the French revolutionists heedlessly take for granted.

To say that Burke has assimilated the idea of divine order to the idea of contract recalls Bolingbroke's deism. For Bolingbroke, the general providence of God operates according to the "first principles" of the original contract. But Burke opposes both Bolingbroke and Dr. Price in regard to "the nature of a contract." The opinion of Dr. Price that the original contract is the source of the rights of man is, in general, the same as the opinion of Bolingbroke that the ruling principles of society are the first principles. Both say that a contract is determined by its origin, although Bolingbroke allows that the first principles of the original contract can be seen best in the operation of society. Both rest their case on "first principles." But Burke opposes the very notion of "first principles" with the theory of prescription, which, contrary to Bolingbroke and Dr. Price, truly describes "the nature of a contract." One can understand Burke's life-long consistency much better by recognizing that both his early "popular" writings and his later antirevolutionary writings oppose the interjection of first principles into politics.

"Prescription" is a term taken from the Roman private law on property, which describes a right based on usage.[46] In Roman law, prescription did not give a positive title to property but was a way of repelling the claims of others to property long used by oneself (acquisitive prescription) or of denying the claims of others to property long unused by those persons (extinctive prescription). For Burke, prescription has a general meaning which grows out of this special meaning in Roman law. It means taking things as they are, with the understanding that the benefits and duties are in rough balance. With this understanding, current usage is the argument against inquiries into origins or original titles; it is a way of repelling claims based on "first principles." Prescription is different from respect for history. It is the opposite of history, when the study of history has the purpose Bolingbroke ascribed to it. Prescription denies the relevance of history as an inquiry into the origins or operation of first principles; it is compatible only with histories like Hume's *History of England,* whose aim is to parade the follies of such inquiries.[47] "The nature of a contract," then, is not first principles, but prescription; and the consent to contract is not the grasping of self-evident first principles but "unison with the predisposed order of things." The order of things is *predisposed;* and Burke's motto is, "No inquiries."

If the moral essence of things is contractual, the nature of a contract must be understood as prescription. The *original* contract gives rise to expectations by its subsequent use and has its force in those expectations, not in its original terms or its first principles. The expectations arise from the natural feeling of men living in the establishments of society; they are the manners and adornments of civilization. The first principles or original terms of the contract refer only to the "naked, shivering nature" of men and recall the fears that first drove men into society. But fear, as we have seen, is not in Burke's view a stable basis for society, however powerful it is as an original motive, for fear gives rise to the "precautions of tyranny." This is why Burke believes that an inquiry into the reason of the first principles serves only to upset the expectations based on their use. He has retained the Aristotelian distinction between the motive for entering and the motive for staying in society. But whereas Aristotle argues that men enter the polis for the sake of life and remain for the sake of the good life, Burke says that men remain in society for the sake of civilized liberty. And whereas the good life, according to Aristotle, is the discovery of reason and, in politics, is the product of a legislator, civilized liberty, according to Burke, has its basis in natural feeling protected by prescriptive right.

Burke has generalized the old right of prescription. But to do this, he has transformed a private right into public law, into the very ground of public law.[48] The ground of public law is the nature of a certain private contract—title by prescription. This title is also the basis of the rule of gentlemen, when virtue is presumed of the holders of settled property; that is, prescription is the basis of presumptive virtue. We can see then why Burke advances both a theory of natural law, which implies natural support for actual virtue, and a theory of presumptive virtue, which implies the lack of such support. Actual virtue is incapable of rule and lacks natural support; for the "first principles" to which men of actual virtue have access by the range of their vision and by the practice of their talents cannot make society secure. Prescription is what makes a society secure, and prescription, Burke says, is a "great fundamental part of natural law."[49] Prescription states neither the natural *end* of society ("the good life" in Aristotle) nor the natural *origin* of society (the "first principles" in Bolingbroke). It states the natural *manner of growth* of society. Nature supports presumptive virtue through prescription; for the rule of gentlemen is secured by the natural way in which they have acquired power. This natural way—"swaddled, and rocked, and dandled into a legislator"—is not the highest way, but it is the safest way.

If prescription is the natural support for presumptive virtue, the problem of presumptive virtue remains that of the transformation of private right into public law. Prescription is the natural growth of natural feeling in the establishments to develop a "natural sense of right and wrong." This "natural sense" differs in two respects from the natural *habitus*, or inclination, which makes natural law effective according to Aquinas: it is feeling to no particular end, rather than inclination to a rational end; and it is private rather than directed to the common good. For Burke, the establishments are natural but private, while the law is public but artificial. Then "natural law," which must mean that the realm of the public is natural to man, is possible only if the public emerges from the private, as by prescription. The private inclinations of men are naturally stronger than their public inclinations, Burke believes; but the private inclinations can be made to support the public inclinations. "So to be patriots, as not to forget we are gentlemen"; such are those who succeed in "grafting public principles on private honor."[50] But a gentleman is a family (or a party) gentleman, in Burke's view; and is it impossible or unlikely for patriotism to conflict with family (or party) loyalty? If patriotism is to be effective, must it not sometimes be imposed upon lesser loyalties, when it will not emerge from them? And how can patriotism be imposed upon lesser loyalties except by contradicting natural feelings with reason? We must next consider the role of prudence in presumptive virtue.

CHAPTER NINE

Statesmanship and Prescription

Presumptive virtue has been considered from the standpoint of its source in natural feeling. But what of the honest gentlemen who lead the people? What is the place of their reason or prudence? According to Burke, reason is involved in prejudice, and the prudent statesman has only to direct the prejudice of the people. Burke's praise of prejudice has been quoted in the discussion of Bolingbroke's attack on prejudice, where it was suggested that they are connected. Bolingbroke's belief that prejudice can be abolished seems to prepare for Burke's belief that prejudice can be made reasonable: if prejudice can be replaced by non-partisan first principles, it can be made reasonable by making it non-partisan. The theory of prescription protects the good-natured non-partisanship of popular prejudice; for the rule of present possession prevents an appeal to partisan principle. Burke thought, contrary to Bolingbroke, that an appeal to first principles was bound to be a partisan appeal. The "men of ability" attracted and concerted by Bolingbroke's program are not a non-party, but the "court party." Thus Burke co-operated in Bolingbroke's intention of making society non-partisan by directly opposing his method, the appeal to first principles. And to oppose Bolingbroke's method, Burke directly opposed his program of anti-partisanship. In Britain, party government had its origin in the conflict of the forces of Burke and Bolingbroke, against the background of their agreement on making society non-partisan.

Presumptive Virtue and Prudence

The reason in prejudice can be seen in what Burke says here of the British constitution:

Profound thinkers will know it in its reason and spirit. The less inquiring will recognise it in their feelings and their experience. They will thank God they have a standard which, in the most essential point of this great concern, will put them on a par with the most wise and knowing.[1]

"The less inquiring" accomplish through prejudice what "profound thinkers" must reason for. Thus there exists a "true moral equality of mankind";[2] for, given the proper circumstances, all men are capable of living under the British constitution. All men are equal, not in fullness of understanding, which is available to only a few of actual virtue, but in their appreciation of "the most essential point," the advantages of the constitution.

Prejudice can be as reasonable as profound wisdom only if it does not involve first principles. Bolingbroke had agreed with Plato and Aristotle that prejudice *does* involve first principles; Plato and Aristotle thought that ordinary people have prejudices or opinions which claim to see the whole truth and which must therefore involve first principles. Upon inquiry, one discovers that claim is false, because ordinary people exaggerate a partial truth; that is to say, their opinion is typically partisan and typically unaware of being partisan. Bolingbroke believed that people could be persuaded to adopt non-partisan first principles if they were made aware of the bad consequences of partisan opinions. Burke believed that opinions need not have bad consequences because they need not involve first principles. Instead of changing the opinions of the people, he tried to sever their connection with first principles by means of the theory of prescription. In this theory, prejudice can be reasonable only when it no longer claims to be true; prejudice must claim no more than to be viable.

Now if prejudice is reasonable, it follows that the role of statesmen is reduced. They do not rule over popular prejudice by virtue of their prudence; they direct popular prejudice. Prudence is "the first of all the virtues, as well as the supreme director of them all."[3] As the characteristic virtue of the "true natural aristocracy," it is the directing element in presumptive virtue. Yet this aristocracy of statesmen consists of the best available public servants. They secure the conditions of civilized liberty and adorn the establishments which attract the patriotism of free men, but they do not set the ends of society. As we have seen, they lead the people because they are part of the people; their prudence finds the means to accomplish the ends rightly sensed by prejudice. When presumptive virtue is expedient, prejudice is raised above prudence. When the "less inquiring" are as intelligent as the "profound thinkers" in the decisive issues, then statesmen use their superior prudence to serve ends within the sight of prejudice. Burke did not blink at the conclusion that moral equality makes the aristocracy into servants of the people. "In effect, to follow, not to force the public inclination; to give a direction, a form, a technical dress, and a specific sanction, to the general sense of the community, is the true end of legislature."[4]

Prudence is thus limited, in Burke's intention, to serving the interests of the people. He does not contrast prudence and prejudice, as Aristotle contrasts prudence and right opinion; prudence and prejudice meet to co-operate. The prudent man sees that the people are right in their feelings.

It is very rare indeed for men to be wrong in their feelings concerning public misconduct; as rare to be right in their speculation upon the cause of it. . . .

. . . the most poor, illiterate, and uninformed creatures upon earth are judges of a *practical* oppression. It is a matter of feeling; and as such persons generally have felt most of it, and are not of an over-lively sensibility, they are the best judges of it. But for the *real cause*, or the *appropriate remedy*, they ought never to be called into council about the one or the other.[5]

It should be repeated that, for Burke, the people's feelings, if well-informed and not inflamed by their imaginations, could be trusted properly to perceive their interests. But the feelings of the people have only the capacity of prejudice. "Prejudice is of ready application in an emergency," having engaged the mind in a "steady course of wisdom and virtue."[6] But because prejudice is ready for application, it is ill-informed about circumstances; it must be supplemented (not contradicted) by the prudence of men who have deliberated on the circumstances. That feelings be moderated and kept in the course of nature is not sufficient for the life of society according to natural law. "The will of the many, and their interest, must very often differ. . . . I conformed to the instructions of truth and nature, and maintained your interest, against your opinions, with a constancy that became me."[7] Feelings as habits give rise to prejudices, which are steady and reliable; but feelings expressed as will or opinions and used to decide upon systems and details of policy are frequently erroneous. Statesmen must seek the various and common interests of the people by means of prudence.

Yet interests have their basis in prejudice, by which the people determine the general end of their interests—liberty—and check the performance of those who tend to these interests. Otherwise, prejudice, even when moderate, could never follow a "steady course of wisdom and virtue"; and the people could not be sure of recognizing "practical oppression." But interests, as distinguished from prejudices, require information about circumstances, hence the need for prudence.[8] The political reason of statesmen, in Burke's view, works within limits set by natural feeling. The hallmark of this typically modern conclusion is Burke's disdain for popular opinions, which is combined with his reliance on popular feelings and interests. The people do not know their interests directly, in their opinions, but only through prudent statesmen, who are their leaders.

Burke finds it possible to avoid an appeal to first principles by the discovery of the reasonableness in prejudice, and this reasonableness reduces the contribution of prudence to government. Yet there is no doubt that Burke's conception of prudence is like the prudence which the classical political philosophers thought to be the virtue of statesmen, and that many of Burke's particular political judgments, whose defense evoked his praise of prudence, would be understandable from the classical position. Whereas the importance of prudence is diminished by the reasonableness of prejudice, it is increased by the danger of an appeal to first principles. Presumptive virtue, in Burke's view, seems to be divided, like Aristotle's moral virtue, between the virtue of those who follow—natural feeling and prejudice—and the virtue of those who lead—prudence. Burke's prudence, unlike Aristotle's prudence, is not sovereign over the prejudice or opinion of the people. But prudence is relied upon more by Burke than by Aristotle as a substitute for first principles or political philosophy. Burke's reliance upon prudence, which has the appearance of Aristotelianism, serves a purpose which denies Aristotle's belief in the possibility of a legislator: in Burke's opinion, it is always prudent to avoid the legislator's appeal to first principles.

The result of this complex relation of prudence and prejudice in Burke is the lawful or legalized prudence which has already been noticed. This notion can be seen more clearly if one seeks to connect a number of Burke's thoughts on prudence.

Burke denies that the lines of morality are "like the ideal lines of mathematics"; they are made by the "rules of prudence."[9] "The rules of prudence . . . are formed upon the known march of the ordinary providence of God."[10] The known march of providence must be what is known by human beings to be beneficial (which is more than what is congenial), since the mysterious part of providence is what does not seem beneficial. Providence is divided into known and unknown dispensations by Burke, as opposed to the orthodox Christian view, which regards Providence as a mysterious whole. The known march of providence must therefore be what Burke calls "prescription," the gradual accumulation and continual provision of benefits in a habit or institution; for prescription is the sufficient standard of goodness known to men for the judging of their habits and institutions. Prescription, to repeat, is a "great fundamental part of natural law." When the "metaphysic" rights of man enter into common life, they are refracted from their straight line by the laws of nature; they cannot be secured except by knowing the laws of nature. Prescription is based on these refracted rights, not on "self-evident" rights. But change is "the most powerful law of nature." Therefore the proper use of prudence is to ensure prescription through the shift of events. To ensure prescription through change is to reform; thus the proper use of prudence is reform.[11]

Change is the most powerful natural law, but natural law is not simply change; it is a refraction of natural rights. Men maintain contact with their original natural rights through natural law, though this connection is not direct. When Burke says that change is by nature the most powerful law, he means that things have a law of change as a nature—that is, in classical terms, they have a law rather than a nature. Then there must be a means of continuity in the agent of natural law, which endows or secures the lawfulness of things, so that society does not drift away from its concern to protect natural rights. Such a means of continuity is the reason of men, the stock of reason, the "collected wisdom of ages." The stock of reason could be made up of laws or prudence. Laws are man-made, according to Burke; "the nature and description of a legislative act" is that "arbitrary discretion leads, legality follows." But laws are also "beneficence acting by a rule"; the laws ensure prescription, which is part of natural law. Thus the laws are man-made rules to effect the ends of natural law, and in this sense, "only declaratory."[12] The laws reach but a little way, however. Prudence must then be beneficence acting by less of a rule than a law, in areas where the laws cannot reach. But prudence needs rules to ensure that its ends are secured according to natural law, for there are no first principles of political things by which prudence may be safely guided. The rules of prudence, not first principles, keep society moving according to law. Consequently the rules of prudence acquire the attributes of natural law, and the result is the "lawful prudence" which has been described. Furthermore, as the obligation to reform is derived from natural rights, however refracted, the task of reform is the protection of those rights, which have been defined by prescription. Prudence accordingly aims at safety first and prosperity second.

Whatever the reasons which deflected Burke from the traditional notion of prudence, two very practical differences between that notion and his can be identified, prescription and political economy. The theory of prescription limits the prudent statesman by requiring that he not attempt to form society's establishments; he may only reform them to answer particular grievances. Moreover, since the establishments raise up men of pre-sumptive virtue, prescription ensures the sovereignty of these men over men of actual virtue. The virtue presumed of these honest men is thus fortunately a limited prudence, suited to their capacity. Honest men—Burke's "true natural aristocracy"—are presumed to have virtue because they stand upon an elevated ground. It is well that prudence, the supreme director of the virtues, can be simplified for their use. Prudence becomes a consequence of place; it is therefore a duty, since there is no possible ex-cuse for not exercising it; and because the supreme director of virtues is a duty, presumptive virtue in general can be considered definitively as duty. Our reason is a "disagreeable yoke," Burke says, in a revealing simile; rea-son does not rule but yokes.[13] Its influence is naturally unpleasant and happily limited.

Secondly, in Burke's view, the statesman's prudence is limited and sys-tematized by the method of political economy. As we have seen in Burke's arguments against Hastings, the natural laws of political economy outline an aspect of life which the legislator is forbidden to enter. Burke would agree that one cannot repeal the law of supply and demand or the law of the multiplier. Whatever the laws of economics may be, they are natural, that is to say, beyond political control. Here again, the leadership of hon-est men is assisted by a limitation on prudence. These men need only the wisdom to watch and to regulate the economy, not to prescribe for its working and its moral effects.

In reckoning the mutual influence of these two limitations on prudence, one can see that the establishment in society of a sanctuary for economics beyond political control, done in the name of liberty, helps the statesman who wishes to keep first principles out of politics. People are distracted from public affairs when they are encouraged to be busy in their private affairs. But the long-term compatibility of prescription and political econ-omy can well be doubted. It became clear in the nineteenth century that the hunger for economic innovation awakes in every subordinate part of society an urge for political innovation against the establishments.

There remains one problem in prudence, which concerns the relation of actual and presumptive virtue. The rules of prudence are formed on the "known march" of the *ordinary* providence of God. But Burke explicitly distinguishes ordinary from extraordinary providence, and it is only from ordinary providence that *rules* of prudence may be formed. He also refers to "prudence of a higher order" at the beginning of the "Reflections," when he violates the usual rule of prudence in private men with regard to poli-tics, which is silence.[14] Burke began the "Thoughts" with a similar deference to the general duty of reserve, but made a particular exception for that occasion. Thus higher prudence has no rules; it is for the use of men of actual virtue on extraordinary occasions. It is also needed for the theoretical defense of presumptive virtue. Prejudice must be endorsed by "our men of speculation" in order to repel the temptation "to trade each on his own private stock of reason."[15] The "sacred rules of prescription" themselves must be established in the public law of every free society, for prescription does not become established by prescription. We shall attempt to understand the activity of higher prudence by explaining the relation of actual and presumptive virtue.

Presumptive Virtue and Providence

Before one can decide whether Burke's conception of natural law is modern or traditional (that is, Christian), his views on Christianity must be examined. Our contemporary perspective hinders this examination, because the present age is so unconcerned with the divine that Burke's frequent references to God, as such or in one of His attributes, will be taken as evidence of a "deeply religious nature." From this perspective, it would be too much to require that a man believe in the truth of Christian revelation, and hence of very little importance to prove that he did not. Nevertheless we shall make this inquiry, first because we cannot agree that a thoughtful man can disbelieve the truth of Christian revelation and at the same time accept Christian natural law. We contend that Burke's belief is in serious doubt, though we cannot prove more; and this fact must be very damaging to any interpretation of Burke that places him in the Christian tradition of natural law. Christian natural law asserts that the revelation of God conforms to the discoveries of unassisted human reason; if Christian revelation is denied, then the content of natural law must be different from traditional natural law, if it is not to contradict whatever revelation (if any) replaces Christian revelation. Or, if Thomist natural law can be matched to non-Christian revelation, then the basis of that conception of natural law, the conformity of Christianity and nature, is absolutely destroyed. The second reason for making this inquiry is that Burke himself thought religion to be very important. He once said, "I never loved impiety or blasphemy: a great portion of my time has been occupied in studying theoretical religion."[16] This forces us to answer another question: If Burke was not an orthodox Christian, what is the meaning of his references to God and providence?

We shall begin with evidence for our doubts of Burke's belief in the truth of Christian revelation;[17] no single item is decisive; yet added together, the succession is impressive. Burke does not have on record, to the knowledge of the present writer, any profession of belief in Christian revelation—although if he had, that too would not be decisive, in view of other remarks to follow. Confessing bewilderment as the result of his study of theological publications, Burke said, "I dropped them, embracing and holding fast a firm faith in the Church of England."[18] He did not mean by this that he preferred the Bible to theology, because he once said, "The Bible is a vast collection of different treatises; a man who holds the divine authority of one, may consider the other as merely human." The Bible is in *need* of human interpretation (a need unacknowledged, not to say repudiated, in the Bible itself); otherwise it may be a source of dangerous fanaticism.[19] The Bible is not so clear, and Christianity is not so clearly true, as is a proposition derived from "our natural rights": "For the Protestant religion, nor . . . the truth of our common Christianity, is not so clear as this proposition; that all men, at least the majority of men in the society, ought to enjoy the common advantages of it."[20]

Burke is an enemy to atheism, but not to closet atheists, to "speculative and inactive atheists."[21] This is an interesting distinction, and it is possible that a Christian would make it in *his* closet; but it is hardly likely that a Christian would find it desirable to make an exception publicly in favor of closet atheism, which Burke here *identifies* with philosophy as a matter of course. Closet atheism, he says, is "more than punished, whenever it is embraced." If one turns to Burke's production in the closet, his *Philosophical Enquiry into the Origin of Our Ideas of the Sublime and Beautiful,* one finds this statement: "Besides, many ideas have never been at all presented to the senses of any men but by words, as God, angels, devils, heaven and hell, all of which have however a great influence over the passions."[22] It is hard to reconcile this statement with a belief in the Christian miracles.

Burke's early schoolmate and lifelong friend, Richard Shackleton, once wrote the following of him in a short biography:

He has not yet been favoured to find that clue which could lead him to the indubitable certainty of true religion, undefiled with the mixture of human inventions, to which his own spirit as a man (though *truly excellent*) can no more guide him, than their *fine parts* and *reasoning* could guide the *ancient poets, philosophers,* etc., who notwithstanding their noble exertion of the rational faculties in investigating the works of nature, remained in the grossest ignorance and absurdity respecting the truths of Christianity.

And surely, in a matter most essentially necessary and interesting, it is not to be imagined that Divine Wisdom and Goodness would leave us destitute of the means of infallible certainty.

Shackleton states the case well for our purpose. It may be objected that, as a Quaker, he would have a special idea of an indubitable clue; but he seems to mean indubitable certainty within the Church of England. Burke was incensed when this biography was published and wrote to Shackleton, objecting in detail to the treatment of his wife, his father, and his debating. But he made no remark on Shackleton's conjecture about his religion.[23]

In the "Reflections," Burke's most important writing, these words occur: "The body of all true religion consists, to be sure, in obedience to the will of the Sovereign of the world; in a confidence in his declarations; and in imitation of his perfections. The rest is our own."[24] Evidently a very great deal of Christianity is "our own" in origin; and "all true religion" is not necessarily Christian. We shall not attempt a minute inspection of this passage, but shall remark only upon its vagueness, as an assertion taken at its own claim to importance. Elsewhere in the "Reflections," Burke says that "man is by constitution a religious animal"[25]—a statement which may not exclude revelation, but which does not obviously include it. "Religious animal" does not have a biblical redolence; if this definition of man is intended as a contrast to Aristotle's definition of man, "by constitution" should be distinguished from "by nature." The previous quotation then leaves it in doubt whether true religion is constituted by God, by man himself, or by both.

In general, when Burke speaks of the value of religion or of Christianity, he has a political purpose in view. His defense of religion in the "Reflections" is a defense of the church as an establishment whose purpose is to consecrate the commonwealth. His defense of monasteries is argued from the benefits of the "surplus product of the soil" owned by monasteries; these are libraries, collections, paintings, monuments, and specimens of nature which "open the avenues to science." That monks serve God, Burke says, is one of "the fictions of a pious imagination."[26] Elsewhere the statement that "God has given the Earth to the Children of Man" is used in an argument for Irish free trade, which was made in a public letter particularly addressed to Dissenters.[27] We have also seen, in his speeches against Hastings, that he does not regard references to God as exempt from use as a rhetorical device.

How to interpret this political emphasis is a problem. Those who believe a religion to be true are not disqualified from thinking it to be useful; but for them, utility is a *consequence* of truth. False religion may indicate a need, or a striving, but it cannot answer the need or fulfil a function. Burke does not exert himself to demonstrate that, for him, the utility of religion is a consequence of its truth. At one point, having described atheism as "the great political evil of the time," he says:

> I hope I need not apologize for this phrase, as if I thought religion nothing but policy; it is far from my thoughts, and I hope it is not to be inferred from my expressions. But in the light of policy alone I am here considering the question. I speak of policy too in a large light; in which large light, policy too is a sacred thing.[28]

This statement does not resolve the issue as Burke appears to wish it resolved; for the question is precisely whether religion can be considered "in the light of policy alone."[29] It may be tentatively concluded that Burke apparently does not subscribe to Christian revelation and that his opinions on religion have a political tendency.

One can improve this understanding by examining more directly what he says about God. "The body of all true religion consists . . . in obedience to the will of the Sovereign of the world. . . ." This is a "resource" found necessary to the strongest minds. But what is His will? Both the learned and the less inquiring parts of the community "conceive, that He who gave our nature to be perfected by our virtue, willed also the necessary means of its perfection.—He willed therefore the state.—He willed its connexion with the source and original archetype of all perfection."[30] One cannot assert that biblical revelation is not also, in Burke's view, a necessary means of perfection; but it is not mentioned. The virtue by which man perfects his nature, since it is his prerogative "to be in a great degree a creature of his own making," is made possible by the original contract. On that occasion, the command of God's will is made known in order to impress men with the truth that, as only supreme necessity can justify the dissolution of contract, so it first forces the making of it.

> Each contract of each particular state is but a clause in the great primaeval contract of eternal society, linking the lower with the higher natures, connecting the visible and invisible world, according to a fixed compact sanctioned by the inviolable oath which holds all physical and all moral natures, each in their appointed place. This law is not subject to the will of those, who by an obligation above them, and infinitely superior, are bound to submit their will to that law. . . . It is the first and supreme necessity only, a necessity that is not chosen, but chooses, a necessity paramount to deliberation, that admits no discussion, and demands no evidence, which alone can justify a resort to anarchy.[31]

But the effect of this doctrine is typically modern: one can secure liberty only when the necessity of obedience is universally recognized. To obey necessity is the first act of liberty. Thus the will of God is that man find it absolutely necessary to perfect his nature by means of his own artificial creation, the state.[32] This is one of the "rational and natural ties that connect the human understanding and affections to the divine."

It is the will of God, further, that men use power "strongly and awfully impressed with an idea that they act in trust." Statesmen should "not look to the paltry pelf of the moment . . . but to a solid permanent existence, in the permanent part of their nature, and to a permanent fame and glory, in the example they leave as a rich inheritance to the world." We observe that "solid permanent existence" for statesmen refers to their example, not to their souls or the afterlife. The people must have "emptied themselves of all the lust of selfish will, which without religion it is utterly impossible that they ever should," so that "they will be more careful how they place power in base and incapable hands."[33] The statement that the people must empty themselves of selfish will by religion implies, given a "state of unconnected nature," that religion takes effect only with the original contract, and that selfish will naturally precedes man's recognition of God. Providence, then, is the necessary condition of prescription; it makes duty possible by awing the passions and allowing their development into natural feeling and by lengthening the vision of statesmen. Burke thinks that to the statesmen and to the people Christianity must seem to be true; but whether it is true is left ambiguous. "Religion, to have any force on men's understandings, indeed to exist at all, must be supposed paramount to laws, and independent for its substance upon any human institution. Else it would be the absurdest thing in the world; an acknowledged cheat."[34] Providence also offers the benefits of existence, while it uses fear to secure them. It is the model for prescription. The eternal order is fixed by the will of God; yet it is also contractual. God has given to man a nature capable of perfection by virtue; He has also given the means of perfection, the state. Men can collect the rewards of God's promise if they carefully conserve the benefits of God's providence. Men should form rules of prudence from the known march of providence; these rules of prudence are Burke's replacement for biblical revelation and for the commands of traditional natural law, which restated revealed law.

In summary of Burke's views on religion, it is not too much to say that God and providence appear to do the work of Hobbes's sovereign. There is no clear reason to deny that Burke believes in a personal God who cares for human affairs, but there is reason to doubt that this God and His providence are specifically Christian. Men do not naturally desire to do good, according to Burke; they can do good only under a sovereign, only with "the principle of a superior law."[35] The law of nature is the command of that Sovereign (and Burke often refers to God abstractly, as

"Sovereign," "Author," "Creator," or "Founder"), but the command is not specific, like the commands of Christian natural law, nor is it Christian natural law.[36] The command of God is not spoken directly to man, through revelation; God speaks through man's fears and feelings, and man must draw the conclusions by himself. It is true that "policy too is a sacred thing." In order to secure the natural rights of man in government, men must be taught more than to grab, more than "the little catechism of the rights of man." They must be taught reverence for the duties and policy which secure those rights. Although this point did not escape the American Founding Fathers, Burke states it with greater insistence and his statement is less clouded by the clear appearance of calculation. But we repeat, this interpretation must be almost as guarded in its claim to proof as is Burke in his expressions of faith.

Natural Law in Summary

We can now come to a conclusion about Burke's conception of natural law and presumptive virtue. Natural law is compatible with presumptive virtue, because the way men presume virtue in their leaders by prescription is natural. Natural law is a way of presuming, a law of reason in operation—not a statement of the fixed end of man, a law for reason to discover. Burke's description of "that wonderful structure Man, whose prerogative it is, to be in a great degree a creature of his own making" has been quoted. Another statement develops this point: "For man is by nature reasonable; and he is never perfectly in his natural state, but when he is placed where reason may be best cultivated, and most predominates. Art is man's nature."[37] Man is never perfectly in his natural state except where reason most predominates. It has been noted that Burke accepts the Hobbesian concept of the state of nature at the beginning as "a savage and incoherent mode of life." Man then becomes more truly natural, not directly by the use of reason to modify his savagery, but "when he is *placed* where reason may be best cultivated." The means of passage from the partly to the fully natural is art, and human nature consists in the manner of effecting this passage. Human nature is a contrivance against the savagery of the natural origins of men. In Burke's formulation, natural law is fundamentally two rules of prudence, prescription and political economy. These two rules guide man in his contrivance against nature, in the construction of his "second nature."[38]

But how does man's civilized second nature emerge from his naked and savage first nature? The answer is, by natural feeling. Natural feeling is "our common nature," a phrase frequent in Burke's writings. "Our common nature" is responsible for "the true moral equality of mankind." It is a highest common factor in human nature, rather than the highest element in human nature; as the standard for living in accordance with natural law (for example, in the Hastings impeachment), "our common nature" enforces an attainable minimum of virtue rather than proposes higher achievements.[39] This minimum is attainable if natural feeling is secured by the establishments and if the establishments are secured by the reason of statesmen. Thus a society made up of establishments is the place where reason most predominates, however much or little that may be. It is the best place for man to live according to his natural feeling. Men are by nature reasonable, because they can, through a natural aristocracy, use their reason to develop their natural feeling. If their reason were more than subordinate to their feeling, natural inequalities in reason would produce a natural aristocracy of rulers. But as reason serves to develop and protect natural feeling in the establishments, natural inequalities in reason (which are of course undeniable) produce a natural aristocracy of leaders, instead of rulers. Natural law is the method of leadership by which man's art perfects man's nature. It therefore coincides with the interests of the people, in contrast to their will or opinions.

Burke's conception of natural law, as compared to traditional natural law, liberates natural feeling. To be sure, natural feeling is not mere selfishness, but it is love of one's own. Liberty, not obedience, is the chief quality of life according to Burke. There is little harshness and constraint in natural law; for art imitates the change and variety in nature or simply permits the free growth of habits and institutions. Art is not legislation, which is based on political science; art is the slow, unplanned growth of manners and establishments, based on collected wisdom or rules of prudence.[40]

The advantage of natural feeling over the fear of violent death as the basis for natural law is that it does not recall first principles. According to Hobbes, the commonwealth is securely constructed by human art when men are inspired by the fear of violent death. This fear reminds men of the dangers of the state of nature and thus of the reason, or first principles, for society. But in Burke's view, society cannot advance beyond the state of nature when it is based upon the same passion which inspires men in the state of nature. Fear cannot be *transformed* into trust; it must be *replaced* by trust. Since Burke agrees with Hobbes that the first principles of society are established by fear, he argues that trust is the result of a certain forgetfulness carefully tended by prudent statesmen. Natural law is the law of reason, by which the early nature of man is forgotten. If there were a fixed, final nature of man, toward which man tends, there would be no problem in forgetting his early nature. But Burke agrees with Hobbes, against Aquinas, that there is no fixed, final nature of man toward which he tends. For him, natural law is liberty disciplined by honesty, or presumptive virtue.

Burke's differences with Aquinas in regard to the end of natural law and with Hobbes in regard to the avoidance of first principles lead him to a low opinion of the use of intellectual virtue or speculative reason in politics. Henry Grattan wrote to Burke at the end of his life, after the death of his son: "You . . . have now no other prospect of immortality than that which is common to Cicero or to Bacon."[41] But Burke would not have been consoled. He once gave a beautiful appreciation of contemplative virtue, asserting it to be higher "in the order of things" than active virtue.[42] Its use in politics, however, is obstructed by the rule of prescription. The man of actual virtue who is the founder of a family would be a man of practical virtue, not a philosopher; and if actual virtue must be mediated through family, intellectual virtue would seem to be subordinated to practical or "active" virtue. It must be allowed that Burke's life shows his belief in this subordination. He wrote for the occasion, not in a narrowly partisan spirit and not without generalizations, but hardly ever with purely theoretical intent, as in his *Philosophical Enquiry into the Origin of Our Ideas of the Sublime and Beautiful*. Living a political life, Burke sensed the importance of politics, but he was unable to find support for its importance by contemplating "the order of things." He could not disdain political things, and he could not connect them to higher things.

In a letter to his first patron, Hamilton, he reserved for himself some time to write for publication, since "whatever advantages I have acquired . . . have been owing to some small degree of literary reputation."[43] Burke thought that a "man of ability" could safely shine in the literary world—his own style was never modest. It was only the attempt to rise rapidly in politics and the meddling of literary men in politics, which he thought dangerous. Yet he sought a literary reputation, not the opportunity to contemplate things that are beyond action. The purpose of a literary reputation may perhaps be found in the encomium to Montesquieu at the end of the "Appeal." Montesquieu, Burke said, collated and compared "all the schemes of government which had ever prevailed among mankind." "Let us then consider, that all these were but *so many preparatory steps* to qualify a man, and such a man, tinctured with no national prejudice, with no domestic affection, to admire, and to hold out to the admiration of mankind, the constitution of England!"[44] Burke presents Montesquieu as an admirer of the British constitution, as the man of actual virtue who admires the constitution because he understands it and whose admiration should be the model for those who can only venerate it.[45] The British constitution, in Burke's thought, replaces the theoretically best constitution of political philosophy. The theoretically best constitution is impossible, because the highest and most civilized state has only natural beginnings and a natural mode of growth, not a natural end.

One can only admire the British constitution in its complexity, that is, in the relations of its establishments. These relations are unplanned; they were not made by a legislator. They must be protected by the prudent statesman who understands from the rule of prescription that he can at most found a family, never a state. In Burke's opinion, the admiration of a Montesquieu for the British constitution can never inspire a founder or new-modeler; his theoretical understanding can only applaud the forbearance and delicacy of British statesmen. When the philosopher must admire unplanned practice, he loses his primacy over the practicing statesman. But the unplanned practices take form in establishments, which are private institutions. And unplanned practice has a good result only if it is protected from planning. The establishments must be kept inviolate, or nearly so; they must be regarded as private institutions, substantially immune from public control. Hence Burke raised the practicing statesman above the political philosopher because he reduced the status of politics below the dignity of private institutions. His depreciation of speculative reason, variously repeated in his writings, was a consequence of his theory of prescription, not the cause of it.

Prescription and Party

The theory of prescription had a more practical result for Burke than his demotion of speculative reason: it made possible the respectability of party. Bolingbroke's attack on partisanship arose from his fear of religious parties and of divisive doctrines in general. He proposed a system of first principles to substitute theoretical certitude for the divisons which arguable doctrines, especially those based on faith in revelation, arouse. Burke is, on the contrary, so vague and so guarded on the first principles of religion that he does not even refute, he ignores, Bolingbroke's first principles.[46] In his "Vindication of Natural Society" he satirizes Bolingbroke's system by revealing its absurd political consequences; similarly, in the "Thoughts" he does not oppose Bolingbroke's program directly but shows the danger from men of ability who are undisciplined by any other principle than the principle of ability. His own statements on "true religion," though not scarce, are limited to what is necessary to support a grave belief in the theory of prescription. "The rest is our own," he says; that is, the rest of religion is a private affair, not the concern of the public. In place of a publicly established theoretical certitude in religion, Burke proposes the greatest possible incertitude, with a bare minimum of divine providence, to protect the most latitudinarian religious establishment. Not only are his first principles of religion latitudinarian, but the minimum of divine providence they endorse is designed to protect the theory of prescription, which is the very soul of latitudinarianism.

The result is that party becomes respectable, that is, the honored practice of gentlemen. Bolingbroke would not have cared if each gentleman had private opinions on religion and first principles; but for him it was necessary to the peace of the constitution that all gentlemen publicly subscribe to his first principles. Bolingbroke believed that his first principles were true, not merely salutary, and that they should be made the public opinion of Britain because of their truth. Yet he shared with the classical political philosophers the belief that certain theoretical or religious principles must be avowed by all the gentlemen in a country. Burke, on the other hand, believed that gentlemen could differ openly on theoretical or religious principles—and therefore on *political* principles. An open difference is a public difference; if gentlemen can differ openly, then the public can be divided. Yet one cannot neglect the lesson of the English civil war, seconded by the reasoning of all previous statesmen and philosophers, that divisions of public opinion can bring on dangerous conflict. How can such conflict be prevented?

Burke's answer is that gentlemen can be presumed to have virtue from their *position*, not from their *opinions*. In a free country a position of great property sufficiently ensures both a common interest with the other parts of the people and an outlook adequately elevated to see the needs of that common interest. This presumptive virtue is obtained by public establishment of the theory of prescription. The theory of prescription does not make a public issue of the private opinions of the leading gentlemen, because it teaches that a country is not founded on opinions or on first principles. A country is not founded at all; it begins and it grows. If the public believes that gentlemen rule by prescription, it will not inquire into the theoretical or religious opinions of gentlemen. As we said, there is a limit to public forbearance from such inquiry. Gentlemen must subscribe to a minimum belief in providence; if they wish to be atheists, they must be closet atheists. But they subscribe to this belief in order to support a belief in prescription, from which they derive liberty of belief in all other matters of religion.

Burke's minimum of religion and his theory of prescription are to be publicly enforced as much as Bolingbroke's first principles, but they are not so restrictive. Burke's religious principles, unlike Bolingbroke's, have been more pleasing to the orthodox than to the unorthodox, as he did not advertise his exceptions to orthodoxy. His religious principles seem designed not to awaken religious parties, whereas Bolingbroke's first principles were designed to settle religious parties. Burke attempted to establish prescription as public law, by helping to pass the Nullum Tempus Act of 1769. This act was proposed after an attempt by the crown to transfer certain property with some electoral influence from the Duke of Portland to Sir James Lowther, a supporter of the ministry. The argument of the crown was that the property was not named in the grant of William III to Portland and that prescription does not apply to the crown (*nullum tempus occurrit regi*). The act provided that the crown could not reclaim, because of a flaw in the title, any estate which had been enjoyed without interruption for sixty years.[47] Burke also defended the theory of prescription in his writings on the French Revolution; yet he defended it not as a theory, but as a practice, especially as a British practice. In seeking to establish prescription he was careful to conform to the spirit of prescription.

Party principle is today so much the standard of political conduct that it is no longer paradoxical. In the traditional view of party, there could be no "party principle." Sound principle could be only temporarily advanced by a party, when prudent men at last saw no other way of upholding it. For the good of the country and of the principle, they tried to make the country conform to the principle, so far as could be. But Burke's forgetful, forbearing statesmen avoid this test of prudence. According to Burke's definition of party, they act on their party principle, almost regardless of what the principle is. "Principledness" becomes the standard of statesmanship when statesmen refrain from attempting to make the country as a whole conform to any particular principle. "Principledness" is viable when it is understood as the opposite of "first principles," as well as the discipline of ambitious abilities. It is understood in both ways in the theory of prescription.

Actual Virtue and Presumptive Virtue

Yet Burke was always dissatisfied with the system of presumptive virtue and party principle which he founded. At the beginning of the "Thoughts" he indicated that a private man of higher prudence must sometimes intervene to save the constitution when honest men are confused. Party government had to be established by a better statesman than a party statesman. And after party government was established, the disastrous inflexibility of the Whig party in face of the French Revolution forced Burke to attempt to destroy his particular party and to limit the general respectability of party, which he had done so much to create. The rule of prudence for men of presumptive virtue must occasionally yield to a higher prudence. The problem is that it is occasionally imprudent to follow the rules of prudence.

It is for men of actual virtue to exercise higher prudence. If Burke considered himself a man of actual virtue, what was his rule for the exercise of prudence, which had been formed from his life as a whole? Fortunately there are two passages in which Burke gives a direct answer to this question. One is the section at the beginning of the "Appeal," the sequel to the "Reflections," where he defends the consistency of his views on the French Revolution with his earlier actions against the attacks of the Foxite Whigs. The other is the last sentence of the "Reflections," which is less open to the charge of reasoning after the fact. It should be no surprise that a man of Burke's quality would not rush or drift from one occasion of life to the next; he would have a plan.[48] But it is noteworthy that he chose to disclose his plan in a defense of himself, because he might have left it for others to discern as best they could.

The last sentence of the "Reflections" says that Burke's opinions come "from one who wishes to preserve consistency; but who would preserve consistency by varying his means to secure the unity of his end; and when the equipoise of the vessel in which he sails may be endangered by overloading it upon one side, is desirous of carrying the small weight of his reasons to that which may preserve its equipoise."[49] This is a nearly faithful rendition of Lord Halifax's definition of the antipartisan "Trimmer":

This innocent word Trimmer signifieth no more than this, that if Men are together in a Boat, and one part of the Company would weigh it down on one side, another would make it lean as much to the contrary; it happeneth there is a third Opinion of those, who conceive it would do as well, if the Boat went even, without endangering the passengers. . . .[50]

Halifax wrote *The Character of a Trimmer* to combat the charge of inconsistency from the parties: hence Burke clearly is not just a party man.

In the "Appeal," Burke argues that for most men,

the danger of anything very dear to us removes, for the moment, every other affection from the mind. When Priam had his whole thoughts employed on the body of his Hector, he repels with indignation, and drives from him with a thousand reproaches, his surviving sons, who with an officious piety crowded about him to offer their assistance. A good critic . . . would say that this is a master-stroke, and marks a deep understanding of nature in the father of poetry.

He would despise a Zoilus, who would conclude from this passage that . . . [Priam] preferred a dead carcass to his living children.[51]

He himself did not go to such lengths; but if he had, he would have deserved the allowance due to Priam.

The reader, or good critic, who would make the proper allowance, appreciates the consistency of Burke's life, which needs no such allowance, but only the understanding that produces it. As Churchill said, any man can sense Burke's consistency.[52] It is a higher consistency than the party consistency of a Zoilus, who in this instance makes the perfect prototype of a party critic. For, when regarded as a whole, Burke's career closely resembles the character of the Trimmer. As a man of actual virtue, he intervened in politics on a series of occasions when the rules of prudence were inapplicable. He cites one example—his "Bristol Speech," whose arguments against compulsive instructions to representatives in Parliament were intended, he says, to have the striking effect that the occasion of their delivery preserved for them. Other interventions were the impeachment of Hastings, intended as an example of impeachment; the attack on the French Revolution, intended as a warning to Englishmen; the defense of party in the "Thoughts"; and the assertion of limits to party in the "Appeal." These interventions are all, in a sense, legislative, because they were meant as examples to others, to honest men of presumptive virtue. But they are not legislative in the sense of the classical legislator; they are only responses to particular grievances that develop. Such interventions do require a balanced perception of the common good on the part of Burke, but they do not attempt an entire and balanced reconstruction of society on the basis of the perception. Hence, as examples for honest men, these interventions seem to require only a perception of some wrong, which is easily learned from popular discontents, and a perception of the remedy that will restore peace and security.

Remedies are fixed in rules for the sake of honest men. But the generality of mankind, misled by history, are fifty years behind hand in their politics. They do not see that at some times the usual remedy will be unavailing; they need the intervention of a man of actual virtue in order to find a particular remedy and to modify the rules of prudence. Prudence must have rules; and every act of prudence, especially by a man of reputation, tends to become a rule. This is the legislative character of the great man's interventions. Yet because these interventions are limited to responses, irregular and unpredictable, they are like the balancing shifts of the Trimmer.

Higher consistency is consistent with lower, or party consistency, only by the restraint of great men. Great men see more clearly than men of presumptive virtue; they see without the aid of appearances. "For madness and wickedness are things foul and deformed in themselves; and stand in need of all the coverings and trappings of fortune to recommend them to the multitude. Nothing can be more loathsome in their naked nature." Honest men must be included among the multitude in this respect; for the coverings and trappings of their own fortune prevent them from seeing clearly the naked nature of wickedness. Honest men are too much impressed by good fortune, and too sensitive to threats against their good fortune.[53] But great men, the true men of ability, are not bemused by success or high position. They have higher prudence because they can see that what has worked in the past will not necessarily work now. Yet as great men, they also recognize that honest men, born to the great families and organized in political parties, must rule in the ordinary course of affairs. Burke requires this recognition not only because supreme virtue is rare (in which all agree) but also because it is essentially incapable of rule. Great men can excel in reason, but reason is dangerous in politics because it recalls the first principles which underlie politics. The appearances of politics, the "solemn plausibilities," are not distinguished from natural law. They are not merely endorsed by natural law; they are caused by natural law. Natural law is the standard from which men perfect their original nature. Men necessarily lose sight of the "naked nature" of politics (that is, the nature of politics in the light of the original contract) when they attempt, by following natural law, to improve upon that nature. Great men must therefore respect the appearances of politics—the ways in which politics appears to the public— not because men of presumptive virtue are more available than they, but because men of presumptive virtue are in a sense wiser than they. "Political arrangement, as it is a work for social ends, is to be wrought only by social means. There mind must conspire with mind. Time is required to produce that union of minds which alone can produce all the good we aim at."[54] Great men must be essentially modest, rather than disdainful. Hence Burke's rhetoric has a familiar style; it attempts to make a great man's wisdom part of the general stock of reason. His respect for the appearances, which we noticed in the discussion of the "Thoughts," is not the respect of a philosopher for those he cannot teach. It is true patience, caused by true modesty. Whether true modesty is possible, when Englishmen need Burke to tell them of their stock of reason or when only Burke perceives the result of mind conspiring with mind, is a problem he apparently did not resolve. But the deference Burke showed to lesser men throughout his life should be traced ultimately to his opinion of the danger of first principles.

One may come to a judgment of Burke's idea of the relation of actual to presumptive virtue by inquiring whether he is properly called a "conservative." Burke's respect for the rules of prudence justifies his title of conservative, but one must question whether this respect has been, or could be, successful in its aim. Burke never called himself a conservative, and it is generally most imprudent to use a name for a thinker not avowed by that thinker (unless he has reason to avoid a stigma). For such a name implies that the namer knows the thinker better than the thinker knows himself. Burke can be called a conservative only in criticism. "Conservative" is usually used in opposition to "liberal," the one systematically supporting the status quo, the other systematically proposing change. Both are *party* positions in that they publicly state a systematic opinion without reference to circumstances, each in opposition to the other. The usage of both terms began only after the introduction of party government.

In the conflict between Bolingbroke and Burke one can see the conflict between liberal and conservative doctrine, or more generally, the conflict between rationalism and empiricism. Rationalism is the modern doctrine which seeks a secured liberty on the basis of natural law understood as true first principles. Its objects are liberty from the bondage of prejudice and superstition and security against the fanaticism raised by prejudice and superstition. The true first principles of rationalism are, generally, that the natural liberty of men teaches them the necessity of security in civil society. Rationalism presents the truth as the way to peace. Burke says the opposite:

> I will not enter into the question how much truth is preferable to peace. Perhaps truth may be far better. But as we have scarcely ever the same certainty in the one that we have in the other, I would, unless the truth were evident indeed, hold fast to peace, which has in her company charity, the highest of the virtues.[55]

Truth presented to the public is not the way to peace. Usually, peace must be preferred to unevident truth. Burke's prescriptive right from usage is the opposite of Bolingbroke's inalienable rights, which are derived from the truth of human nature. Prescriptive right is gained or lost, but an inalienable right is neither gained nor lost. Burke advances a theory of prescription; Bolingbroke simply dismisses prescription.[56] Accordingly, as the theory of prescription makes party principle tenable, Burke proposes party government; Bolingbroke simply and fiercely opposes it.

Yet behind this contradiction there is an agreement that the aim of the state is peace. Burke's party government rests on the assumption that the great parties are entirely dissolved. According to Burke in the "Appeal," the Settlement of 1688–89 was not based on doctrine, but on absolute necessity; therefore it cannot be a source of partisanship. According to Bolingbroke, that Settlement was based on true doctrine; therefore it cannot be a source of partisanship. This flat contradiction regarding an event of great importance to each man reveals their most fundamental agreement. They agree that peace in liberty is the proper *result* of state action, not its *aim*, for as liberty is natural to men, the state can secure it by aiming at peace. The supposed truths of rationalism and the evasions of empiricism have the common purpose of producing quiet—the one by stilling disputes, the other by shrugging off inquiry. That is why party government, which was prepared for by Bolingbroke's rationalism and flowered as Burke's empiricism, alternates today between rationalism and empiricism, between liberalism and conservatism.

Now it might seem that Burke transcended this alternation when he said, "A state without the means of some change is without the means of its conservation."[57] Besides, the founder of party as a *system* (not as a single "country party") might seem to stand above identification with one of the parties within the system. Nor did Burke envisage a party system composed of parties of opposed doctrine, conservative and liberal; he hoped that all parties would be conservative. But we may reply that Burke did not specify what, apart from the natural rights of man of his opponents' doctrine, he wished to conserve *without* change. He did not say where the British constitution should stop developing, having attained a theoretically best state. It is well known that conservatives of a later period are as liberals, or radicals, to conservatives of an earlier period. From this truth one might infer that ever since conservatism received a name it has been uniformly unsuccessful. In Burke's thought one could find the reason: Burke fundamentally agrees with the ends of rationalism; he merely wants to further its ends less precipitously. What is fundamental in Burke is his substitution of the rules of prudence, or of conservatism, for statesmanship—not his attempted anticipation of Bolingbrokian party government by a party system based on the rules of prudence. It might be said, then, that if Burke wanted nothing more than a prudential rationalism, his aim and that of conservatism generally have been successfully achieved, at least in Britain. But Burke did not succeed even in modifying the doctrine of first principles with the rules of prudence. He was able to inspire only one part of the party system with the rules of prudence. His present influence is as a founder of one party, not of the party system. Thus his doctrine of party is now used to tolerate those rationalist "Jacobins" whom he meant to extirpate. Such was the case, as we have noted, in his own time; and we believe this to be a necessary result of his position.

Burke intended to maintain a tension between actual and presumptive virtue, or between statesmanship and party government. He left a record of party and of higher, non-partisan, consistency. But his idea of actual virtue was a statesmanship reduced to correcting the errors of inflexible statesmen. Statesmanship in Burke has lost its culmination in the classical idea of the legislator, and thence its connection to political philosophy; it accepts popular desires as its limit and takes the present discontents as its signal. When the people come to accept their natural rights as the basis of government, statesmen will have to adapt to this great change. But their adaptation will have to include tolerance of a popular party or parties led by Bolingbroke's "men of ability." The people, knowing their rights, will be receptive to leaders who ask them to return to the original contract and to ignore or destroy the establishments. Burke's statesmen may oppose such leaders with the rules of prudence and the strength of the establishments, but they can only retreat so long as they accept "the *real* rights of men" and fear to appear "to resist the decrees of Providence itself."[58] We conclude that Burke was a conservative, not by intention, but by his preparation for conservatism as a party doctrine. By intention, he reduced statesmanship to the rules of prudence, in order to serve the needs of party government. In effect, he demoted statesmanship to conservatism.

Notes

Works and collections listed in the Bibliography are cited in short form in the Notes. Citations to Burke's *Works* are to the Bohn Library edition and those to his *Correspondence* are to the Copeland edition, unless otherwise indicated.

CHAPTER ONE

1. Edmund Burke, *Works*, I, 185.
2. *Discourses*, I, 2–8; cf. John Plamenatz, review of Burke's "Thoughts" in *Parliamentary Affairs*, V (1951), 211.
3. Thomas Babington Macaulay, *The History of England from the Accession of James the Second* (10 vols.; New York, 1908), I, 294–95; Winston S. Churchill, *Marlborough, His Life and Times* (2 vols.; London, 1947), I, 161; emphasis in the original. Cf. Thomas DeQuincey, *Politics and Political Economy* (New York, 1877), pp. 497, 502–6.
4. J. R. Jones, *The First Whigs: The Politics of the Exclusion Crisis, 1678–1683* (London, 1961), pp. 213–15, 222.
5. Macaulay, *History of England*, IV, 351, 387–97; George M. Trevelyan, *The English Revolution, 1688–1689* (London, 1938), pp. 240, 245; but cf. W. E. H. Lecky, *A History of England in the Eighteenth Century* (12 vols.; New York, 1878), I, 6, 13, and David Hume, *The History of England* (6 vols.; Boston, 1854), VI, 363.
6. Burke, "Thoughts," *Works*, I, 308; cf. Burke, *Correspondence*, II, 279. The distinction between great and small parties is explained by Alexis de Tocqueville, *Democracy in America*, trans. H. Reeves (2 vols.; New York, 1945), I, 175.
7. Cf. G. M. Trevelyan, "The Two-Party System in English Political History," in *An Autobiography and Other Essays* (London, 1949), p. 197.
8. M. Ostrogorski, *Democracy and the Organization of Political Parties*, trans. F. Clarke (2 vols.; New York, 1902), Part I, chaps. 1–4; Part II, chaps. 1–2; Max Weber, "Politics as a Vocation," in H. Gerth and C. W. Mills (eds.), *From Max Weber* (New York, 1946), pp. 100–107. Weber's thoughts on parties have been gathered in the fourth edition of *Wirtschaft und Gesellschaft* (2 vols.; Tübingen, 1956), II, 845–58; see also I, 167–69; II, 675–78, 865–76.
9. Ostrogorski, *Political Parties*, I, 22.
10. David Hume, "Of Parties in General," *Essays Moral, Political, and Literary* (2 vols.; Edinburgh, 1817), I, 54; emphasis in the original.
11. See Plato, *Laws*, 803d–803e; 828d.
12. Livy, *History of Rome*, ii. 24, 32–33, 44, 65; iv. 2–6; cf. Machiavelli, *Discourses*, I, 5–6.

13. E.g., Aristotle, *Politics*, iii, iv, vi, esp. 1281a9–11, 1296a7–13; Polybius, vi. 3, 10, 18, 26, 43, 46–47; Plutarch, *Praecepta Gerendae Reipublicae*, 824b–825b; cf. J. S. Mill, *On Liberty* ("Everyman Edition," [London, 1936]), pp. 105–7; and *Representative Government*, chap. 2.

14. Weber, in *Wirtschaft und Gesellschaft*, II, 676. Cf. Ostrogorski, *Political Parties*, I, 25–28; Ernst Troeltsch, *Protestantism and Progress*, trans. W. Montgomery (Boston, 1958), pp. 105, 125; and *The Social Teaching of the Christian Churches*, trans. O. Wyon (2 vols.; London, 1931), II, 636–39, 690, 1011; Guido de Ruggiero, *The History of European Liberalism*, trans. R. G. Collingwood (Boston, 1959), pp. 162–63.

15. R. H. Tawney, *Religion and the Rise of Capitalism* (New York, 1947), pp. 234–35, 261–63. Consider this reasoning of John Toland: "The People of both sides are dispos'd to be quiet, as long as their priests will let them: They think not a jot the worse of one another, for not walking the same way to Church on *Sunday*, because they joyn'd company the *Saturday* before to market: They judge of one another's Honesty by their Dealings and not from their Notions: Trade is vigorously carried on without Distinction. . . ." *The Art of Governing by Partys* (London, 1701), p. 21; emphasis in original.

16. Kurt Kluxen, *Das Problem der politischen Opposition* (Freiburg, 1956), pp. 1–64, 157–64; cf. Jones, *The First Whigs*, p. 17; Francis Lieber, *Manual of Political Ethics* (2 vols.; Boston, 1839), II, 435.

17. L. B. Namier, *England in the Age of the American Revolution* (London, 1930), pp. 55–58; Kluxen, *Das Problem*, p. 179.

18. W. R. Fryer, "Namier and the King's Position in English Politics, 1744–1784," *The Burke Newsletter*, V (1963), 248–49; J. B. Owen, *The Rise of the Pelhams* (London, 1957), p. 299.

19. Richard Pares, *King George III and the Politicians* (Oxford, 1953), pp. 94–97, 207.

20. Cf. Aristotle, *Politics*, 1303b17–1304b8; and Machiavelli, *Prince*, chap. 19; *Discourses*, III, 6.

21. *The Writings of Thomas Jefferson*, ed. P. J. Ford (10 vols.; New York, 1896), VII, 128; cf. VII, 43, IX, 425. Carl J. Friedrich, *Constitutional Government and Democracy* (rev. ed.; Boston, 1950), p. 414.

22. See *The Complete Works of George Saville First Marquess of Halifax*, ed. Walter Raleigh (Oxford, 1912), p. 225.

23. Philip C. Yorke, *Life of Hardwicke* (3 vols.; Cambridge, 1913), II, 392; III, 362, 496.

24. Robert M. MacIver, *The Web of Government* (New York, 1948), p. 208; Austin Ranney, *The Doctrine of Responsible Party Government* (Urbana, Ill., 1954), p. 4; Sigmund Neumann (ed.), *Modern Political Parties* (Chicago, 1956), p. 1.

25. Hume, "Of the Coalition of Parties," *Essays*, I, 472; cf. James Harrington, *The Commonwealth of Oceana* (London, 1887), pp. 30–40, 135, 171, 200–201.

26. Caroline Robbins, "Discordant Parties—a Study of the Acceptance of Parties by Englishmen," *Political Science Quarterly*, LXXIII (1958), 505–29.

27. Wilfred A. Binkley and Malcolm C. Moos, *A Grammar of American Politics* (3d ed.; New York, 1958), p. 195; D. W. Brogan, preface to Maurice Duverger, *Political Parties*, trans. B. & R. North (London, 1954), p. vi; Neumann, *Modern Political Parties*, p. 1; Neil A. McDonald, *The Study of Political Parties* (New York, 1955), p. 3.

28. Avery Leiserson, *Parties and Politics* (New York, 1958), p. 316.

CHAPTER TWO

1. Consider Sir Lewis Namier's assertion: "The foremost task of honest history is to discredit and drive out its futile or dishonest varieties." In his opinion the futile and dishonest varieties of history about this period are based in good part upon "the literary afterthoughts of Edmund Burke." Namier, *Avenues of History* (London, 1952), p. 6, and *The Structure of Politics at the Accession of George III* (2d ed.; London, 1957), pp. 9, 238. Namier is criticized by this writer, H. C. Mansfield, Jr., "Sir Lewis Namier Considered," *Journal of British Studies*, II (November, 1962), 28–55; see also Robert Walcott, "Sir Lewis Namier Considered Considered," *ibid.*, III (May, 1964), 85–108. Other historians with a similar understanding of Burke's "Thoughts" are: Herbert Butterfield, *George III and the Historians* (London, 1957), pp. 54–56; Richard Pares, *King George III and the Politicians* (Oxford, 1953), pp. 31 n., 80 n., 84; John Brooke, *The Chatham Administration, 1766–1768* (London, 1956), pp. 225, 276, 281.
2. "Thoughts," *Works*, I, 306; the next sentence explains the danger in coming near persons of weight and consequence.
3. *Ibid.*, p. 310.
4. *Ibid.*, pp. 310–11; cf. p. 476. Burke said in a letter relating to the American problem: "I cannot think the people at large wholly to blame; or if they were, it is to no purpose to blame them." *Correspondence*, III, 217–18.
5. "Thoughts," *Works*, I, 311; cf. Sir Henry Cavendish, *Debates of the House of Commons*, I, 306, 308.
6. Plato, *Laws*, 683e; cf. 631b, 660e; Aristotle, *Politics*, 1277b25–31; *Rhetoric*, i. 8.
7. "Thoughts," *Works*, I, 311; cf. "Remarks on the Policy of the Allies," *Works*, III, 456; Leo Strauss, *Natural Right and History*, p. 306.
8. "Thoughts," *Works*, I, 313.
9. *Ibid.*, pp. 314–15; emphasis in original.
10. *Ibid.*, p. 330. Walpole thought that the "Thoughts" was impolitic for discharging Bute of present influence, "for while the book thus removed from the people's attention an odious and ostensible object, it presented them with nothing but a vague idea, which it called *a Double Cabinet*." Horace Walpole, *Memoirs of the Reign of King George the Third* (4 vols.; New York, 1894), IV, 89; so also the Duke of Portland, Rockingham MSS, R1 1249.
11. "Thoughts," *Works*, I, 317.
12. Namier did not investigate the rhetoric of Burke's "Thoughts," but he was bold enough to regard Burke's specific exclusion of George III from the inner magistracy of the court system as mere humbug. He said that Burke "constructed the theory that it was George III's deliberate policy and established practice to withhold . . . support from ministers." L. B. Namier, *England in the Age of the American Revolution* (London, 1930), p. 182; cf. Namier, *Monarchy and the Party System* ("Romanes Lecture" [Oxford, 1952]), p. 11.
13. Burke, *Correspondence*, II, 53.
14. *Ibid.*, pp. 41, 45; see also pp. 260–63, where Burke strongly denies that he ever slandered the King's character; cf. Sir George Savile, in Burke, *Correspondence*, II, 119.
15. "Thoughts," *Works*, I, 318; emphasis supplied.
16. *Ibid.*, p. 320; emphasis in original.
17. Burke, *Correspondence*, II, 336.

18. "Thoughts," *Works,* I, 324–25; emphasis supplied.
19. In the only explicit reference to actual events in this section on the court system, after he describes one of the least vague and most recognizable of the cabal's actions, Burke does not claim to offer more than an *application* of his remarks: "They who remember the riots which attended the Middlesex election, the opening of the present parliament, and the transactions relative to St. George's Fields, will not be at a loss for an application of these remarks." *Ibid.,* p. 327.
20. *Ibid.,* p. 331; emphasis in original. Cf. p. 329: Burke hints that this system is a French system by calling it a *"double cabinet,* in English or French as you choose to pronounce it." This is the ancient furniture of tyranny, *style Louis XIV,* and may serve to conceal the indigenous origin of the danger in Bolingbroke's theory—just as Burke's "Reflections on the Revolution in France" does not mention the English origin of the Jacobin doctrine of the rights of man.
21. *Correspondence,* I, 169, 170, 265, 277, 284, 285, 290, 297, 311, 316, 317, 339, 342; II, 5, 43, 44, 55, 59, 101, 144, 176, 198. On December 29, 1770, Burke wrote: "It is clear to me, that Lord Bute is no longer the *adviser,* but that his system is got into firmer and abler hands"; cf. *Works,* I, 183–84. But see Namier, "The Character of Burke," *The Spectator,* December 19, 1958, p. 895.
22. "Thoughts," *Works,* I, 336.
23. *Ibid.,* p. 351.
24. Cf. Cavendish, *Debates,* I, 231.
25. "Thoughts," *Works,* I, 340; cf. p. 351.
26. *Ibid.,* p. 329.
27. *Ibid.,* p. 331.
28. Butterfield, *George III and the Historians,* pp. 54–57; Namier, *England in the Age of the American Revolution,* p. 179; Brooke, *The Chatham Administration, 1766–1768,* pp. 232–33.
29. *Correspondence,* II, 108, 122. Walpole and Chatham believed that the "Thoughts" weakened opposition to the court; see Walpole, *Memoirs of George III,* IV, 83; and Earl of Albemarle, *Memoirs of the Marquis of Rockingham* (2 vols.; London, 1852), II, 194–95.
30. Burke, *Correspondence,* II, 136, 139.
31. Burke from Dr. Leland, June 11, 1770, Fitzwilliam MSS. The reader will note Burke's concern for what survived of himself. He sifted his correspondence, destroying many letters, leaving it in the nature of a public record.

CHAPTER THREE

1. W. Murison (ed.), *Thoughts on the Cause of the Present Discontents* (Cambridge, 1930), p. xxii; E. J. Payne (ed.), *Burke, Select Works,* I, xvi–xvii; F. G. Selby (ed.), *Burke's Thoughts on the Cause of the Present Discontents,* pp. 104, 152.
2. "Thoughts," *Works,* I, 308.
3. L. B. Namier, *England in the Age of the American Revolution* (London, 1930), pp. 61–64, 70; Romney Sedgwick (ed.), *Letters from George III to Lord Bute, 1756–1766* (London, 1939), pp. xii–xix.
4. Namier, *England in the Age of the American Revolution,* p. 225, and *Monarchy and the Party System* (Oxford, 1952), p. 9.
5. Bolingbroke, *Works* (4 vols.; Philadelphia, 1841), II, 10, 22.
6. "Thoughts," *Works,* I, 307.
7. Cf. "Remarks on the History of England," Letter 1, *Works,* I, 293.

8. Hume has a similar difficulty in his first essays on parties, published in 1742. He distinguishes "personal" and "real" parties or factions, the former founded on personal friendship or animosity, and the latter undefined but divided into parties of interest, principle, and affection. Parties of interest are the most reasonable and excusable, since states have distinct orders, and distinct orders have distinct interests. But parties from interest are not serious or dangerous, because they do not differ on the fundamentals of government. Parties from principle, which may differ on these fundamentals or on religion, are "known only to modern times, and are, perhaps, the most extraordinary and unaccountable *phenomenon* that has yet appeared in human affairs." But parties from religious principle, though they are founded in the absolutizing tendency of human nature, are frivolous because different religions need not produce contrariety of conduct. Hume cites modern wars of religion as an example of ridiculous and unreal controversy. Moreover, parties from political principle can be reconciled, as Hume shows in his discussion of the Whigs and Tories in his essay "Of the Coalition of Parties," published in 1752. Lastly, parties from affection are founded "on the different attachments of men towards particular families and persons, whom they desire to rule over them." But these attachments are an "imaginary interest" and do not seem to be distinct from the personal parties which Hume has distinguished from real parties. Where then are parties based on real differences? See David Hume, *Essays Moral, Political and Literary* (2 vols.; Edinburgh, 1817), I, Essays 8, 9; II, Essay 14.
9. Bolingbroke, *Works*, II, 25.
10. *Ibid.*, p. 48.
11. *Ibid.*, p. 54.
12. *Ibid.*, p. 67.
13. *Ibid.*, pp. 67, 71, 76.
14. *Ibid.*, pp. 27, 37.
15. *Ibid.*, pp. 80–81.
16. "A Letter to Sir William Windham," *Works*, I, 113–15, 118, 131–32; cf. "Of the State of the Parties," *Works*, II, 433.
17. Bolingbroke's relations with the other deists can be pursued in Walter Merrill, *From Statesman to Philosopher: A Study in Bolingbroke's Deism* (New York, 1949); and John Leland, *A View of the Principal Deistical Writers* (3 vols.; London, 1754–56); see also the stylish remarks of Leslie Stephen, *History of English Thought in the Eighteenth Century* (2 vols.; London, 1902), I, chap. 3, 82–88; II, chap. 10, 43–54.
18. Bolingbroke, *Works*, IV, 142, 162, 318, 333, 423–24; cf. Spinoza, *Theologico-Political Treatise*, chap. 4.
19. Cf. Kant, "On the Impossibility of the Psycho-theological Proof," *Critique of Pure Reason*.
20. Bolingbroke, *Works*, IV, 142.
21. *Ibid.*, III, 399.
22. Shaftesbury's deism, which is more subtle and problematic than Bolingbroke's, is associated with a direct attack on Locke's theory of ideas. See *The Life, Unpublished Letters and Philosophical Regimen of Anthony, Earl of Shaftesbury*, ed. B. Rand (London, 1900), pp. 13–47, 415; Shaftesbury, *Characteristicks* (4th ed., 3 vols.; London, 1727), I, 109–14; II, 6–20, 68, and *Second Characters*, ed. B. Rand (Cambridge, 1914), pp. 105–6; Bolingbroke, *Reflections Concerning Innate Moral Principles* (London, 1752).
23. Bolingbroke, *Works*, III, 81, 102–3, 158–63; Locke, *An Essay Concerning Human Understanding*, Bk. 2, chap. 30; Bk. 4, chap. 4.
24. Bolingbroke, *Works*, III, 225, 235.

25. *Ibid.*, p. 487.
26. *Ibid.*, IV, 14–15, 84, 480.
27. Bolingbroke accepts this argument of Locke. Bolingbroke, *Works*, IV, 43–44; see also II, 201; III, 421; IV, 172–3; Locke, "The Reasonableness of Christianity," *Works* (3 vols.; London, 1740), III, 522–27, 545–46; cf. Spinoza, *Theologico-Political Treatise*, chaps. 4, 5.
28. Bolingbroke, *Works*, III, 328.
29. *Ibid.*, pp. 405–6; IV, 263.
30. *Ibid.*, III, 374–77.
31. Similarly, Bolingbroke indicates that knowledge of duty is separable from the "reasonableness of Christianity" presented in Parts III and IV of Hobbes's *Leviathan*, although he seems to adopt much of that reasonableness: "The kingdom of [artificial] theology is the kingdom of darkness; and to enjoy the true light of the gospel, we must fly from it. To believe that Jesus was the Messiah is said by some to be the 'unum necessarium' of faith; but to observe the laws of nature is certainly the 'unum necessarium' of duty. About this summary of faith and duty there can be no very reasonable doubt." *Works*, III, 485; cf. III, 418. Locke, *Works*, III, 573–79.
32. Bolingbroke, *Works*, III, 148, 189, 232 n.; IV, 431; Locke, *Two Treatises of Government*, II, §§ 12, 63, 124.
33. Bolingbroke, *Works*, III, 327; IV, 142, 160.
34. *Ibid.*, IV, 374.
35. *Ibid.*, p. 146.
36. *Ibid.*, III, 67; IV, 147.
37. But see Locke, *Two Treatises of Government*, II, § 110. Bolingbroke's criticism of Hobbes is also not pertinent. *Leviathan*, chaps. 13, 30.
38. Bolingbroke, *Works*, IV, 167–68, 190, 426; Bolingbroke follows Shaftesbury in supposing that men are naturally sociable, but, unlike Shaftesbury, argues that their sociability is derivative from self-love. See Shaftesbury, *Characteristicks*, I, 109–14; II, 23–25.
39. Bolingbroke, *Works*, IV, 151.
40. In seeking to distinguish his system from that of Hobbes, Bolingbroke gives an imperfect rendering of Hobbes, as if Hobbes denied a difference between natural and positive law, rather than affirmed that they were co-extensive in civil society. To secure this difference, Bolingbroke frequently quotes Cicero, somewhat in the spirit of Shaftesbury and Spinoza, and not because he would "take Tully for my guide in matters of the first philosophy." *Works*, IV, 147 n. Bolingbroke has none of Shaftesbury's appreciation for the ancients; see Shaftesbury, *Characteristicks*, I, 268.
41. Bolingbroke, *Works*, III, 103.
42. *Ibid.*, IV, 187.
43. Hobbes, *Leviathan*, chap. 30; Bolingbroke, *Works*, IV, 193.
44. Bolingbroke seems to recognize this need. *Works*, IV, 217.
45. *Ibid.*, pp. 203, 217–22.
46. *Ibid.*, III, 294, 485.
47. *Ibid.*, II, 90; IV, 196.
48. *Ibid.*, IV, 146.
49. Cf. *ibid.*, p. 199.
50. "Letters on the Study and Use of History," *Works*, II, 177, 222, 229; Dionysius of Halicarnassus, *Roman Antiquities*, xi. 1. 4.
51. Bolingbroke, *Works*, IV, 149, 197–203.
52. *Ibid.*, I, 316, 319; II, 196, 211; Michael Geddes, *Miscellaneous Tracts* (3 vols.;

London, 1706), III, 16–21; Nathaniel Bacon, *An Historical and Political Discourse* (London, 1760), Part I. See also James Harrington, *The Commonwealth of Oceana* (London, 1887), pp. 19, 51, 55, 156, 246; Algernon Sidney, *Discourses Concerning Government* (2 vols.; Edinburgh, 1750), II, 245–46, 259; Montesquieu, *De l'esprit des lois*, XI, 8, and *Lettres persanes*, nos. 131, 136; and Burke's criticism, "Abridgment of English History," *Works*, VI, 415. As indicated, the Gothic constitution becomes important for Bolingbroke only in the context of Hobbes's conception of the state of nature.

53. Bolingbroke, *Works*, II, 121, 140. In the "Letters on the Study and Use of History," *Works*, II, 239, Bolingbroke says that modern politics began an era so generally new at the end of the fifteenth century with the anti-aristocratic and anti-ecclesiastical policies of kings, that close study of previous eras is needless. See also "On the Power of the Prince," *Works*, I, 511. Yet it remains true that the Gothic constitution was reinstituted in Queen Elizabeth's time. *Ibid.*, I, 360–63.
54. *Ibid.*, IV, 141–42; cf. III, 398–99.
55. *Ibid.*, IV, 415–16.
56. *Ibid.*, pp. 108–9.
57. *Leviathan*, chap. 39.
58. Bolingbroke, *Works*, II, 43.
59. Burke, "Reflections on the Revolution in France," *Works*, II, 359.

CHAPTER FOUR

1. Bolingbroke, *Works*, II, 168.
2. Burke, "Thoughts," *Works*, I, 367–68; cf. Halifax, "A Rough Draught of a New Model at Sea," *The Complete Works of George Savile, Marquess of Halifax* (Oxford, 1912); *see* Joseph Cropsey, *Polity and Economy* (The Hague, 1957), p. 69.
3. Bolingbroke, *Works*, II, 353–55, 358, 369.
4. *Ibid.*, p. 352.
5. *Ibid.*, p. 379.
6. Cf. Shaftesbury, *Characteristicks* (4th ed.; 3 vols.; London, 1727), III, 143–47.
7. Bolingbroke, *Works*, II, 360.
8. Locke, *Two Treatises of Government*, II, § 225.
9. Bolingbroke, *Works*, II, 374.
10. *Ibid.*, p. 370.
11. Yet Bolingbroke chose to open a literary quarrel with Alexander Pope, then dead but defended by Warburton, over the premature publication. See the Printer's Advertisement to the first edition of *The Idea of a Patriot King* (London, 1749); George H. Rose (ed.), *Papers of the Earls of Marchmont* (3 vols.; London, 1831), II, 181, 185–89, 284–85; *Letters of Lady Luxborough to William Shenstone* (London, 1775), pp. 104–5; *Walter Sichel, Bolingbroke and His Times, The Sequel* London, 1902), pp. 284, 384–91, 556, 583.
12. Bolingbroke, *Works*, II, 372, 390.
13. *Ibid.*, p. 381; Burke, *Works*, II, 397.
14. Bolingbroke, *Works*, II, 384.
15. Machiavelli, *Discourses*, I, 10, 17, 25, 52.
16. Bolingbroke, *Works*, II, 392.
17. *Ibid.*, pp. 393, 395–96; Machiavelli, *Discourses*, I, 18.
18. Bolingbroke, *Works*, II, 396.
19. *Ibid.*, p. 401; Francis Bacon, "Of Simulation and Dissimulation," "Of Cunning,"

Essays; cf. Shaftesbury, *Philosophical Regimen,* p. 182. Bolingbroke has simplified Bacon's distinctions.

20. Bolingbroke, *Works,* II, 353.
21. *Ibid.,* p. 428.
22. *Ibid.,* p. 398.
23. *Ibid.,* p. 355.
24. *Ibid.,* pp. 364, 397.
25. The "Patriot King" was first entitled "Patriot Prince," perhaps a nicer address to Prince Frederick as well as to Machiavelli. See Herbert Butterfield, *The Statecraft of Machiavelli* (London, 1940), pp. 135–65.
26. Bolingbroke, *Works,* II, 365.
27. *Ibid.,* p. 401. Cf. John Toland, *The Art of Governing by Partys* (London, 1701), p. 41: "Divisions ought carefully to be avoided in all good Governments, and a King can never lessen himself more than by heading of a Party; for thereby he becomes only the King of a faction, and ceases to be the common Father of his people."
28. Bolingbroke, *Works,* II, 405.
29. *Two Treatises of Government,* II, § 235; cf. Burke, "Reflections on the Revolution in France," *Works,* II, 302–3.
30. Bolingbroke, *Works,* II, 408–10.
31. *Ibid.,* p. 415.
32. *Ibid.,* p. 412.
33. *Ibid.,* p. 428; see Bolingbroke's "On the Policy of the Athenians," *Works,* I, 496–508.
34. *Ibid.,* II, 424. Hobbes also used "popularity" in an estimable sense. *Leviathan,* chaps. 10, 30 (end).
35. Bolingbroke, *Works,* II, 419.
36. Burke, "Thoughts," *Works,* I, 320.
37. The "Thoughts" seems to have been written from July, 1769, to February, 1770; Burke, *Correspondence,* II, 39–40, 49, 52, 92, 101, 122.
38. *Politics,* 1313b39–1314a10.
39. Bolingbroke, *Works,* II, 396–97. Queen Elizabeth made a near approach to the model of the Patriot King. Bolingbroke says that no reign "deserves to be more studied, or to be oftener called to remembrance both by those who govern, and by those who are governed, than the reign of Queen Elizabeth." *Ibid.,* I, 363. She falls short of the Patriot King perhaps in her willingness to encourage parties at court (cf. *ibid.,* I, 372; II, 406), and more importantly (one must suppose) in her failure to avow the first principles. Saving the constitution requires educating the people, in Bolingbroke's opinion; and the people are properly educated, not by a noble example, but by being enlightened about their rights and duties. Only system is safe, and system must be taught in principles. Elizabeth stilled the parties of her time but failed to spread the principles which would prevent parties from arising in the future.
40. *Ibid.,* II, 379.
41. Thomas Babington Macaulay, *Miscellaneous Works* (10 vols.; Boston, n.d.), VI, 326 (Essay on Chatham); D. A. Winstanley, *Personal and Party Government* (Cambridge, 1910), pp. 22–23; H. N. Fieldhouse, "Bolingbroke and the Idea of Non-Party Government," *History,* XXIII (1938), 50; Kurt Kluxen, *Das Problem der politischen Opposition* (Freiburg, 1956), p. 111.
42. Bolingbroke, *Works,* II, 381.
43. Horace Walpole, *Memoirs of the Reign of King George the Third* (4 vols.; New York, 1894), I, 42.
44. Burke published "A Vindication of Natural Society" in 1756 to show the subversive

effect on government of those principles Bolingbroke used for the destruction of religion, implying by his assumption of Bolingbroke's style that Bolingbroke should have foreseen this effect but that he did not foresee it. Then Bolingbroke's attack on religion would be franker than his politics.

CHAPTER FIVE

1. "Thoughts," *Works*, I, 320; emphasis in original.
2. London, 1761. Cf. F. G. Selby (ed.), *Burke's Thoughts*, p. 104, and E. J. Payne (ed.), *Burke, Select Works*, I, 247–48.
3. Douglas, *Seasonable Hints*, pp. 7–8, 4, 61, 12.
4. *Ibid.*, pp. 23, 13, 14.
5. *Ibid.*, pp. 15, 33–35, 9.
6. *Ibid.*, p. 28.
7. *Ibid.*, pp. 61, 41.
8. Burke said only that the pamphlet "had all the *appearance* of a manifesto preparatory to some considerable enterprise." "Thoughts," *Works*, I, 320; emphasis supplied.
9. *Ibid.*, I, 322.
10. John Brown, *An Estimate of the Manners and Principles of Our Times* (2 vols.; London, 1757–58), and *Thoughts on Civil Liberty* (London, 1765).
11. *Thoughts on Civil Liberty*, p. 12.
12. *Ibid.*, pp. 24, 28, 29; *Estimate*, I, 72; II, 173.
13. *Estimate*, I, 72.
14. *Nicomachean Ethics*, 1123b16–24, 1124a12–20, 1159a22–27.
15. *Thoughts on Civil Liberty*, p. 92; *Estimate*, I, 137, 141; II, 154.
16. *Nic. Ethics*, 1124b6–9.
17. *Thoughts on Civil Liberty*, pp. 34, 81, 113.
18. *Ibid.*, pp. 31, 93; *Estimate*, I, 53, 59, 61; *Honour: A Poem* (London, 1743). Cf. *Nic. Ethics*, 1124a10–12, 1124b24–26.
19. Dr. Brown changed his mind about whether avarice or ambition and avarice causes faction (*Estimate*, I, 122, and *Thoughts on Civil Liberty*, p. 111) and about whether faction must be tolerated, following Montesquieu, or abolished, following Bolingbroke (*Estimate*, I, 104; II, 185; *Thoughts on Civil Liberty*, pp. 56, 92, 160).
20. *Thoughts on Civil Liberty*, pp. 160–62, 167; cf. Bernard de Mandeville, *An Enquiry into the Origin of Honour and the Usefulness of Christianity in War* (London, 1732), who with the same general understanding of honor as Dr. Brown, allows some social utility to "modern honour," the propensity to resent an affront.
21. *Thoughts on Civil Liberty*, p. 112. Cf. Burke's "Thoughts," *Works*, I, 337: the "natural strength of the kingdom" is "the great peers, the leading landed gentlemen, the opulent merchants and manufacturers, the substantial yeomanry."
22. *Estimate*, I, 114–15, 151–219; II, 203, 214–50.
23. *Ibid.*, II, 252.
24. "Thoughts," *Works*, I, 323.
25. The reader is advised that the names of authors of these pamphlets are often only conjectural.
26. For example, consider the attack of Catharine Macaulay on Burke's "Thoughts," as he said, "the patriotick scolding of our republican Virago." She castigates the "dangerous manoeuvres of aristocratic faction and party," as a consequence of "his present majesty's having displayed the independent greatness of his situation." Here is Bolingbroke's influence clearly; but Mrs. Macaulay requires, contrary to

Bolingbroke and to Locke, that government which provides "full security of the rights of nature" to be republican. Catharine Macaulay, *Observations on a Pamphlet, Entitled Thoughts on the Cause of the Present Discontents* (London, 1770), pp. 6, 8, 13; Burke, *Correspondence*, ed. Copeland, II, 150.

27. [Owen Ruffhead], *Reasons Why the Approaching Treaty of Peace Should Be Debated in Parliament* (London, 1760); *Ministerial Usurpation Displayed, and the Prerogatives of the Crown, with the Rights of Parliament and of the Privy Council, Considered* (London, 1760), pp. 5, 21, 26; *Considerations on the Present Dangerous Crisis* (London, 1763), p. 45.

28. [Sir John Marriot], *Political Considerations* (London, 1762), pp. 15, 16, 29, 41.

29. [Tobias Smollett], *The Briton* (London, 1762–63), pp. 2, 21, 26, 184–85, 216.

30. Arthur Murphy (ed.), *The Auditor* (London, 1762–63), pp. 6, 12, 27–28, 30, 43, 47, 65, 80, 175–80.

31. Thomas Pownall, *Principles of Polity* (London, 1752), pp. 7, 13, 31; *The Administration of the Colonies* (London, 1764); Locke, *Two Treatises of Government*, II, § 132.

32. [Charles Lloyd], *The Anatomy of a Late Negotiation* (London, 1763), pp. 1, 8, 15; *A Defence of the Majority* (London, 1764); *A Critical Review of the New Administration* (London, 1765); and *The Conduct of the Late Administration Examined Relative to the Repeal of the Stamp Act* (London, 1767).

33. [John Almon], *A Review of the Reign of George the Second* (London, 1762), pp. 8–9, 29 n., 113, 258; *A Review of Mr. Pitt's Administration* (London, 1763), p. 130; *A Review of Lord Bute's Administration* (London, 1763); and *A Letter to the Right Hon. George Grenville* (London, 1763).

34. [John Almon], *History of the Late Minority* (London, 1766), pp. 10, 14, 38–41, 74, 329; Burke said that "we should have been tried" with the court system "if the Earl of Bute had never existed." "Thoughts," *Works*, I, 330.

35. [William Pulteney, Earl of Bath], *Reflections on the Domestic Policy Proper To Be Observed on the Conclusion of a Peace* (London, 1763), pp. 2, 44, 65, 85, 97.

36. ———, *A Letter from a Gentleman in Town to His Friend in the Country* (London, 1763), p. 9.

37. [Ruffhead?], *The Conduct of the Administration in the Prosecution of Mr. Wilkes* (London, 1764), pp. 13, 16, 25.

38. "Observations," *Works*, I, 187.

39. Lloyd wrote a pamphlet called *The Conduct of the Late Administration Examined Relative to the Repeal of the Stamp Act.*

40. "Observations," *Works*, I, 248; in a letter, Burke refers to the Grenvilles as "that Political School." *Correspondence*, II, 85. See the review of *The Present State* in *The Political Register* (4 vols.; London, 1767–69), IV, 161–66, 304–5, 312.

41. "Observations," *Works*, I: Introduction, pp. 185–87; analysis, pp. 187–266; defense, pp. 267–90; remedy, pp. 290–305.

42. *Ibid.*, I, 188; [William Knox and George Grenville], *The Present State of the Nation* (London, 1768), p. 99.

43. "Observations," *Works*, I, 234, 291; [Knox and Grenville], *The Present State*, p. 32.

44. *The Present State*, p. 67.

45. *Ibid.*, pp. 7, 29; Burke, "Observations," *Works*, I, 199; [Sir Grey Cooper], *The Merits of the New Administration Truly Stated* (London, 1765), p. 18. Cooper was a member of the Rockingham party.

46. *The Present State*, pp. 64, 94; Burke, "Observations," *Works*, I, 290, 294–95; "Letters on a Regicide Peace," *Works*, V, 339.

47. Albert von Ruville, *William Pitt, Earl of Chatham*, trans. H. Chayter (3 vols.; Lon-

don, 1907), I, 75, 88, 104, 130, 289; Basil Williams, *The Life of William Pitt, Earl of Chatham* (2 vols.; London, 1914), I, 40, 51, 54.

48. See Romney Sedgwick (ed.), *Letters from George III to Lord Bute, 1756–66* (London, 1939), Introduction; and H. C. Mansfield, Jr., "Sir Lewis Namier Considered," *Journal of British Studies,* II (November, 1962), 28–55. See also Sir George Young, *Poor Fred: The People's Prince* (London, 1937), pp. 60–62, 172–75, 210–14.

49. Burke, "Thoughts," *Works,* I, 315; L. B. Namier, *England in the Age of the American Revolution* (London, 1930), p. 433; James Boswell, *The Life of Samuel Johnson* ("Modern Library" [New York, n.d.]), p. 528.

50. Burke, *Works,* II, 361.

51. This is Kurt Kluxen's argument in *Das Problem der politischen Opposition* (Freiburg, 1956), chap. 10. Kluxen mistakes Bolingbroke's intention, in supposing that he desired national unity without parties only as his highest and impracticable ideal (pp. 111–16).

52. See Bolingbroke, "Party and Faction defin'd and distinguish'd," *Craftsman,* No. 674, June 9, 1739, and in *Gentleman's Magazine,* IX, 313–14.

53. [Ruffhead?], *The Conduct of the Administration,* p. 27; [Marriot], *Political Considerations,* p. 41; [Ruffhead], *Considerations on the Present Dangerous Crisis,* p. 44; see also [Nathaniel Forster], *A Defence of the Proceedings of the House of Commons in the Middlesex Election* (London, 1770), p. 1; and [————], *The Principles of the Late Changes Impartially Examined* (London, 1765), pp. 38–39; cf. Burke, "Not men but measures," "Thoughts," *Works,* I, 376.

54. Burke, "Observations," *Works,* I, 259.

55. Burke's argument differs from Aristotle's famous argument against innovation. Suppose the improvements were not hastily and publicly proposed but privately presented to the rulers, and then publicly adopted only after careful reflection. Aristotle shows that such innovations, even as real improvements, might be bad; for since virtue is the result of habituation and since innovations destroy the power of habit, all innovations will attack virtue, even when their effect is on balance for good. Aristotle, *Politics,* 1268b23–1269a29. Compare Burke, ". . . authority depending on opinion at least as much as on duty," with Aristotle, ". . . for the law has no power over obedience besides the force of custom. . . ." Burke, *Works,* I, 260; Aristotle, *Politics,* 1269a21. Burke is friendlier to innovation than is Aristotle because he holds a doctrine of natural law, even though his version of natural law concedes much to the force of habit.

56. Burke, "Observations," *Works,* I, 330; Douglas, *Seasonable Hints,* p. 14; Murphy (ed.), *The Auditor,* p. 179.

57. "Thoughts," *Works,* I, 322, 354, 372, 378.

58. The case was different with the plausible doctrine that inspired the French Revolution; its progress was more advanced and had to be met with direct refutation, at any hazard. "Appeal," *Works,* III, 104.

59. Oliver Goldsmith, *The Life of Henry St. John, Lord Viscount Bolingbroke* (London, 1770), p. 96, and *The Citizen of the World* (2 vols.; London, 1762), I, 84, 131; II, 226; Samuel Johnson, *The False Alarm* (London, 1770); [Nathaniel Forster], *A Defence of the Proceedings of the House of Commons in the Middlesex Election,* pp. 1–2, *An Enquiry into the Causes of the Present High Price of Provisions* (London, 1767), p. 41, and *A Letter to the Author of an Essay on the Middlesex Election* (London, 1770), p. 2; [Charles Jenkinson], *A Discourse on the Conduct of the Government* (London, 1759), pp. 9, 87; Josiah Tucker, *The Case of Going to War for the Sake of Procuring, Enlarging or Securing of Trade* (London, 1763), pp. 13, 21; Catharine Macaulay, *Observations on a Pamphlet;* Joseph

Priestley, *An Essay on a Course of Liberal Education for Civil and Active Life* (London, 1765), pp. 35, 150, 196; Andrew Henderson, *Considerations on the Question, Relating to the Scots Militia* (London, 1769), p. 1; [Dr. Robert Wallace], *A View of the Internal Policy of Great Britain* (London, 1764), pp. vii, 11, 68, 100; [Sir John Dalrymple], *An Appeal to Facts* (London, 1763), p. 18; and *The Appeal of Reason to the People of England* (London, 1763), pp. 8, 16–17, 19, 39; [———], *A Letter from the Cocoa Tree to the Country Gentlemen* (London, 1762), pp. 4, 8, 13.

CHAPTER SIX

1. "Thoughts," *Works,* I, 312.
2. *Ibid.,* pp. 308, 328, 331, 343–44, 359; see also "Reflections," *Works,* II, 303, 327, 396–97; "A Letter to a Member of the National Assembly," *ibid.,* p. 545; "Appeal," *ibid.,* III, 8, 25, 33, 37, 115; "Remarks on the Policy of the Allies," *ibid.,* p. 429.
3. *Politics,* 1285a4–1285b4; cf. 1286a5.
4. *Ibid.,* 1286a13–14, 1287b8–12, 1286a8–1288a32.
5. *Ibid.,* 1261b6–7, 1276b37–9, 1279a8–17, 1287a17.
6. Aristotle also asserts, on the other side of the argument, that the best man cannot rule without laws. *Ibid.,* 1286a22–3, 1287b8–12.
7. "Thoughts," *Works,* I, 331–37, 342–46.
8. *Ibid.,* pp. 342–43.
9. *Ibid.,* pp. 331–32.
10. Cf. Locke, *Two Treatises of Government,* II, § 159.
11. "Thoughts," *Works,* I, 331–34.
12. See the following pamphlets on the idea of a prime minister: [Owen Ruffhead], *Ministerial Usurpation Displayed* (London, 1760), p. 28; [———], *Political Disquisitions Proper for Public Consideration in the Present State of Affairs* (London, 1763), pp. 4–9; [———], *The Conduct of a Rt. Hon. Gentleman* (London, 1761), p. 52; [———], *A Letter to the Right Honourable Author of a Letter to a Citizen* (London, 1761), pp. 9–10.
13. "Thoughts," *Works,* I, 332.
14. *Politics,* 1278b9–15, 1288a27–29.
15. Lester J. Cappon (ed.), *The Adams-Jefferson Letters* (2 vols.; Chapel Hill, N.C., 1959), II, 388.
16. "Thoughts," *Works,* I, 343.
17. *Ibid.,* p. 343.
18. *Ibid.,* p. 348.
19. *Ibid.,* p. 346.
20. *Ibid.,* pp. 359–65.
21. Betty Kemp, *King and Commons, 1660–1832* (London, 1957), pp. 73–76; Burke, "A Letter to a Noble Lord," *Works,* V, 122; "Speech on Economical Reform," *ibid.,* II, 55–126.
22. Perhaps his application of the principle goes as far as modern practice, since modern parliamentary control of expenditure hardly amounts even to the enforcement of a ceiling on government expenditure, otherwise unexamined, or if examined, examined ex post facto.
23. "Thoughts," *Works,* I, 364; emphasis in original.
24. *Ibid.,* p. 314. See "Reflections," *ibid.,* II, 396, where Burke translates, or endorses the translation of, "absolute monarch" for Aristotle's *turannis,* and wrongly denies that absolute monarchy is one of the "legitimate" forms of government (*Politics,* 1288a32–36). Cf. Locke, *Two Treatises of Government,* II, §§ 90, 138, 153.

25. "Appeal," *Works,* III, 37.
26. Bolingbroke, *Works,* II, 420–22, 425.
27. "Thoughts," *Works,* I, 347.
28. *Ibid.,* pp. 313–14, 322.
29. *Ibid.,* pp. 314–15; emphasis in original.
30. *Ibid.,* p. 333.
31. *Ibid.* "Representatives and grandees" apparently refers not only to Commons and Lords, but also to Parliament and ministers.
32. *Ibid.;* emphasis in original.
33. *Ibid.,* p. 337.
34. *Ibid.,* pp. 347–65.
35. *Ibid.,* pp. 347–48. For the "late pernicious doctrine," see [Jeremiah Dyson], *The Case of the Late Election* (London, 1769), p. 1; [————], *Some Considerations upon the Late Decision of the House of Commons* (London, 1769), p. 13.
36. The consistency of this speech with Burke's "popular" writings is considered in H. C. Mansfield, Jr., "Rationality and Representation in Burke's *Bristol Speech,*" *Nomos,* VII (1964), 197–216.
37. "Thoughts," *Works,* I, 347, 349–50; emphasis in original.
38. *Ibid.,* pp. 335–36, 350.
39. Burke discusses it in "Observations," *Works,* I, 293–96.
40. *The Federalist* No. 48, Earle ed. ("Modern Library" [New York, n.d.]), p. 323; cf. Montesquieu, *De l'esprit des lois,* XI, 6. For the agreement with Burke, see *The Federalist* No. 39, p. 243.
41. Walter Bagehot, *The English Constitution* ("World's Classics" [London, 1929]), pp. 116, 129.
42. W. E. H. Lecky, *A History of England in the Eighteenth Century* (12 vols.; New York, 1878), IV, 332–36; Kemp, *King and Commons,* pp. 78–80; W. T. Laprade, "Public Opinion and the General Election of 1784," *English Historical Review,* XXXI (1916), 224–37.
43. "Motion Relative to the Speech from the Throne," *Works,* II, 252–53.
44. "Thoughts," *Works,* I, 334.
45. Erskine May, *The Constitutional History of England* (3 vols.; London, 1889), II, 92–94; A. V. Dicey, *The Law of the Constitution* (London, 1902), p. 398.
46. Sir William Blackstone, *Commentaries on the Laws of England* (1765–69), IV, 19, 1.
47. "Thoughts," *Works,* I, 347.
48. Cf. Montesquieu, *De l'esprit des lois,* XI, 6.
49. (1) *Works,* IV, 222, 233, 247, 355, 494, 526; V, 13, 22, 28, 49, 50; (2) IV, 258; (3) IV, 251, 260, 327; (4) IV, 259; (5) IV, 271; (6) IV, 275; (7) IV, 279, 300–301, 321–22; (8) IV, 401; see Articles VII, XI, XII; (9) V, 7; (10) V, 36.
50. "Speech on Mr. Fox's East India Bill," *Works,* II, 205; "Speech on Hastings," *ibid.,* VIII, 141.
51. Peter J. Stanlis, *Edmund Burke and the Natural Law,* pp. 63–64.
52. "Speech on Hastings," *Works,* VII, 2–3 (emphasis added); cf. *ibid.,* p. 11: "the enlarged and solid principles of state morality"; p. 92: "the spirit of the laws of this country"; p. 93: "the spirit of equity"; VIII, 11: "principles of natural equity and of the law of nations."
53. *Ibid.,* VIII, 141; VII, 94, 504, 231; cf. *ibid.,* VII, 99–105, and VIII, 309.
54. In the following list of Burke's references to God in his speeches and writings on Hastings, the first number is the number of oaths, the second, the number of references to the works of God and the duties He has imposed, and the third, the number of pages. Burke's speeches in the Lords: 55, 61, 945; Speech of July 30,

1784: 2, 13, 21; Speech on Fox's East India Bill: 0, 1, 75; Speech on the Nabob of Arcot's Debts: 1, 2, 81; other speeches in Commons: 1, 1, 65; Articles of Charge: 0, 1, 365; Ninth Report from the Select Committee: 0, 0, 126; Eleventh Report from the Select Committee: 0, 0, 50. The high score on the first item may be owing to the fact that bishops sit in the House of Lords; Burke on that occasion called them "representatives of that religion which says that their God is Love." *Works,* VII, 230. The high score on the second item consists of threats of the wrath of Providence against a group of hecklers, recently elected after the dissolution of 1784 which Burke had so vehemently opposed.

55. *Works,* VIII, 5; VII, 100; cf. William Cobbett, *The Parliamentary History of England,* XXIV, 1273; and *Works,* II, 176–79.

56. *Works,* VII, 231, 312; cf. *ibid.,* II, 220; VII, 190, 232; and Cobbett, *Parliamentary History,* XXV, 162.

57. *Works,* IV, 29, 32, 52; "Motion Relative to the Speech from the Throne," *ibid.,* II, 267.

58. *Ibid.,* IV, 52; emphasis in original; cf. "Speech on Mr. Fox's East India Bill," *ibid.,* II, 227–28, where Burke lists six commercial principles violated by the company.

59. *Ibid.,* IV, 84.

60. Engaging in commerce also requires trust between commercial factors, based on reputation for keeping bargains. See "Speech on the Nabob of Arcot's Debts," *Works,* III, 160; and Cobbett, *Parliamentary History,* XXVI, 41. Cf. *The Federalist* No. 3, pp. 14–15.

61. *Works,* VII, 10–11; Cobbett, *Parliamentary History,* XXV, 1387, 1397.

62. "Speech on Hastings," *Works,* VIII, 407; cf. *The Correspondence of the Right Honourable Edmund Burke,* ed. Charles William, Earl Fitzwilliam, and Sir Richard Bourke, III, 41–42. See "Speech on Mr. Fox's East India Bill," *Works,* II, 210; Cobbett, *Parliamentary History,* XXV, 1092–93; XXVI, 40. Burke supported Fox's India Bill as a remedy for British misrule in India, a bill whose aim was to extend strict control over the governor-general by a board of commissioners appointed by the crown.

63. *Works,* VII, 10–11. Cf. Alexis de Tocqueville, *Democracy in America,* trans. Henry Reeves (2 vols.; New York, 1945), chap. 7; *The Federalist* No. 65.

64. "Thoughts," *Works,* I, 351.

65. This is in contrast to Cicero, who condemns Verres on much broader grounds than those on which Burke condemns Hastings. *In Verrem,* I. 4. 13; I. 5. 13; II. iii. 1. 5; II. iv. 40. 87.

66. "Thoughts," *Works,* I, 334.

67. In the "Reflections" Burke distinguishes the "practical claim of impeachment," usable not only to protect constitutional liberty but also to correct "vices of administration," from the ceremony of "cashiering their governors," advocated to the people by Dr. Price. *Works,* II, 302.

68. "Thoughts," *Works,* I, 351, 357, 354.

69. *Ibid.,* p. 356.

70. *Ibid.,* p. 355.

71. *Ibid.,* pp. 351, 356; cf. *ibid.,* II, 250.

72. *Ibid.,* I, 359.

73. In the "Thoughts," Burke has his eye chiefly on the House of Commons; in his "Motion Relative to the Speech from the Throne" (June 14, 1784) (*Works,* II, 252), he denies that the House of Lords is the representative of the people—a doctrine that would permit the ministers to deflect the disapprobation of the House

of Commons. The House of Lords is nonetheless indirectly connected and ultimately subordinate to the people, as seen in the previous chapter. Its situation,
in Burke's view, seems similar to that of the United States Senate, originally connected to the people (though by election) but not direct representatives of them.
If we follow Burke's thought, it becomes a question whether American government is more popular as a whole (stability and wisdom aside) because the Senate
is now popularly elected. See "Reflections," *Works*, II, 330; "Observations on the
Conduct of the Minority," *ibid.*, III, 500.

74. "Letters on a Regicide Peace," *Works*, V, 190.
75. *Politics*, 1298a20–25, 1318b27–33; cf. "A Letter to Sir Hercules Langrishe,"
Works, III, 305: "Franchises were supposed to belong to the *subject*, as a *subject*,
and not *as a member of the governing part of the state*"; emphasis in original.
76. "Thoughts," *Works*, I, 331–32.
77. *Ibid.*, p. 353.
78. *Works*, I: p. 307, composing minds of subjects; p. 308, description of disorder,
not injustice; p. 317, singular advantages of the present king—security and wealth;
p. 321, glory, power, and commerce of England; pp. 324–25, weakness is consequence of cabal; p. 336, good humor in people, security of government; p. 337,
disorder and confusion; p. 338, security of a free government; p. 341, order; p.
342, our public peace; p. 349, difficulty of reconciling liberty under monarchical
government with external strength and internal tranquillity; p. 369, enfeebling the
regular authority of the state; p. 371, public peace and all the ends of good government; p. 375, the whole fabric of public strength; p. 380, faction weakens all
powers of executory government, weight of country added to force of executory
power.
79. "A Letter to a Noble Lord," *Works*, V, 124; cf. "Thoughts and Details on Scarcity,"
ibid., p. 85.
80. "Thoughts," *Works*, I, 337–38.
81. "The active, awakened, and enlightened principle of self-interest will provide a
better system for the guard of that interest, than the cold, drowsy wisdom of those
who provide for a good out of themselves ever contrived for the public." *Works*,
VII, 36.
82. "Thoughts," *Works*, I, 332–33, 337–38, 364–65; cf. the alternative of England and
France, *ibid.*, pp. 310, 321, 329, 338, 339, 340, 364.
83. *Ibid.*, pp. 345, 368. But see "Appeal," *ibid.*, III, 25, where Burke says that the
three parts have "three very different natures" which have to be defended on
"totally different" grounds. We cannot but regard this passage as rhetorical exaggeration; taken literally, it would make the constitution theoretically indefensible,
which Burke denies (*ibid.*, p. 113). The context is the defense of his own consistency, which, he claims, requires a one-sided concern with the most urgent
problem, and hence the appearance of inconsistency. Thus, applying his explanation to his own defense, we see that he may have exaggerated the appearance of
inconsistency in order to show its inevitability.
84. Bolingbroke, *Works*, II, 88–89, 119. Cf. Locke, *Two Treatises of Government*, II,
chap. 10.
85. Bolingbroke, *Works*, II, 424; *ibid.*, pp. 114, 118–21, 126, 148. Cf. Burke, "Reflections," *Works*, II, 334: "The simple governments are fundamentally defective, to
say no worse of them." See "Thoughts," *ibid.*, I, 331; "Reflections," *ibid.*, II, 294;
"A Letter to Sir Hercules Langrishe," *ibid.*, III, 302.
86. Bolingbroke, *Works*, II, 119.
87. *The Federalist* No. 14, ed. Earle, p. 81.

CHAPTER SEVEN

1. "Reflections," *Works,* II, 363. For evidence of the orderliness of this defense and of the "Reflections" as a whole, see J. T. Boulton, "The *Reflections:* Burke's Preliminary Draft and Methods of Composition," and John Morley, *Burke,* p. 149.
2. "Thoughts," *Works,* I, 375.
3. *Paradise Lost,* Book I, l. 392; Moloch, the proud warrior-king, sought adherents to the claims of honor with grand disregard of distracting connections, such as Burke believes to be the necessary support of honor. In his Trinity College debating club, Burke once spoke the speech of Moloch (II, 43) and received applause, the secretary noted, "It being in character"; but for the Whigs, it seems that the example of Moloch is too stern and demanding. See Arthur P. I. Samuels, *The Early Life, Correspondence, and Writings of Burke,* p. 266.
4. "Reflections," *Works,* II, 290, 301; "Appeal," *ibid.,* III, 66.
5. "Thoughts," *Works,* I, 323.
6. "Appeal," *Works,* III, 42; cf. "Letter to the Sheriffs of Bristol," *ibid.,* II, 37–38.
7. *Correspondence,* I, 250, 267, 307; II, 41, 51, 72, 86, 100, 116; cf. *ibid.,* II, 373–74, 376; III, 382–84, 388–89.
8. "Thoughts," *Works,* I, 318, 370.
9. Cf. "Appeal," *Works,* III, 107; "A Letter to a Noble Lord," *ibid.,* V, 140.
10. Winston S. Churchill, *Marlborough, His Life and Times* (2 vols.; London, 1947), I, 349.
11. "Appeal," *Works,* III, 3.
12. "I have reason to be persuaded that it was in this country, and from English writers and English caballers, that France herself was instituted in this revolutionary fury." "Letters on a Regicide Peace" (1796), *Works,* V, 397. Cf. "Reflections," *ibid.,* II, 279; "Appeal," *ibid.,* III, 108; and "A Letter to a Noble Lord," *ibid.,* V, 124.
13. Burke did favor a limited opposition union with the Grenvilles, for a time prior to the publication of the "Thoughts." But this union was only a brief tactic in the service of his party policy. See *Correspondence,* II, 85, 89, 101, 105, 113, 115.
14. But see "Reflections," *Works,* II, 518 (to be discussed).
15. "Appeal," *Works,* III, 43.
16. *Ibid.*
17. Cf. Locke, *Two Treatises of Government,* II, § 242.
18. "Thoughts," *Works,* I, 323.
19. *Ibid.,* p. 311; cf. "Remarks on the Policy of the Allies," *ibid.,* III, 456–57.
20. "Thoughts," *Works,* I, 336.
21. *Ibid.,* p. 379.
22. *Ibid.,* p. 373; cf. *Correspondence,* II, 373; III, 89–90, 381.
23. Cf. "Appeal," *Works,* III, 81: ". . . such devious proceedings [as determining the just occasion for revolution] . . . must be ever on the edge of crimes."
24. "Observations," *Works,* I, 293, 188.
25. *Ibid.,* pp. 295–96; emphasis in original.
26. *Ibid.,* p. 294.
27. "Appeal," *Works,* III, 97.
28. "Thoughts," *Works,* I, 372.
29. *Ibid.,* p. 377; emphasis in original.
30. There is a hint of the necessity in the "Observations," where Burke says that those who renounce the principle of adherence to connections advertise their treachery to their connections. *Works,* I, 296.
31. Cf. "Reflections," *Works,* II, 336.

32. "Thoughts," *Works*, I, 378. Note the "general principles upon which the party is founded"—i.e., founded in particular; the difficulty is repeated.
33. "Letter to the Sheriffs of Bristol," *Works*, II, 38.
34. *Correspondence*, II, 101.
35. *Ibid.*, p. 377.
36. "Observations," *Works*, I, 295.
37. "Letters on a Regicide Peace," *Works*, V, 291.
38. "Thoughts," *Works*, I, 371.
39. *Ibid.*, p. 373.
40. *Ibid.*
41. *Ibid.*, pp. 318, 323; cf. "Appeal," *ibid.*, III, 85–86, and "Reflections," *ibid.*, II, 323.
42. "Thoughts," *Works*, I, 323.
43. "Reflections," *Works*, II, 331–33.
44. Cicero, *In Verrem*, II. i. 15.
45. "Thoughts," *Works*, I, 378; emphasis in original.
46. "Appeal," *Works*, III, 16; *Correspondence*, II, 372.
47. "Thoughts," *Works*, I, 378–79.
48. *Ibid.*, p. 376. This is further proof that party adherence is not caused by a natural law that is the standard of virtue, but by some principle, perhaps the natural law, which states the means of overcoming weakness.
49. Burke regards ambition as a greater menace than avarice. "Speech on the Nabob of Arcot's Debts," *Works*, III, 192–93; Cavendish, *Debates*, I, 312–13. Cf. "Thoughts and Details on Scarcity," *Works*, V, 89 and "Speech on Hastings," *ibid.*, VII, 131.
50. It is Burke's argument against a Place Bill, the third proposed remedy for the present discontents, that the aristocracy needs a tolerable outlet for ambition. "Thoughts," *Works*, I, 367–68.
51. "Letters on a Regicide Peace," *Works*, V, 315.
52. See Alfred de Grazia, *Public and Republic* (New York, 1951), pp. 40–41.
53. John Brooke, *The Chatham Administration, 1766–68* (London, 1956), pp. 85, 96–98.
54. *Correspondence*, II, 109.
55. "Thoughts," *Works*, I, 372.
56. *Ibid.*, p. 373.
57. See *The Complete Works of George Savile First Marquess of Halifax*, ed. Walter Raleigh (Oxford, 1912), pp. 157–58, 225–27.
58. "Thoughts," *Works*, I, 369; cf. the argument against the second proposed remedy for the present discontents, a triennial parliament. *Ibid.*, p. 367. Before the "Thoughts" was published, Burke preferred petitions from the people to the crown over representations from the people to M.P.'s, because the latter implied a submission by the people to the Commons. See *Correspondence*, II, 51, 66–67, 73.
59. "Thoughts," *Works*, I, 379.
60. "Appeal," *Works*, III, 78.
61. "Reflections," *Works*, II, 331, 335–36, 368–69; "Appeal," *ibid.*, III, 98–99; "A Letter to a Noble Lord," *ibid.*, V, 120.
62. "Appeal," *Works*, III, 113–14.
63. *Ibid.*, pp. 82, 85, 87.
64. "Reflections," *Works*, II, 333.
65. "Appeal," *Works*, III, 82–83; "Reflections," *ibid.*, II, 332.
66. "Appeal," *Works*, III, 79–80.
67. *Ibid.*, p. 45.
68. "As no water can rise higher than its spring, no establishment can have more authority than it derives from its principle; and the power of government can

with no appearance of reason go further coercively than to bind and hold down those who have once consented to their opinions. The consent is the origin of the whole." "Tracts on the Popery Laws," *Works,* VI, 33.

69. "Reflections," *Works,* II, 323. This passage will be discussed in the next chapter.
70. "Appeal," *Works,* III, 99.
71. "Tracts on the Popery Laws," *Works,* VI, 43; "Reflections," *ibid.,* II, 332, 442; cf. Charles Parkin, *The Moral Basis of Burke's Political Thought,* p. 46.
72. "Appeal," *Works,* III, 77, 83.
73. *The Writings of Thomas Jefferson,* ed. P. J. Ford (10 vols.; New York, 1896), VII, 38, 43, 170, 265, 333, 355, 373, 464; VIII, 7, 22; IX, 387, 425. Cf. William N. Chambers, *Political Parties in a New Nation* (New York, 1963), pp. 106–7.
74. "Appeal," *Works,* III, 92–93; "Reflections," *ibid.,* II, 515.
75. "Appeal," *Works,* III, 76, 83–85; "Reflections," *ibid.,* II, 332.
76. *Correspondence,* IV, 80.

CHAPTER EIGHT

1. "Reflections," *Works,* II, 323.
2. L. B. Namier, *The Structure of Politics at the Accession of George III* (2d ed.; London, 1957), pp. 10–11.
3. *Correspondence,* I, 196; see Thomas W. Copeland, "Burke's First Patron."
4. *Correspondence,* I, 163–66, 185.
5. "A Letter to a Noble Lord," *Works,* V, 124–25." Cf. "My merits, whatever they are, are original and personal; his are derivative." *Ibid.,* p. 130; also "Reflections," II, 517; *Correspondence,* II, 131.
6. "A Letter to a Noble Lord," *Works,* V, 130.
7. *Ibid.,* p. 131; emphasis in original.
8. *Ibid.,* pp. 117, 126–27.
9. *Ibid.,* p. 133; *Correspondence,* II, 263.
10. *Works,* V, 135.
11. Quoted in Thomas H. D. Mahoney, *Edmund Burke and Ireland,* p. 226; see *The Epistolary Correspondence of Edmund Burke and Dr. French Laurence,* p. 31; "A Letter to a Noble Lord," *Works,* V, 136; and James Prior, *Life of the Right Honourable Edmund Burke,* pp. 405–6.
12. Cf. Ernest Barker, *Essays on Government* (2d ed.; Oxford, 1951), pp. 173, 176.
13. "Reflections," *Works,* II, 324; cf. "Thoughts," *ibid.,* I, 313.
14. Leo Strauss, *Natural Right and History,* p. 315 n.
15. "Reflections," *Works,* II, 331–32; "Thoughts and Details on Scarcity," *ibid.,* V, 100; cf. Charles Parkin, *The Moral Basis of Burke's Political Thought,* pp. 31–33.
16. "Appeal," *Works,* III, 80; Persius, *Satires,* No. III, l. 72; *Correspondence,* IV, 79; cf. J. J. Rousseau, *Second Discourse,* Preface.
17. "Appeal," *Works,* III, 85–86. Note that Burke's "true natural aristocracy" seems to demand a large society; cf. *The Federalist* Nos. 10, 14.
18. "A Letter to a Noble Lord," *Works,* V, 147.
19. "Letters on a Regicide Peace," *Works,* V, 227; *Correspondence,* III, 218.
20. *Works,* V, 164, 342.
21. "Reflections," *Works,* II, 332; cf. St. Thomas Aquinas, *Summa theologica,* I–II, 94, 2.
22. "Appeal," *Works,* III, 78–79.
23. This identification is implied in "Reflections," *Works,* II, 310, 335, 353–54; "Letters on a Regicide Peace," *ibid.,* V, 266.

24. "Letters on a Regicide Peace," *Works*, V, 326. The temperate man is he who does not have evil passions to control. Aristotle, *Nicomachean Ethics*, 1152a1–3.
25. "Appeal," *Works*, III, 77.
26. Cf. H. V. F. Somerset (ed.), *A Note-book of Edmund Burke*, pp. 71–73, 117.
27. Hobbes, *Leviathan*, chaps. 5, 8; Aquinas, *Summa theologica*, I–II, 94, 4.
28. "Reflections," *Works*, II, 333.
29. "Thoughts," *Works*, I, 377. "That secret tribunal" is clearly "conscience" in this paragraph.
30. Cf. "Appeal," *Works*, III, 78, 106; "Remarks on the Policy of the Allies," *ibid.*, III, 444; "Reflections," *ibid.*, II, 484; "Letters on a Regicide Peace," *ibid.*, V, 429.
31. "Appeal," *Works*, III, 76–77.
32. "Reflections," *Works*, II, 349–50; cf. Montesquieu, *De l'esprit des lois*, III, 6, 7; IV, 2; Hobbes, *Leviathan*, chaps. 11, 13.
33. "Reflections," *Works*, II, 350.
34. "Appeal," *Works*, III, 80.
35. "Reflections," *Works*, II, 353. Cf. this passage from a speech against Hastings: "It is wisely provided in the constitution of our hearts, that we should interest ourselves in the fate of great personages. They are therefore made everywhere the objects of tragedy, which addresses itself directly to our passions and our feelings. And why? Because men of great place, men of great rank, men of hereditary authority, cannot fall without a horrible crash upon all about them. Such towers cannot tumble without ruining their dependent cottages." Note that the people, when they see tragedy, do not see greatness directly, but only indirectly, through the effect upon their own interest. *Works*, VIII, 59. Cf. "Hints for an Essay on the Drama," *ibid.*, VI, 179–81; Burke, *A Philosophical Enquiry into the Origin of Our Ideas of the Sublime and Beautiful*, ed. J. T. Boulton, pp. 44–47.
36. "Reflections," *Works*, II, 332.
37. "Appeal," *Works*, III, 99.
38. *Ibid.*, p. 88 n.
39. "Thoughts and Details on Scarcity," *Works*, V, 107–9.
40. "Appeal," *Works*, III, 78.
41. *Ibid.*, p. 79.
42. *Ibid.*, pp. 79–80; cf. "Tracts on the Popery Laws," *ibid.*, VI, 20–21.
43. "Thoughts and Details on Scarcity," *Works*, V, 100.
44. C. B. Macpherson, "Edmund Burke," p. 26.
45. "Reflections," *Works*, II, 354.
46. Burke gives his source as Jean Domat, who says, according to Burke, that prescription is a part of natural law. This statement was not found. "Reflections," *Works*, II, 422; Domat, *The Civil Law in the Natural Order*, Part I, Book III, Title VII, §§ 4, 5.
47. David Hume, *The History of England* (6 vols.; New York, 1878), II, 429, 514; V, 38, 145–46; VI, 214–15, 361, 363–65; and *A Treatise of Human Nature*, ed. L. A. Selby-Bigge (Oxford, 1896), p. 563.
48. Cf. Locke, *Two Treatises of Government*, II, § 110. J. G. A. Pocock says that Burke transforms a principle of legal order into a principle of the natural order of society. "Burke and the Ancient Constitution," p. 131. But this transformation brings prescription from private into public law, and Burke apparently took the principle of prescription from Roman law, not from the English common lawyers. "An Abridgment of English History," *Works*, VI, 414; *Correspondence*, II, 217.
49. "Reflections," *Works*, II, 422; cf. *ibid.*, VI, 146: "Prescription is the most solid of all titles, not only to property, but, which is to secure that property, to government. . . . It is accompanied with another ground of authority in the constitution

of the human mind—presumption." See also *ibid.*, II, 26; VI, 80, 117; and Francis P. Canavan, *The Political Reason of Edmund Burke*, pp. 127–28.
50. "Letter to the Sheriffs of Bristol," *Works*, II, 38.

CHAPTER NINE

1. "Appeal," *Works*, III, 112; cf. "Reflections," *ibid.*, II, 369.
2. "Reflections," *Works*, II, 310. In this context also, Burke repels a wrong conclusion from the rights of man that all walks of life deserve equal political power.
3. "Speech on Hastings," *Works*, VII, 161.
4. "Letter to the Sheriffs of Bristol," *Works*, II, 27; cf. "Reflections," *ibid.*, II, 314.
5. "Thoughts," *Works*, I, 311; "A Letter to Sir Hercules Langrishe," *ibid.*, III, 326; cf. Locke, *Two Treatises of Government*, II, §§ 223–25; Aristotle, *Politics*, 1277b25–29.
6. "Reflections," *Works*, II, 359.
7. *Ibid.*, p. 325; "Speech at Bristol" (1780), *ibid.*, p. 138; cf. "Two Letters to Gentlemen in Bristol," *ibid.*, II, 51.
8. In his "Letter to the Sheriffs of Bristol," *Works*, II, 41, Burke says that "superior understandings" ought to "correct vulgar prejudice"—which assumes that vulgar prejudice is corrigible.
9. "Appeal," *Works*, III, 16.
10. "Letters on a Regicide Peace," *Works*, V, 236.
11. "Reflections," *Works*, II, 334; "A Letter to Sir Hercules Langrishe," *ibid.*, III, 340; Francis P. Canavan, *The Political Reason of Edmund Burke*, p. 177; Howard White, "Edmund Burke on Political Theory and Practice."
12. "Thoughts," *Works*, I, 357; "Reflections," *ibid.*, II, 331; "Tracts on the Popery Laws," *ibid.*, VI, 22.
13. Burke, *A Philosophical Enquiry into the Origin of Our Ideas of the Sublime and Beautiful*, ed. J. T. Boulton, p. 25.
14. "Reflections," *Works*, II, 284; cf. "Letters on a Regicide Peace," *ibid.*, V, 278.
15. "Reflections," *Works*, II, 359.
16. Cavendish, *Debates*, I, 181.
17. He does profess "in common" a belief in "revealed religion." "Speech on a Bill for the Relief of Protestant Dissenters," *Works*, VI, 110; cf. *Correspondence*, I, 32–33; IV, 84.
18. Cobbett, *Parliamentary History*, XXII, 126.
19. "Speech on the Acts of Uniformity," *Works*, VI, 101–2.
20. "Tracts on the Popery Laws," *Works*, VI, 29–30. "True humility, the basis of the Christian system, is the low, but deep and firm, foundation of all real virtue." "Letter to a Member of the National Assembly," *ibid.*, II, 536. Thus all real virtue does not seem to be comprised by the Christian system.
21. "Reflections," *Works*, II, 414.
22. Burke, *Sublime and Beautiful*, ed. Boulton, p. 174.
23. *Correspondence*, I, 271; II, 129–31, 133–36; Arthur P. I. Samuels, *The Early Life, Correspondence, and Writings of Burke*, pp. 402–4.
24. "Reflections," *Works*, II, 430.
25. *Ibid.*, p. 363.
26. *Ibid.*, pp. 364, 430–33.
27. *Correspondence*, III, 442; cf. Locke, *Two Treatises of Government*, II, § 25.
28. "Remarks on the Policy of the Allies," *Works*, III, 444. Cf. H. V. F. Somerset (ed.), *A Note-book of Edmund Burke*, pp. 8, 70; Samuels, *The Early Life*, p. 252.

29. Burke said that "all the principal religions in Europe" are "humanly speaking . . . prescriptive religions." To know more would be to know "the secret dispensations of Providence," not true revelation. "Letter to William Smith," *Works*, VI, 52.
30. "Reflections," *Works*, II, 370; cf. "Thoughts," *ibid.*, I, 348.
31. *Ibid.*, II, 368–69.
32. "Letters on a Regicide Peace," *Works*, V, 153.
33. "Reflections," *Works*, II, 364–66; cf. *ibid.*, p. 373.
34. "Tracts on the Popery Laws," *Works*, VI, 32.
35. *Ibid.*, p. 21.
36. "Letters on a Regicide Peace," *Works*, V, 209.
37. "Appeal," *Works*, III, 86.
38. "Reflections," *Works*, II, 454; Burke, *Sublime and Beautiful*, ed. Boulton, p. 104.
39. "Reflections," *Works*, II, 352; *Sublime and Beautiful*, ed. Boulton, p. 11.
40. "Reflections," *Works*, II, 310; Morton J. Frisch, "Burke on Theory" and "Rational Planning *versus* Unplanned Becoming."
41. *Correspondence*, ed. Fitzwilliam, IV, 229.
42. *Correspondence*, II, 355; cf. Aristotle, *Politics*, 1282b14–23.
43. *Correspondence*, I, 165.
44. "Appeal," *Works*, III, 113; emphasis added. Yet Burke spoke of Montesquieu as "a man who could spend twenty years in one pursuit" (see *De l'esprit des lois*, Preface); such a remark indicates some appreciation of theory. Burke was a careful reader of Montesquieu; he once said: ". . . we must not forget that the excellent author himself, through an extreme refinement, was not wholly free from obscurity." *Annual Register*, 1758, p. 311.
45. Cf. Montesquieu's own description of his purpose in *De l'esprit des lois*, Preface (end); see also "Reflections," *Works*, II, 351.
46. *Works*, VI, 107–13.
47. "Thoughts," *Works*, I, 326; VI, 80; *Correspondence*, I, 344; II, 38.
48. *Correspondence*, II, 263.
49. "Reflections," *Works*, II, 518.
50. *The Complete Works of George Savile First Marquess of Halifax*, ed. Walter Raleigh (Oxford, 1912), p. 48.
51. "Appeal," *Works*, III, 26; "A Letter to William Elliot," *ibid.*, V, 79.
52. Winston S. Churchill, *Amid These Storms* (New York, 1932), p. 40.
53. "Appeal," *Works*, III, 92; "Letters on a Regicide Peace," *ibid.*, V, 315.
54. "Reflections," *Works*, II, 439; cf. "Appeal," *ibid.*, III, 114.
55. *Works*, VI, 98.
56. Bolingbroke, *Works*, II, 81–82.
57. "Reflections," *Works*, II, 295.
58. *Ibid.*, p. 331; "Thoughts on French Affairs," *ibid.*, III, 393.

Bibliography

The bibliography has been restricted to writings of Burke and writings about Burke.

WRITINGS OF BURKE

Annual Register, 1758–70.

BURKE, EDMUND. *Burke, Select Works*. Edited by E. J. PAYNE. 2 vols. Oxford: Clarendon Press, 1922.

——. *The Correspondence of the Right Honourable Edmund Burke*. Edited by CHARLES WILLIAM, EARL FITZWILLIAM, and SIR RICHARD BOURKE. 4 vols. London: F. and J. Rivington, 1844.

——. *The Correspondence of Edmund Burke*. Edited by THOMAS W. COPELAND. 5 vols. to date. Chicago: University of Chicago Press, 1958——.

——. *The Epistolary Correspondence of Edmund Burke and Dr. French Laurence*. London: C. and J. Rivington, 1827.

——. Fitzwilliam Manuscripts. Sheffield Central City Library.

——. *A Note-book of Edmund Burke*. Edited by H. V. F. SOMERSET. Cambridge: Cambridge University Press, 1957.

——. *A Philosophical Enquiry into the Origin of Our Ideas of the Sublime and Beautiful*. Edited by J. T. BOULTON. London: Routledge and Kegan Paul, 1958.

——. *The Speeches of the Right Honourable Edmund Burke in the House of Commons and in Westminster Hall*. 4 vols. London: Longman, 1816.

——. *Thoughts on the Cause of the Present Discontents*. Edited by W. MURISON. Cambridge: Cambridge University Press, 1930.

——. *Thoughts on the Cause of the Present Discontents*. Edited by F. G. SELBY. London: Macmillan & Co., 1951.

——. *Works*. 8 vols. Bohn Library edition. London, 1854.

CAVENDISH, SIR HENRY. *Debates of the House of Commons*. 2 vols. London: J. Wright, 1848.

COBBETT, WILLIAM. *The Parliamentary History of England*. London, 1782, 1786.

SAMUELS, ARTHUR P. I. *The Early Life, Correspondence, and Writings of Burke*. Cambridge: Cambridge University Press, 1923.

WRITINGS ABOUT BURKE

BOOKS

BARKER, ERNEST. *Essays on Government.* 2d ed. Oxford: Clarendon Press, 1951.
BISSET, ROBERT. *The Life of Edmund Burke.* 2 vols. 2d ed. London: G. Cawthorn, 1800.
CANAVAN, FRANCIS P. *The Political Reason of Edmund Burke.* Durham, N.C.: Duke University Press, 1960.
COBBAN, ALFRED. *Edmund Burke and the Revolt against the Eighteenth Century.* London: G. Allen and Unwin, 1929.
CONE, CARL B. *Burke and the Nature of Politics: The Age of the American Revolution.* Lexington, Ky.: University of Kentucky Press, 1957.
COPELAND, THOMAS W. *Our Eminent Friend, Edmund Burke.* New Haven, Conn.: Yale University Press, 1949.
DILKE, CHARLES W. *Papers of a Critic.* 2 vols. London: John Murray, 1875.
FAY, C. R. *Burke and Adam Smith.* Belfast: Queen's University of Belfast, 1956.
HOFFMAN, ROSS J. S. *Edmund Burke, New York Agent.* Philadelphia: American Philosophical Society, 1956.
LENNOX, RICHMOND. *Edmund Burke und sein politisches Arbeitsfeld.* Berlin: R. Oldenbourg, 1923.
MACCUNN, JOHN. *The Political Philosophy of Burke.* London: E. Arnold, 1913.
MAGNUS, PHILIP. *Edmund Burke: A Life.* London: John Murray, 1939.
MAHONEY, THOMAS H. D. *Edmund Burke and Ireland.* Cambridge, Mass.: Harvard University Press, 1960.
MORLEY, JOHN. *Burke.* New York: Macmillan, 1879.
MURRAY, ROBERT H. *Edmund Burke.* Oxford: Oxford University Press, 1931.
NEWMAN, BERTRAM. *Edmund Burke.* London: G. Bell and Sons, 1927.
PARKIN, CHARLES. *The Moral Basis of Burke's Political Thought.* Cambridge: Cambridge University Press, 1956.
PRIOR, JAMES. *Life of the Right Honourable Edmund Burke.* 5th ed. London: G. Bell and Sons, 1878.
Rockingham Manuscripts. Sheffield Central City Library.
SKALWEIT, STEPHAN. *Edmund Burke und Frankreich.* Cologne: Westdeutscher Verlag, 1956.
STANLIS, PETER J. *Edmund Burke and the Natural Law.* Ann Arbor, Mich.: University of Michigan Press, 1958.
STRAUSS, LEO. *Natural Right and History.* Chicago: University of Chicago Press, 1953.
WECTER, DIXON. *Edmund Burke and His Kinsmen.* Boulder, Colo.: University of Colorado Studies, 1939.

ARTICLES

BOULTON, J. T. "The *Reflections:* Burke's Preliminary Draft and Methods of Composition," *Durham University Journal,* XIV (1953), 114–19.
The Burke Newsletter (Detroit), 1959 to date.

COPELAND, THOMAS W. "Burke's First Patron," *History Today*, II (1952), 394–99.

EINAUDI, MARIO. "The British Background of Burke's Political Philosophy," *Political Science Quarterly*, XLIX (1934), 576–96.

FRISCH, MORTON J. "Burke on Theory," *Cambridge Journal*, VII (1954), 292–97.

———. "Rational Planning *versus* Unplanned Becoming," *Classical Journal*, XLVII (1952), 288–90.

MACPHERSON, C. B. "Edmund Burke," *Transactions of the Royal Society of Canada*, LIII (1959), 19–26.

POCOCK, J. G. A. "Burke and the Ancient Constitution," *Historical Journal*, III (1960), 125–43.

SEWALL, RICHARD B. "Rousseau's Second Discourse in England from 1755 to 1762," *Philological Quarterly*, XVII (1938), 97–114.

SMITH, GOLDWIN. "Burke on Party," *American Historical Review*, XI (1905), 36–41.

WHITE, HOWARD B. "Edmund Burke on Political Theory and Practice," *Social Research*, XVII (1950), 106–27.

Index

and corruption, 45, court and country, 47–48, 66, "great," 41–42, and society, 62–63; on *party:* and anti-party, 113, and corruption of court, 67, and country, 112, defined, 78, his, 118–19, last, 113, philosophic view of, 112–13, and program of, 112, and traditional view of, 112–13; and passions, 76; and patriotism, 59; patriotism of, 84; and Patriot King, 58, 137, 146; on peers and people, 162; and philosophy, natural, 53; "political school" of, 175; on prejudice, 224–25; principles from interests, distinguished by, 119; and program of Patriot King, 75–80; on progress, moral and technological, 53; and providence, God's, 53–54, 59–62, 68; and public opinion, 46; on reason, 50–51, 53, 54; and religion, natural, 61–62; and revelation, 55; rhetoric of, 118; on sociability, natural, of men, 54, 56, 57, 75; on society, natural vs. civil, 54; on society and truth, 63; and sovereignty, natural and artificial, 56, 57; and "spirit of patriotism," 68; on state action, 245; on state of nature, 56; on state of war, 55; and statesmanship, 69–70; theory of, as cause of present discontents, 41; and toleration, religious, 61–63; and virtue, public, 73; and virtue, "supernatural," 84; and Whig families, 85; on wisdom and cunning, 73–74

Boswell, James, 111, 257
Boulton, J. T., 262, 265, 266
Bourke, Sir Richard, 260
British constitution, 210–11; aristocratic branch, 93–94; "best constitution" replaced by, 238; Burke on, 123, 245; classification of, 124 ff., 160–61; and contract, 162; and crown's powers, 130; end of, 159, 160; and gentlemen, rule of, 164–200; and government, 162; and impeachment, 146; and monarchy, 136–37; without parties, 48; and people, 158; and popular government, 123–62, 163, 164; private character, 38; private and public, 3, 14–15; and prudent statesmen, 238; republican parts and crown, 137; spirit of, 73; and standing government, 158, 162; three elements of, 124; and true principles, 49; and who rules, 160–67
Brogan, D. W., 248
Brooke, John, 249, 250, 263
Brown, Dr. John, 86, 87, 90–98, 109, 121, 217, 255

Burke, Edmund: acts respecting party, 198–200; and Aristotle on virtue, 214–15; on association, 187; and atheism, 231; and *Bolingbroke:* concessions to, 161–62, criticism of, 207, influenced by, 123, on party system, 183, on peace, 245, on peers and people, 162, and political school, 175–77, and program, 11; on British constitution, 123–24, 238, 245; and Dr. Brown, 86, 96; and Christian revelation, 230–35; on classification of British constitution, 124–25; on conscience, 216; as conservative, 244–46; consistence of, 241, 246; and conspiracy, 174; correspondence of, 168; and "court cabal," 30–36; and court system, 46, 136–40; on crown's honor, 135; on duties and rights, 58; on duty, 213; on equality of opportunity, 202; on establishments as natural, 223; on fame, family, 205, 207; on fame, personal, 203; on first principles, 221–22, 238; as founder of party, 2; on "free state," 160; on God, 233–35; and group action, 189–90; on Hastings, charges against, 148–49; on himself, 17; and history, 58; on honor, 87; on impeachment, 146–54; and innocent gentlemen, 89; on "king's men," 88; on law over discretion, 135; on laws, 228; on legislator, 213–14; as man of ability, 199; as man of actual virtue, 203, 241; on man and British constitution, 136–37; on mixed government, 128, 157–63; and monarchical principle, 126, 143; on monarchy, 129–33; on monarchy and despotism, 135–36; and natural law, 58, 212–23; on natural rights, 220, 245; and *necessitudo sortis,* 183–86; on Old Whigs, 171–73, 175–81, 182; on parties, "great," 41–42; on *party:* attack on revolutionary, 196–97, as chief remedy, 39, competition, 122, defined, 17, divisions, 106, as establishment, 196, his, 198–200, as natural, 190, respectability of, 85, Rockingham, 168, skeptical of claims, 181, system, 183; on Patriot King, 120; on peers, influence of, 95–96; on political principles, 239; on popular favor, 155–57; on popular government, 157–63; on prejudice, 224–25; on private man in politics, 106; on prudence and statesmanship, 163, 245–46; on religion, 230–35; rhetoric of, 21, 26, 30–31, 154–55; on separation of powers, 161; on state action, 245; as statesman, 27, 40; on "supernatural virtue," 84; "Thoughts,"

Lightning Source UK Ltd.
Milton Keynes UK
UKHW010250140223
416945UK00006B/623